INTERNATIONAL NARCOTICS CONTROL BOARD

Report

of the
International Narcotics Control Board
for 2015

UNITED NATIONS
New York, 2016

E/INCB/2015/1

UNITED NATIONS PUBLICATION
Sales No. E.16.XI.1
ISBN: 978-92-1-148283-6
eISBN: 978-92-1-057741-0
ISSN 0257-3717

Foreword

Currently, there is a global debate taking place on "the right way in drug policy". The International Narcotics Control Board (INCB) will participate in this debate, given its mandate to monitor implementation of and compliance with the three international drug control conventions.

The General Assembly has decided to convene a special session on the world drug problem in April 2016 to review progress in the implementation of the 2009 Political Declaration and Plan of Action on International Cooperation towards an Integrated and Balanced Strategy to Counter the World Drug Problem and to assess the achievements and challenges in countering the world drug problem, within the framework of the three international drug control conventions and other relevant United Nations instruments. The special session, which will examine world drug policy, should lead to a rethinking and refocusing of the world's drug control priorities and promote global cooperation in countering drug abuse and drug-related crime, while affirming that the global capacity to resolve these issues requires commensurate global political and legal commitment.

The International Narcotics Control Board is uniquely placed to contribute to current discussions on international trends and emerging threats in drug control. It will contribute the insight and experience it has accumulated over decades of monitoring the implementation of the drug control conventions and identifying achievements, challenges and weaknesses in drug control. INCB will engage in the special session and its preparation by highlighting and clarifying the approaches and principles underlying the international system of drug control and making recommendations based upon the conventions. In its annual reports, published pursuant to the treaties, INCB has been addressing, particularly in the thematic chapters, most of the relevant aspects of the global drug problem and most of the critical points in the ongoing debate on the "right way in drug policy". Equally, the release of the present annual report of the Board for 2015, the annual report on precursors[1] and the supplementary report on the availability of internationally controlled drugs[2] is part of our contribution to the special session and the forthcoming policy discussions.

The present report of the Board for 2015 contains a thematic chapter on the health and welfare of mankind and the international drug control system. It shows that concern for health and welfare is at the core of the international drug control system. INCB emphasizes that the system in place, when fully implemented, contributes to protecting the health and welfare of people worldwide and ensures balanced national approaches that take into account local socioeconomic and sociocultural conditions.

Even with the reality of the constantly shifting contours of the drug problem, the 1961, 1971 and 1988 conventions have proved their value as the cornerstone of international cooperation in drug policy. The fact that the conventions have been almost universally ratified by States underscores that the desire to counter the world's drug problem is shared globally. States have regularly reaffirmed their commitment to working within the framework of the three international drug control conventions and the political declarations.

Assessing the achievements and challenges of the current drug control system, INCB believes that the control of the international licit trade in narcotic drugs, psychotropic substances and precursors has been an undeniable success, as today no noteworthy diversion of those substances from licit to illicit channels is taking place. On the other hand, the availability and accessibility of narcotic drugs and psychotropic substances for medical purposes is not at all satisfactory at the global level. Equally, the goal of a noticeable reduction in the illicit demand for and supply of drugs has not been reached. Finally, there are numerous new challenges emerging, such as new psychoactive substances.

---

[1] E/INCB/2015/4.

[2] E/INCB/2015/1/Supp.1.

However, INCB is convinced that these challenges can be met by fully implementing the conventions and the principles of the political declarations. The drug control system is a balanced system, driving towards improving public health and welfare, based on the underlying principles of proportionality, collective responsibility and compliance with international human rights standards. Implementing this system means putting the health and welfare of mankind at the core of drug policies, applying comprehensive, integrated and balanced approaches to elaborating drug control policy, promoting human rights standards, giving higher priority to prevention, treatment, rehabilitation and the reduction of the negative consequences of drug abuse, and strengthening international cooperation based on shared responsibility.

States parties to the treaties have a certain flexibility in their interpretation and implementation of the treaties, within the boundaries that they themselves set out and agreed upon during treaty negotiations. The treaties provide for alternatives to punishment: they do not require the incarceration of drug users for drug use or minor offences. Instead of or in addition to conviction or punishment, States can take measures for the prevention of abuse of drugs and for education, early identification, treatment, aftercare, rehabilitation and social reintegration of affected persons. In addition, States have a certain latitude regarding the sanctions they apply against unlawful behaviour, subject to their constitutional principles and the basic concepts of their legal systems.

Thus, it remains imperative that Governments give due regard to the letter and spirit of the drug control conventions in the elaboration of future policies. States will continue to have their own practical and operational approaches to addressing local drug problems, but compliance with the conventions means fully implementing the underlying principles and obligations.

The special session should reaffirm these principles. Governments should demonstrate that drug control is a shared responsibility among all States and that together Governments can focus on identifying measures to ensure full implementation of the conventions.

Recognizing that the framework of the conventions has sometimes been misinterpreted, INCB believes that the special session will provide an opportunity to emphasize that the spirit of the conventions and political declarations—namely, promoting the health and welfare of mankind—rests upon the ability of States to enact policies and practices that are grounded in evidence. The first chapter of this publication, the Board's annual report for 2015, shows that the current framework is both comprehensive and cohesive, promoting the application of scientific knowledge, proportionally and in moderation.

The present report, together with the supplementary report on the availability of internationally controlled drugs and the report on precursors, provides an update on the functioning of the international drug control system and delivers an analysis of developments in the world drug situation. These reports promote greater understanding of the role and work of the Board as the treaty-monitoring body and the importance of compliance by Member States with the conventions. Any proposals to work outside the framework of the treaties undermine the broad-based consensus upon which the drug-control system is founded.

INCB looks forward in the coming year to the continuing global dialogue and elaboration, through the special session of the General Assembly on the world drug problem, of a set of practical actions to address emerging challenges.

Werner Sipp
President
International Narcotics Control Board

Contents

Explanatory notes

Data reported later than 1 November 2015 could not be taken into consideration in preparing this report.

The designations employed and the presentation of the material in this publication do not imply the expression of any opinion whatsoever on the part of the Secretariat of the United Nations concerning the legal status of any country, territory, city or area or of its authorities, or concerning the delimitation of its frontiers or boundaries.

Countries and areas are referred to by the names that were in official use at the time the relevant data were collected.

References to dollars ($) are to United States dollars, unless otherwise stated.

The following abbreviations have been used in this report:

APAAN	*alpha*-phenylacetoacetonitrile
ASEAN	Association of Southeast Asian Nations
ATS	amphetamine-type stimulants
BZP	*N*-benzylpiperazine
CSTO	Collective Security Treaty Organization
CICAD	Inter-American Drug Abuse Control Commission
ECOWAS	Economic Community of West African States
EMCDDA	European Monitoring Centre for Drugs and Drug Addiction
Europol	European Police Office
GHB	*gamma*-hydroxybutyric acid
ha	hectare
I2ES	International Import and Export Authorization System
INCB	International Narcotics Control Board
INTERPOL	International Criminal Police Organization
IONICS	Project Ion Incident Communication System
LSD	lysergic acid diethylamide
MDMA	methylenedioxymethamphetamine
MDPV	methylenedioxypyrovalerone
OAS	Organization of American States
PEN Online	Pre-Export Notification Online
PICS	Precursors Incident Communication System
THC	tetrahydrocannabinol
UNODC	United Nations Office on Drugs and Crime
WCO	World Customs Organization
WHO	World Health Organization

Chapter I.

The health and welfare of mankind: challenges and opportunities for the international control of drugs

A. Health and welfare as the main objectives of the international drug control treaties

1. The ultimate goal of the three international drug control conventions is to protect public and individual health and welfare. All three treaties—the Single Convention on Narcotic Drugs of 1961,[3] the Convention on Psychotropic Substances of 1971[4] and the United Nations Convention against Illicit Traffic in Narcotic Drugs and Psychotropic Substances of 1988[5]—make reference to that concern. Along with the limitation of the use of narcotic drugs and psychotropic substances exclusively for medical and scientific purposes, the conventions require Governments to take all practicable measures for the prevention of drug abuse and for the early identification, treatment, education, aftercare, rehabilitation and social reintegration of the persons involved (article 38 of the 1961 Convention and article 20 of the 1971 Convention).

2. With the special session of the General Assembly on the world drug problem to be held in 2016, the time has come to make a critical assessment of the global drug situation and drug control policies and to review how the main principles of the drug control treaties and the inherent balanced approach have been implemented in practice. The world has changed, as have drug policies, and it is therefore necessary to consider how policy changes to address emerging challenges can be achieved within the existing international legal drug control framework, which continues to enjoy almost universal support, although its objectives have sometimes been misunderstood or misinterpreted. Building on its findings with respect to the implementation of a comprehensive, integrated and balanced approach, as examined in the annual report of the Board for 2014 and previous years, the Board presents in this thematic chapter a number of additional considerations on the subject of drugs and health.

B. Drugs and the health and welfare of mankind

3. The use of substances to influence mood, sensation, perception and cognition is a near-universal human phenomenon. The substances so used, whether consumed in the form of naturally occurring plant material, extracts, derivatives or pure synthetics, are generically referred to as "drugs" (this term will be used in the present chapter for the sake of brevity). Many of those substances pose the risk of addiction or, more largely, problematic patterns of use and abuse among people who take them.

4. The use of a substance liable to abuse—regardless of whether the substance is controlled—has characteristic risks, with the level and combination of risks varying widely depending on the substance, the individual, the social setting and the mode of administration. The abuse of any substance poses a risk to the health and welfare of

---

[3] Single Convention on Narcotic Drugs of 1961 as amended by the 1972 Protocol (United Nations, *Treaty Series*, vol. 976, No. 14152).

[4] United Nations, *Treaty Series*, vol. 1019, No. 14956.

[5] Ibid., vol. 1582, No. 27627.

the users and those around them. Drugs are placed under international and national control precisely because they can seriously endanger the health and welfare of individuals. Similarly, all Governments have chosen to distribute most medications in pharmacies and by prescription because many of those substances may have seriously toxic and noxious effects when administered without expert supervision.

5. Psychoactive substances—whether or not they are under international control—are no ordinary commodities in the sense that a large fraction of the revenue to the sellers comes from users whose habits and addiction are not under voluntary rational control. Even in a hypothetical political, social and legal system that assumed that the consumption choices of adults should be left unconstrained and that producers should be free to supply and foster consumer demand with the use of marketing, an exception might reasonably be made for psychoactive substances. This would be done to protect consumers against gaps in their knowledge and defects in their own decision-making (which can be impaired by the consumption of the substance itself), to minimize avoidable disease and death and to protect others from the consequences of drug-influenced behaviour.

6. In recent years, there have been additional challenges such as the appearance of new psychoactive substances. Governments acknowledge the complexity of dealing with an ever-changing spectrum of substances made especially to circumvent controls. In most cases, such substances have unknown short- and long-term effects and may have highly addictive and toxic profiles. A growing number of those substances are now being manipulated and peddled to people, especially youth, at the expense of their health. It is therefore a matter of health and welfare to ensure that those substances are kept away from potential users and that the targeted population groups are provided with information on the risks associated with such substances and primary prevention services.

7. The international drug control conventions recognize and promote the medical use of narcotic drugs and psychotropic substances, which serve as an indispensable source of relief from pain and suffering and other medical conditions. However, although these drugs can be a source of great benefit, they also have the potential to be a source of harm. The conventions therefore oblige States parties to properly regulate, control and limit exclusively to medical and scientific purposes the production, manufacture, export, import and distribution of, trade in, and use and possession of drugs, which, if inappropriately administered, can also be subject to abuse.

8. Globally, access to medicines containing controlled substances is still very uneven, with consumption concentrated primarily in some developed countries. Three quarters of the world's population live in countries with low levels of access, or no access, to medicines containing scheduled substances. The International Narcotics Control Board (INCB) has long pointed out such major discrepancies and has repeatedly stressed that the situation could be improved through corrective action by States to address the regulatory, attitudinal, knowledge-related, economic and procurement-related problems identified as the main causes of inadequate availability. The present annual report of the Board is accompanied by a supplement devoted exclusively to the analysis of this issue.[6]

9. The imbalance in the availability of opioid analgesics is particularly worrying, as the latest data show that many of the conditions that require pain management, particularly cancer, are prevalent and increasing in low-income and middle-income countries.[7] At the same time, in recent years there has been an increase in the abuse of prescription drugs and related overdose deaths in countries with high per capita levels of consumption of opioid analgesics.

10. The conventions do not require any specific modality for the treatment of drug addiction; INCB urges States parties to base any such practice on scientific evidence. The provision of appropriate treatment services for drug abuse is as much an obligation for States parties as is the suppression of drug trafficking. Failure to provide appropriate treatment can exacerbate the health and social damage resulting from drug abuse and contribute to illicit demand for substances of abuse. It is therefore generally recognized that medically accepted standards of care for opioid dependence, including for opioid-dependent persons under criminal justice supervision, advance the goals of the international drug control treaties. The use of substitution therapy for the treatment of opioid dependence has a substantial evidence base, but its application varies among Member States.

11. The Board considers that programmes for the treatment of drug abuse should be held to the same standards of safety and efficacy as programmes for the treatment of other ailments. Inhumane or degrading forms of treatment of drug users should be eliminated.

---

[6] Availability of Internationally Controlled Drugs: Ensuring Adequate Access for Medical and Scientific Purposes (E/INCB/2015/1/Supp.1).

[7] World Health Organization and Worldwide Palliative Care Alliance, Global Atlas of Palliative Care at the End of Life (Worldwide Palliative Care Alliance, 2014).

C. The conventions and their results

12. The achievements of the conventions are difficult to measure because of the difficulty of predicting what would have happened in the absence of international agreement on drug control measures. In 1906/7, prior to the adoption of any international drug control agreement, global opium production was estimated at 41,600 tons, with a world population of less than 2 billion. The most recent estimate of global illicit opium production, published in the 2015 edition of the UNODC *World Drug Report*,[8] was 7,554 tons, a fraction of what was produced 100 years ago, whereas the world's population today is over 7 billion. In addition, the difficulty of diverting from licit international trade narcotic drugs, psychotropic substances and precursor chemicals can be attributed, at least partly, to the effective implementation of the treaties by Governments.

13. Moreover, the abuse of drugs has been contained in comparison with the consumption of other substances that are more easily available, such as alcohol and tobacco. The prevalence of abuse of drugs is much lower than that of alcohol and tobacco. Alcohol causes more violence, and tobacco more harm to health, than all the controlled drugs combined, mainly due to the greater availability of and exposure to those two substances and the prevalence of their use and abuse. Indeed, alcohol and tobacco kill many times more the number of people than controlled substances do. These examples from commercially regulated markets underline the dangers of the use of controlled substances for non-medical purposes. The conventions are designed to protect the health and well-being of populations by avoiding these dangers.

14. The challenge for States when implementing their treaty obligations is to determine the appropriate balance of their drug control efforts. States ought to ensure that their control efforts do not result in unwanted side effects. Problem users, who constitute only a minority of all drug users, consume the overwhelming majority of drugs, typically more than 80 per cent by volume. Furthermore, drug users who are continuously or regularly intoxicated account for a larger proportion of the total health and social damage. One of the most efficient ways to deter traffickers would be to reduce their user base. Removing a significant portion of the source of demand by implementing effective prevention and treatment measures would have a significant impact upon any illicit drug market. Such action should include efforts to prevent drug use in an effective and systematic manner.

15. Although integrated and balanced approaches have existed since the inception of the treaties, they have come to the forefront of international drug control only in recent decades. There are some historical and legal factors for this. International conventions, by definition, deal with cross-border issues of mutual interest to sovereign States, such as international trade. Hence, the conventions, as adopted, focused largely on international trade and trafficking, whereas the development and implementation at the national level of the measures that we now call "demand reduction"—while mandated by the conventions—were left to the discretion of each sovereign State.

D. Socioeconomic and sociopolitical context of drug control

16. Addressing social, economic and political issues that can create opportunities for violence and drug use may be as valuable as the efforts directly targeting the drugs themselves. As the Board has noted in the past, both the supply and demand sides of the drug problem are affected by socioeconomic factors such as poverty, hunger, economic inequality, social exclusion, deprivation, migration and displacement, limited access to education and employment prospects, and exposure to violence and abuse. Those factors are important drivers of the drug problem and need to be taken into consideration as part of a comprehensive approach. When designing and implementing policies to assist people living with substance abuse disorders, States must look deeper at socioeconomic factors such as poverty, marginalization, gender and child development. The role and responsibility of families and society in protecting children by creating environments that are conducive to prevention of drug abuse cannot be overemphasized.

17. The drug problem has many contributing factors and can be influenced by policies in other areas not aimed specifically at illicit drug supply and use. For example, policies that strengthen resiliency at the individual, family and community levels can reduce vulnerability to drug abuse and enhance the prospects for the speedy and lasting recovery of those who have developed drug abuse problems. Robust public institutions that are transparent and accountable can help minimize corrupting efforts of drug trafficking organizations. Likewise, strong communities with rich economic potential are more likely to withstand the deleterious impact of illicit drug crop cultivation and the corrupting influence of drug dealing and drug trafficking.

---

[8] United Nations publication, Sales No. E.15.XI.6.

E.   Social health and challenges

18.   Promoting the welfare of mankind requires the prevention and reduction of social harm. Some drug users suffer health damage due to the drugs themselves, impurities in the drugs or the means by which the drugs are administered. Other drug users cause harm to themselves or to others by acting carelessly, negligently or criminally while under the influence of drugs, and some users find that their drug use has escaped voluntary control and has become an unwanted and in some cases persistent and recurrent addiction that can result in significant health and personal costs, not to mention the costs to family and society. Even people with no diagnosable drug abuse disorder may contribute to a social problem both by supporting illicit drug markets and by engaging in risky behaviour while under the influence of the drug. An important social harm is the impact of the incarceration of drug users, for whom incarceration can have significant financial, familial and occupational repercussions.

19.   In addition to the damage drugs cause to the users and the people around them, activities and circumstances related to the illicit production and supply of drugs also threaten the health and welfare of the individual, the community and the State. In the case of substances sold on illicit markets, product quality is unknown, as illicit drugs can be of unknown or deleterious quality. Illicitly supplied drugs may be adulterated or may contain dangerous impurities, and drug users typically have little capacity to ascertain what they are actually consuming. These factors all increase the risk of accidental overdose and other forms of toxicity.

20.   Some drug-taking behaviour particularly compounds the problem of drug abuse. An example is the spread of HIV and the hepatitis C virus through the use of non-sterile injecting equipment. Since those viruses can also be transmitted in other ways, persons who never use controlled substances may also become infected as an indirect consequence of the drug-taking activities of others.

21.   The cost of drugs can impoverish, or further impoverish, persons dependent on the drug in question. This leads some drug users to become involved in criminal activity to support their drug addiction, leading to further harm not only for the drug user but also for others and society as a whole.

22.   The behaviour of illicit drug markets generates harm for society, most notably violence by, among and against drug traffickers. Criminal elements meet the illicit demand for drugs, and illicit drug markets are controlled by organized criminal groups. Violence, social disorder and corruption associated with the illicit production and supply of drugs threatens the security of citizens and undermines the rule of law. Weak governance provides, in turn, ground for the development of the illegal drug industry and markets.

23.   Law enforcement efforts targeting illicit markets may either reduce or exacerbate such violence and also generate harm: violence against and by law enforcement agents; incarceration and other forms of punishment; and corruption among, and human rights violations by, law enforcement agencies.

24.   Violence is perhaps the most visible and pernicious outcome of drug trafficking. The lucrative economic opportunities generated by the illicit demand for drugs attract criminals and enhance their willingness and capability to use violence to protect their illicit drug operations. Territorial disputes among rival drug trafficking organizations, score-settling and intimidation lead to the use of violence to dominate the illicit trade in drugs; this is especially true for communities situated in or near illicit drug production areas, along drug trafficking routes and in neighbourhoods where drug dealing openly occurs. Also, there are many transit countries in which violence associated with drug trafficking takes place. High levels of violence may result when one group of drug traffickers challenges another, or the State, for control of an area. When drug dealing becomes intertwined with political conflicts, horrific levels of violence may ensue.

25.   Drug-related corruption undermines national and global efforts to combat lawlessness. At the national level, corruption threatens the legitimacy of political institutions and industries. The corruption of political parties, state agencies, officials, professionals and leaders of the community obstructs political and economic development in many countries. Drug trafficking organizations understand this well and seek to undermine state capacity by means of corruption and violence. Corruption and drug-related problems are mutually reinforcing, and corruption and other social problems greatly contribute to the development of the illicit drug industry.

26.   Corruption of state officials continues to be a constant challenge in drug control efforts, undermining public welfare. States must seek ways to ensure that public and law enforcement officials, as well as politicians, can fulfil their duties honestly. Citizens need to demand more from their elected representatives and state officials. Nothing has a more debilitating effect on efforts to curtail the illicit drug trade than the successful attempts of criminal organizations to intimidate and corrupt public officials.

27.   One of the most serious challenges includes the loss of state control to organized criminal groups. Impunity and ungovernability pose a challenge to the collective security and well-being of any State, as well as the regional and global community. When state structures become involved with and affected by violence and systemic corruption, drug trafficking can further weaken the efficacy of Governments to the point of creating "failed State" conditions at the national or subregional level. Given the enormous amounts of money available to drug traffickers, law enforcement agencies are especially vulnerable to the threat of corruption, and that threat is greatly exacerbated when law enforcement agents are inadequately paid.

28.   One of the most recent challenges to the international drug control system is that posed by the use of the Internet for drug trafficking. States must do more to enable the investigation of such illegal operations in order to ensure that such operations are identified, restricted and eliminated and that the international postal system is not used for illicit drug shipments. Internet pharmacies and other dispensing methods that physically separate the prescriber or provider from the patient pose a particular risk and require the development of more effective regulatory approaches. In such systems of supply, it is more difficult for prescribers and dispensers to evaluate the needs of patients to ensure that the prescriptions will be used for legitimate medical purposes so as to protect the health and well-being of the individual. States should be mindful of the challenges that such methods for the supply of medications may pose.

F.   Supply reduction efforts and their limitations

29.   In any drug control system, supply reduction and the enforcement of regulations will always be an important element of an integrated and balanced approach. Efforts to suppress the illicit production and supply of drugs, when properly designed and implemented, are essential tools for reducing the social and health damage resulting from illicit drug markets.

30.   In recent years, some criticisms have singled out efforts to suppress the illicit supply and use of drugs, claiming that they are failed policies on the grounds that drug abuse remains prevalent. The logic behind that argument is questionable. Nobody has advocated abandoning the global response to AIDS or hunger because those problems have not been eliminated. Rather, those efforts

are held to be the more reasonable standards for improving the situation, compared with the alternative of inaction.

31.   All other things being equal, higher prices—which may result from a more restricted illicit supply due to law enforcement efforts—will lead to reduced demand. But higher drug prices can affect not only the problems associated with drug-taking but also the problems associated with drug trafficking and with law enforcement efforts. Where the extent of the trafficking falls less than proportionally to the increase in prices, more vigorous law enforcement activity may increase the total revenue available to traffickers and thus increase the incentive to engage in that illicit trade and to struggle for dominance within that trade.

32.   Law enforcement policy therefore needs to be carefully designed, keeping in mind both the objective of drug control and the possible unintended results. It is not the case that the world must choose between "militarized" drug law enforcement and the legalization of non-medical use of internationally controlled drugs. The conventions do not mandate a "war on drugs".

G.   The principle of proportionality

33.   Incorporating the provisions of the international drug control conventions into national law is subject to the internationally recognized principle of proportionality. That principle guides a State's response to acts prohibited by law or custom. When applied to the criminal justice system, the principle permits punishment as an acceptable response to crime, provided that it is not disproportionate to the seriousness of the crime.

34.   Whether or not a response to drug-related offences is proportionate depends in turn on how the legislative, judicial and executive arms of government respond in both law and practice. Given their limited resources, Governments should ensure that law enforcement and justice systems accord high priority to investigating, prosecuting and convicting the most violent of actors and those involved in the illicit supply chain, such as those who control, organize, manage or provide inputs, production and other services for drug trafficking organizations.

35.   The deterrent effect of criminalizing drug possession depends on the specific circumstances of countries. The conventions oblige States to ensure that possession

of drugs—even in small quantities—shall be a punishable offence. At the same time, the conventions offer alternatives to conviction or punishment including treatment, education, aftercare, rehabilitation and social reintegration. The 1988 Convention allows a certain flexibility regarding sanctions for possession for personal consumption, making that obligation subject to the constitutional principles and the basic concepts of the legal system of States. As the Board has stated on numerous occasions, the international drug control conventions do not require the incarceration of drug users. Rather, they oblige States parties to criminalize supply-related behaviour while encouraging them to consider prevention, treatment and rehabilitation as alternatives to punishment.

H.   Respect for human rights

36.   Drug control action must be consistent with international human rights standards. States parties need to make full use of international legal instruments to protect children from drug abuse and ensure that national and international drug control strategies are in the best interests of the child. The Board has also advised all countries that continue to retain the death penalty for drug-related offences to consider abolishing capital punishment for this category of offences.

37.   In addition to indirect and unintentional consequences for human rights via lawless, corrupt and arbitrary governance, violence can threaten efforts to safeguard human rights. This is especially true when drug trafficking and corruption weaken legitimate institutions of governance and contribute to the failure of national authorities or prevent weak States from developing robust structures.

I.   Unintended consequences

38.   There are a number of unintended consequences that can flow from a variety of factors, including the unbalanced implementation of national and international drug control measures. However, the argument that the unintended consequences of implementation of the drug control system are evidence that currently scheduled substances should be authorized for non-medical purposes is based on the incorrect assumption that those undesired consequences cannot be addressed within the framework of the international drug control system. While these consequences are unintended, they are not unexpected, and they may be prevented or managed. The challenge that States parties face is to implement their treaty obligations in a balanced way that minimizes the negative impact of drug abuse and measures to control drug trafficking, and to educate and treat victims of such trafficking.

39.   Most of the discussion surrounding the non-medical use of scheduled substances ignores the nature of drug abuse and addiction and the particularities of drug law implementation. This ignores the realities of many countries, in which the Governments are already overwhelmed by the negative effects, particularly the negative social effects, of loosely controlled or poorly regulated alcohol and tobacco products and in which narcotic drugs for medical use are either too scarce or overconsumed and abused.

J.   Conclusions and recommendations: how drug control can promote human health and welfare

40.   Drugs can be used as medicines but can also cause serious harm to health. Drug control policies can prevent harm but can also result in unintended damage. The international drug control system should therefore promote the application of scientific knowledge, humane thinking, proportionality and moderation to the set of problems related to drugs. Use of scheduled substances for non-medical purposes is not an adequate solution to the existing challenges.

41.   States parties have made important strides towards a more cohesive and coherent drug control strategy as envisioned in the conventions. However, the evolving nature of this complex social problem requires that States be cognizant of the challenges and opportunities they face. The special session of the General Assembly on the world drug problem to be held in 2016 is a timely opportunity to reaffirm drug control policies and practices grounded in evidence and science. Some of the existing policies in some countries, such as militarized law enforcement, policies that disregard human rights, over-incarceration, the denial of medically appropriate treatment and inhumane or disproportionate approaches, are not in accordance with the principles of the conventions. It is recommended that States approach this review with

the goal of reinforcing what works while modifying what does not and expanding the range of interventions to cope with new psychoactive substances, marketing technologies used to promote and facilitate drug abuse such as the use of the Internet and social media. Simplistic calls for permitting and regulating the non-medical use of scheduled substances should be seen as inadequate to remedy the drug-related problems to be faced in a globalized and unequal world.

42.   The continued threat of transnational organized crime needs to be managed in a more focused, cohesive and international manner. States need to improve the quality and transparency of government institutions and agencies so as to confront corruption. Destination countries need to assume their share of responsibility and take more effective action to suppress domestic drug trafficking and demand.

43.   States are reminded of their obligations to employ effective drug abuse prevention, treatment and rehabilitation programmes. Such programmes can involve more than drug-specific policies; interventions that strengthen social ties and individuals' capacity for self-determination and resilience tend to reduce the prevalence of drug abuse.

44.   States should provide effective and humane help to people affected by drug abuse, including both medically appropriate and evidence-based treatment. Drug users should be offered alternatives to punishment. Harsh treatment programmes, including any that involve the use of physical punishment, should be discontinued. Evidence-based treatment modalities that have been found to reduce drug abuse behaviour deserve consideration. Reducing drug abuse is a major step towards protecting and improving the health and well-being of individuals and societies. Reducing the adverse health and social consequences of drug abuse is a complementary element of a comprehensive demand reduction strategy. However, prevention of substance abuse in society in general, and in particular among young people, should remain the primordial objective of government action.

45.   The international drug control system, as established by the conventions and built upon by the relevant political declarations, provides a comprehensive and cohesive framework which can be effective only if States fulfil their treaty obligations, taking into account their domestic situation, including realities of drug supply and demand, the capacity of state institutions, social considerations and the scientific evidence of the effectiveness of existing and future policy options.

Chapter II.

Functioning of the international drug control system

A. Promoting the consistent application of the international drug control treaties

46. In its capacity as custodian of the three international drug control conventions, the International Narcotics Control Board (INCB) works closely with Governments to ensure that the conventions receive the widest possible ratification. Reflecting this fact, INCB has continued to engage the Governments of States parties and non-parties alike in an effort to promote the universal ratification and comprehensive implementation of the conventions.

47. As in the past, this has been accomplished through regular consultations in the form of sustained dialogue with Governments, including high-level meetings, country missions, extensive correspondence on technical and policy matters and the delivery of training activities.

48. INCB has urged Governments, in their implementation of the treaty obligations incumbent upon them, to take a balanced approach to the formulation of drug policy. Such an approach should have the welfare of humankind at its centre and should reflect the following imperatives: the need to control licit trade in controlled substances to prevent their diversion for trafficking purposes while not hindering their availability for legitimate medical and scientific purposes; the need to have structures in place for the prevention of drug abuse, the early identification and treatment of drug abuse and the education, aftercare, rehabilitation and social reintegration of persons affected by drug abuse; and the need to have drug policies that respect human rights and penal policies that

are proportionate and measured, in keeping with the 2009 Political Declaration and Plan of Action on International Cooperation towards an Integrated and Balanced Strategy to Counter the World Drug Problem.

Status of adherence to the international drug control treaties

49. Reflecting the widespread consensus they enjoy among States, the international drug control treaties are among the most widely ratified international legal instruments.

50. Following the accession of Afghanistan, as at 1 November 2015, the number of States parties to the 1961 Convention as amended by the 1972 Protocol was 185. Prior to that accession, Afghanistan had been a party to the Single Convention on Narcotic Drugs of 1961 in its unamended form. Chad is now the only State party to the 1961 Convention that has not yet acceded to the 1972 Protocol. Only 11 States have yet to accede to the 1961 Convention as amended: 2 States in Africa (Equatorial Guinea and South Sudan), 2 in Asia (State of Palestine and Timor-Leste) and 7 in Oceania (Cook Islands, Kiribati, Nauru, Niue, Samoa, Tuvalu and Vanuatu).

51. In 2015, the number of States parties to the 1971 Convention remained 183, with 14 States not yet parties to that Convention: 3 States in Africa (Equatorial Guinea, Liberia and South Sudan), 1 State in the Americas (Haiti), 2 States in Asia (State of Palestine and Timor-Leste) and 8 in Oceania (Cook Islands, Kiribati, Nauru, Niue, Samoa, Solomon Islands, Tuvalu and Vanuatu).

52. The 1988 Convention has been ratified or acceded to by a total of 189 States. As at 1 November 2015, nine States were not party to the 1988 Convention: three States in Africa (Equatorial Guinea, Somalia and South Sudan), one in Asia (State of Palestine) and five in Oceania (Kiribati, Palau, Papua New Guinea, Solomon Islands and Tuvalu).

53. INCB welcomes the near universal ratification of the drug control conventions by States and reminds those States that have not yet acceded to one or more of the conventions of the importance of doing so without further delay and of ensuring their comprehensive implementation within the national legal order.

B. Ensuring the implementation of the provisions of the international drug control treaties

54. The fundamental goal of the international drug control systems is assuring the health and welfare of humankind. This goal is to be achieved through two, twin actions: ensuring the availability of internationally controlled substances for medical and scientific purposes; and preventing the diversion of controlled substances into illicit channels or, in the case of precursor chemicals, for use in the illicit manufacture of narcotic drugs and psychotropic substances.

55. To monitor compliance with the international drug control treaties, the Board examines action taken by Governments to implement the treaty provisions aimed at achieving the overall goals of the conventions. Over the years, the treaty provisions have been supplemented with additional control measures adopted by the Economic and Social Council and the Commission on Narcotic Drugs to enhance their effectiveness. In the present section, the Board highlights action that needs to be taken to implement the international drug control system, describes problems encountered in that regard and provides specific recommendations on how to deal with those problems.

1. Preventing the diversion of controlled substances

(a) Legislative and administrative basis

56. Governments have to ensure that national legislation complies with the provisions of the international

drug control treaties. They also have the obligation to amend lists of substances controlled at the national level when a substance is included in a schedule of an international drug control treaty or transferred from one schedule to another. Inadequate legislation or implementation mechanisms at the national level or delays in bringing lists of substances controlled at the national level into line with the schedules of the international drug control treaties will result in inadequate national controls being applied to substances under international control and may lead to the diversion of substances into illicit channels. The Board is therefore pleased to note that, as in previous years, Governments have continued to furnish information to the Board on legislative or administrative measures taken to ensure compliance with the provisions of the international drug control treaties.

57. In its decision 58/3 of 13 March 2015, the Commission on Narcotic Drugs decided to include AH-7921 in Schedule I of the 1961 Convention as amended. In accordance with article 3, paragraph 7, of the 1961 Convention as amended, that decision was communicated by the Secretary-General to all Governments, to the World Health Organization (WHO) and to the Board on 8 May 2015, and became effective with respect to each party on the receipt of that notification. **INCB therefore requests all Governments to amend the lists of substances controlled at the national level accordingly and to apply to those substances all control measures required under the 1961 Convention as amended.**

58. The Board also wishes to draw the attention of Governments to the fact that nine substances were put under international control under the 1971 Convention by the Commission on Narcotic Drugs in March 2015. The substances concerned are 25B-NBOMe (2C-B-NBOMe), 25C-NBOMe (2C-C-NBOMe) and 25I-NBOMe (2C-I-NBOMe), which were added to Schedule I of the 1971 Convention, and AM-2201, JWH-018, 3-4-methylenedioxypyrovalerone (MDPV), mephedrone (4-methylmethcathinone), methylone (*beta*-keto-MDMA) and N-benzylpiperazine (BZP), which were added to Schedule II of that Convention in accordance with Commission decisions 58/1, 58/6, 58/7, 58/8, 58/9, 58/10, 58/11, 58/12 and 58/13 of 13 March 2015. In accordance with article 2, paragraph 7, of the 1971 Convention, those decisions of the Commission were communicated by the Secretary-General to all Governments, to WHO and to the Board on 8 May 2015, and became fully effective with respect to each party on 4 November 2015. **INCB therefore requests all Governments to amend the lists of substances controlled at the national level accordingly and to apply to those substances all control measures required under the 1971 Convention.**

59. The Board wishes to remind Governments that *gamma*-hydroxybutyric acid (GHB) was transferred from Schedule IV to Schedule II of the 1971 Convention, in accordance with Commission on Narcotic Drugs decision 56/1 of 13 March 2013. The decision of the Commission became fully effective with respect to each party on 4 December 2013. The Board notes that some States parties have not yet reflected this change in their national regulatory systems. **INCB therefore reminds all Governments of their obligations to amend the list of substances controlled at the national level accordingly, and to apply to GHB all control measures foreseen for the substances in Schedule II of the 1971 Convention, including the introduction of an import and export authorization requirement.**

60. In accordance with Economic and Social Council resolutions 1985/15, 1987/30 and 1993/38, Governments are required to introduce an import authorization requirement for zolpidem, a substance that was included in Schedule IV of the 1971 Convention in 2001. In response to the Board's request made in its annual reports for 2012 and 2013, a number of additional Governments have provided the requisite information. Thus, as at 1 November 2015, relevant information is now available for 128 countries and territories. Of those, 118 countries and territories have introduced an import authorization requirement, and 2 countries (Indonesia and the United States of America) require a pre-import declaration. Six countries and territories do not require an import authorization for zolpidem (Cabo Verde, Ireland, New Zealand, Singapore, Vanuatu and Gibraltar). Imports of zolpidem into Azerbaijan are prohibited, and Ethiopia does not import the substance. At the same time, information on the control of zolpidem remains unknown for 86 countries and territories. **INCB therefore again invites the Governments of those countries and territories to supply it with information on the control status of zolpidem as soon as possible.**

61. With regard to precursor chemicals, the Board notes that in a number of countries, the necessary legislation and control measures are still not in place or fully implemented. As a Government's domestic regulatory system is also a prerequisite for being able to notify importing countries of exports of chemicals prior to their departure, Governments are requested to adopt and implement national control measures to effectively monitor the movement of precursor chemicals. Governments are also requested to further strengthen existing precursor control measures, should any weaknesses be identified. By implementing those measures, countries will limit their exposure to the risk of being targeted by drug traffickers.

(b) Prevention of diversion from international trade

Estimates and assessments of annual requirements for controlled substances

62. The system of estimates and assessments of annual licit requirements for narcotic drugs and psychotropic substances is the cornerstone of the international drug control system. It enables exporting and importing countries alike to ensure that trade in those substances stays within the limits determined by the Governments of importing countries and that diversions of controlled substances from international trade are effectively prevented. For narcotic drugs, such a system is mandatory under the 1961 Convention, and the estimates furnished by Governments need to be confirmed by the Board before becoming the basis for calculating the limits on manufacture or import. The system of assessments of annual requirements for psychotropic substances was adopted by the Economic and Social Council and the system of estimates of annual requirements for selected precursors was adopted by the Commission on Narcotic Drugs, in its resolution 49/3, to help Governments to prevent attempts by traffickers to divert controlled substances into illicit channels. The assessments of annual requirements for psychotropic substances and estimates of annual requirements for selected precursors help Governments to identify unusual transactions. In many cases, the diversion of a controlled substance has been prevented when the exporting country refused to authorize the export of the substance because the quantities of the substance to be exported would have exceeded the quantities required in the importing country.

63. The Board regularly investigates cases involving possible non-compliance by Governments with the system of estimates or assessments, as such non-compliance could facilitate the diversion of controlled substances from licit international trade into illicit channels. In that connection, the Board provides advice to Governments on the details of the system for estimates or assessments, as necessary.

64. Governments have the obligation to comply with the limits on imports and exports of narcotic drugs provided for under articles 21 and 31 of the 1961 Convention. Article 21 stipulates, inter alia, that the total of the quantities of each drug manufactured and imported by any country or territory in a given year shall not exceed the sum of the quantity consumed for medical and scientific purposes; the quantity used, within the limits of the

relevant estimates, for the manufacture of other drugs, preparations or substances; the quantity exported; the quantity added to the stock for the purpose of bringing that stock up to the level specified in the relevant estimate; and the quantity acquired within the limit of the relevant estimate for special purposes. Article 31 requires all exporting countries to limit the export of narcotic drugs to any country or territory so that the quantities imported fall within the limits of the total of the estimates of the importing country or territory, with the addition of the amounts intended for re-export.

65. As in previous years, the Board found that the system of imports and exports generally continues to be respected and works well. In 2015, a total of 14 countries were contacted regarding possible excess imports or excess exports identified with regard to international trade in narcotic drugs that had been effected during 2014. Most of the cases were clarified as: *(a)* a result of errors in reporting on imports or exports; *(b)* substances imported for re-export; *(c)* a result of errors in the reporting of the substance or trading partner; and *(d)* seized drugs imported as court evidence. However, four countries confirmed that excess exports or excess imports had actually occurred and they were reminded of the need to ensure full compliance with the relevant treaty provisions. The Board continues to pursue the matter with those countries that have failed to respond.

66. Pursuant to Economic and Social Council resolutions 1981/7 and 1991/44, Governments are requested to provide to the Board assessments of annual domestic medical and scientific requirements for psychotropic substances in Schedules II, III and IV of the 1971 Convention. The assessments received are communicated to all States and territories to assist the competent authorities of exporting countries when approving exports of psychotropic substances. As at 1 November 2015, the Governments of all countries and territories, except for South Sudan, for which assessments were established by the Board in 2011, had submitted at least one assessment of their annual medical requirements for psychotropic substances.

67. The Board recommends that Governments review and update the assessments of their annual medical and scientific requirements for psychotropic substances at least every three years. However, 24 Governments have not submitted a revision of their legitimate requirements for psychotropic substances for at least three years. The assessments valid for those countries and territories may therefore no longer reflect their actual medical and scientific requirements for psychotropic substances.

68. When assessments are lower than the actual legitimate requirements, the importation of psychotropic substances needed for medical or scientific purposes may be delayed. When assessments are significantly higher than legitimate needs, the risk of psychotropic substances being diverted into illicit channels may be increased. In its interaction with State parties, the Board has repeatedly reminded countries that it is important that Governments estimate and assess correctly and accurately the initial needs of their country. **Therefore, INCB calls upon all Governments to review and update their assessments and estimates on a regular basis and to keep it informed of all modifications, with a view to preventing any unnecessary importation and, at the same time, facilitating the timely importation of psychotropic substances needed for medical purposes.**

69. As in previous years, the system of assessments of annual requirements for psychotropic substances continues to function well and is respected by most countries and territories. In 2014, the authorities of eight countries issued import authorizations for substances for which they had not established any such assessments or for quantities that significantly exceeded their assessments. Only two countries exported psychotropic substances in quantities exceeding the relevant assessment.

Requirement for import and export authorizations

70. One of the main pillars of the international drug control system is the universal application of the requirement for import and export authorizations. Such authorizations are required for transactions involving any of the substances controlled under the 1961 Convention or listed in Schedules I and II of the 1971 Convention. Competent national authorities are required by those conventions to issue import authorizations for transactions involving the importation of such substances into their country. The competent national authorities of exporting countries must verify the authenticity of such import authorizations before issuing the export authorizations required to allow shipments containing the substances to leave their country.

71. The 1971 Convention does not require import and export authorizations for trade in the psychotropic substances listed in Schedules III and IV of the Convention. However, in view of the widespread diversion of those substances from licit international trade in the 1970s and 1980s, the Economic and Social Council, in its resolutions 1985/15, 1987/30 and 1993/38, requested Governments to extend the system of import and export authorizations to cover those psychotropic substances as well.

72.   Most countries and territories have already introduced an import and export authorization requirement for psychotropic substances in Schedules III and IV of the 1971 Convention, in accordance with the above-mentioned Economic and Social Council resolutions. By 1 November 2015, specific information had been made available to the Board by 206 countries and territories, showing that all major importing and exporting countries now require import and export authorizations for all psychotropic substances in Schedules III and IV of the 1971 Convention. A table showing the import authorization requirements for substances in Schedules III and IV applied pursuant to the relevant Economic and Social Council resolutions by individual countries is disseminated by the Board to all Governments twice a year. That table is also published in the secure area of the Board's website, which is accessible only to specifically authorized Government officials so that the competent national authorities of exporting countries may be informed as soon as possible of changes in import authorization requirements in importing countries. **INCB urges the Governments of the few States in which national legislation does not yet require import and export authorizations for all psychotropic substances, regardless of whether they are States parties to the 1971 Convention, to extend such controls to all substances in Schedules III and IV of the 1971 Convention as soon as possible and to inform the Board accordingly.**

Developing an international electronic import and export authorization system for narcotic drugs and psychotropic substances

73.   Import and export authorizations are required for narcotic drugs in all Schedules of the 1961 Convention and for psychotropic substances listed in Schedules I and II of the 1971 Convention. Furthermore, pursuant to the relevant Economic and Social Council resolutions, Governments are urged to apply an import and export authorization requirement to substances listed in Schedules III and IV as well. As part of its endeavours to harness technological progress to the effective and efficient implementation of the import and export authorization regime for licit international trade in narcotic drugs and psychotropic substances, the Board has spearheaded efforts to develop an electronic tool to facilitate and expedite the work of competent national authorities and to reduce the risks of diversion of those drugs and substances. The new tool, called the International Import and Export Authorization System (I2ES), is an innovative, web-based application that was developed by the Board in cooperation with UNODC and with the support of Member States. I2ES allows Governments to electronically generate import and export authorizations for

licit imports and exports of narcotic drugs and psychotropic substances, to exchange those authorizations in real time and to instantly verify the legitimacy of individual transactions while ensuring full compliance with the requirements of the international drug control conventions. I2ES significantly reduces the risk of drug consignments being diverted into illicit channels.

74.   As all participating Government officials are individually pre-screened by the INCB secretariat before being given "administrator" access to I2ES, Governments can know with certainty that any I2ES-generated authorization is legitimate and authentic. I2ES automatically checks the amount(s) to be imported against the estimates and assessments of importing countries and alerts users to excess imports. I2ES also sends electronic alerts when the amounts actually received in the importing country are smaller than the amounts that were authorized for export.

75.   Designed to complement, but not replace, existing national electronic systems, I2ES is able to link with other national electronic systems so that Governments do not need to abandon their own domestic electronic monitoring systems. For countries without national electronic monitoring systems, it is possible to generate import and export authorizations in I2ES and to download and print them as necessary. The system is expected to streamline and facilitate the process of verification of import and export authorizations by the competent national authorities. In developing I2ES, the Board has ensured that the format of and the types of information to be included in those electronic authorizations meet all the requirements provided for in the international drug control conventions.

76.   I2ES was officially launched on the margins of the fifty-eighth session of the Commission on Narcotic Drugs, held in Vienna in March 2015. In its resolution 58/10, the Commission welcomed the launch of I2ES, urged Member States to promote and facilitate the fullest possible use of the system and invited Member States to provide voluntary financial contributions for its administration and maintenance. Since its launch, I2ES has been open for registration by competent national authorities. So far, competent national authorities from 15 countries (Algeria, Australia, Bangladesh, Brazil, Canada, Chile, Colombia, Germany, Malaysia, Peru, Singapore, Switzerland, Thailand, Turkey and Zambia) have registered. The Board stands ready to provide further information on I2ES to interested Governments at any time. Detailed information on I2ES is also available on the Board's website (www.incb.org), in the secure area for Governments. **INCB wishes to encourage all competent national authorities that have not yet done so to register and start using I2ES as soon as possible, as only through its widespread application will Governments be able to avail themselves**

of all the advantages that the tool provides. The Board stands ready to assist in that regard. The Board reiterates the call to Member States contained in Commission on Narcotic Drugs resolution 58/10 to provide the fullest possible financial support to enable the secretariat of the Board to continue administering and monitoring the system.

Pre-export notifications for precursor chemicals

77.   To help prevent the diversion of precursor chemicals from international trade, the 1988 Convention, and specifically its article 12, paragraph 10 *(a)*, allows the Governments of importing countries to make it mandatory for exporting countries to inform them of any planned export of precursors to their territory. The importing country has the opportunity to verify the shipment's legitimacy using that pre-export notification. Currently, 113 States and territories have invoked the provision and have formally requested pre-export notifications. Although this represents an increase compared with the previous year, there is still a significant number of Governments and regions that remain unaware of, and vulnerable to, precursors entering their territory. **INCB encourages the remaining Governments to invoke article 12, paragraph 10 *(a)*, of the 1988 Convention without further delay.**

78.   To help Member States easily provide each other with information on planned exports of precursor chemicals, the Board established Pre-Export Notification Online (PEN Online) in 2006. PEN Online allows users to raise alerts when the legitimacy of a given shipment is suspect. A total of 151 countries and territories have registered to use PEN Online, and increasing use has led to an average of more than 2,600 pre-export notifications communicated each month. The Board is aware that some countries continue to export scheduled chemicals without sending pre-export notifications via the PEN Online system, in some cases despite the fact that the importing country requires such pre-export notifications. **INCB calls on Governments to actively and systematically use PEN Online and urges the remaining States that have not registered to use the system to do so as soon as possible.**

(c)   Effectiveness of the control measures aimed at preventing the diversion of controlled substances from international trade

79.   The system of control measures laid down in the 1961 Convention provides effective protection to international trade in narcotic drugs against attempts to divert such

drugs into illicit channels. Similarly, as a result of the almost universal implementation of the control measures stipulated in the 1971 Convention and the related Economic and Social Council resolutions, in recent years there have been no identified cases involving the diversion of psychotropic substances from international trade into illicit channels. In addition, the 1988 Convention obliges parties to prevent the diversion of precursor chemicals from international trade to the manufacture of narcotic drugs and psychotropic substances. The Board has developed various systems to monitor compliance with that aspect of the 1988 Convention and has recorded limited cases of diversion from licit international trade.

80.   Discrepancies in Government reports on international trade in narcotic drugs and psychotropic substances are regularly investigated with the competent authorities of the relevant countries to ensure that no diversion of narcotic drugs and psychotropic substances from licit international trade takes place. Those investigations may reveal shortcomings in the implementation of control measures for narcotic drugs and psychotropic substances, including the failure of companies to comply with national drug control provisions.

81.   Since May 2015, investigations regarding discrepancies for 2014 related to the trade in narcotic drugs have been initiated with 32 countries. The responses indicated that the discrepancies were caused by clerical and technical errors in preparing the reports, reporting on exports or imports of preparations in Schedule III of the 1961 Convention without indicating it on the form, and inadvertent reporting of transit countries as trading partners. In some cases, countries confirmed the quantities reported by them, resulting in follow-up investigations with their respective trading partners being initiated. Reminder letters were sent to the countries that did not reply.

82.   Similarly, with regard to international trade in psychotropic substances, investigations into 549 discrepancies related to 2013 data were initiated with 74 countries. As at 4 September 2015, 28 countries had provided replies relating to 393 cases involving discrepancies, leading to the resolution of 107 of those cases. In all cases in which the data provided were confirmed by the responding countries, follow-up actions with the counterpart countries were initiated. All responses received so far indicate that the discrepancies were caused by clerical or technical errors, in most cases either the failure to convert amounts into anhydrous base or "overlapping", i.e. an export in a given year was received by the importing country only at the beginning of the following year. None of the cases investigated showed a possible diversion of psychotropic substances from international trade.

83. INCB calls upon Governments to continue to monitor international trade in narcotic drugs, psychotropic substances and precursors by using the tools mentioned above. Competent national authorities are encouraged to request the Board to assist in verifying the legitimacy of suspicious individual transactions.

(d) Prevention of diversion of precursors from domestic distribution channels

84. Diversion from domestic distribution channels has become a major source of precursors used for illicit drug manufacture, including methamphetamine. The control measures applied to domestic trade in and distribution of chemical substances often lag behind those used in international trade, and the extent of control over domestic trade and distribution varies significantly from one country to another. More information on diversion from domestic distribution channels can be found in the report of the Board for 2015 on precursors. INCB encourages Governments to actively participate in the activities under Project Prism and Project Cohesion, the two international initiatives focusing on precursors used in the illicit manufacture of amphetamine-type stimulants, and cocaine and heroin, respectively. The Board also recommends that all Governments regularly review their annual legitimate requirements for the import of pseudoephedrine and ephedrine, as published, amend them as necessary utilizing the most recent market data and inform the Board accordingly.

2. Ensuring the availability of internationally controlled substances for medical and scientific purposes

85. In line with its mandate to ensure the availability of internationally controlled substances for medical and scientific purposes, the Board carries out various activities related to narcotic drugs and psychotropic substances. The Board monitors action taken by Governments, international organizations and other bodies to support the availability and rational use of controlled substances for medical and scientific purposes.

(a) Supply of and demand for opiate raw materials

86. INCB regularly examines issues affecting the supply of and demand for opiates for licit requirements, and endeavours to ensure a standing balance between that supply and demand on the basis of data provided by Governments.

87. To establish the status of the supply of and demand for opiate raw materials, the Board analyses the data provided by Governments on opiate raw materials and on opiates manufactured from those raw materials. In addition, INCB also analyses information on the utilization of those raw materials, estimated consumption for licit use and stocks at the global level. A detailed analysis of the current situation with regard to the supply of and demand for opiate raw materials is contained in the 2015 technical report of the Board on narcotic drugs.[9] The following paragraphs provide a summary of that analysis.

88. INCB recommends that global stocks of opiate raw materials be maintained at a level sufficient to cover global demand for approximately one year, in order to ensure the availability of opiates for medical needs in case of an unexpected shortfall in production, for example, caused by adverse weather conditions in producing countries, and, at the same time, limit the risk of diversion associated with excessive stocks.

89. In 2014, the area sown with opium poppy rich in morphine in major producing countries decreased compared with the levels of the previous year in Australia and France, but increased slightly in Turkey and stayed at the same level in India and Spain. In Hungary, the actual area harvested more than doubled in 2014. The advance data for 2015 show a 12 per cent increase in the total estimated area of opium poppy rich in morphine harvested in major producing countries. That may be attributed to the expected increase in Turkey (131 per cent). In 2016, the cultivation of opium poppy rich in morphine will increase relative to 2015 in Spain, but it will decrease in most of the other main producing countries. It is expected to stay at the same level in Turkey.

90. India is the only opium-producing country that exports opium. It reduced its cultivation of opium poppy by 75 per cent in 2013, and its cultivation in 2014 remained at that 2013 level, with 5,329 ha actually harvested in 2014.

91. In 2014, the cultivation of opium poppy rich in thebaine increased in France and Spain and decreased in Australia. In 2015, the cultivation of opium poppy rich in thebaine measured in terms of area harvested is expected to decrease in Australia and to increase in Spain. France is not expected to cultivate opium poppy rich in thebaine in 2015.

---

[9] E/INCB/2015/2.

92.   The actual area harvested for opium poppy rich in codeine in 2014 was 2,117 ha for Australia and 1,859 ha for France. Both Australia and France, being the only countries among the main producers that cultivate opium poppy rich in codeine, are expected to increase their cultivation in 2015. However, Australia has forecast a dramatic decrease in the cultivation of opium poppy rich in codeine, from 5,220 ha in 2015 to 662 ha in 2016, while France has forecast an increase in the cultivation of that variety of opium poppy.

93.   The total production of morphine-rich opiate raw materials in the main producing countries increased to 534 tons[10] in morphine equivalent in 2014 and it is expected to be about 626 tons in morphine equivalent in 2015. Of that quantity, poppy straw will account for 596 tons (95 per cent) and opium will account for 30 tons (5 per cent). In 2016, it is estimated that global production will increase further, to 739 tons in morphine equivalent. In 2014, the global production of opiate raw materials rich in thebaine was 364 tons[11] in thebaine equivalent. It is expected to increase to about 376 tons in thebaine equivalent in 2015 but to decrease to about 309 tons in 2016. As in previous years, the actual production of opiate raw materials in 2015 and 2016 may differ considerably from the estimates, depending on weather and other conditions.

94.   INCB measures demand for opiates in two ways: (a) in terms of the utilization of opiate raw materials, in order to reflect demand by manufacturers; and (b) in terms of global consumption of all opiates controlled under the 1961 Convention for medical and scientific purposes.[12]

95.   Stocks of opiate raw materials rich in morphine in the form of poppy straw, concentrate of poppy straw and opium amounted to about 495 tons in morphine

equivalent at the end of 2014. Those stocks were considered to be sufficient to cover 13 months of expected global demand by manufacturers at the 2015 level. Stocks of opiate raw materials rich in thebaine (poppy straw, concentrate of poppy straw and opium) increased to about 287 tons in thebaine equivalent by the end of 2014. Those stocks would be sufficient to cover the expected global demand by manufacturers in 2015 for about 14 months.

96.   Global stocks of opiates based on morphine-rich opiate raw material, mainly in the form of codeine and morphine, held at the end of 2014 (574 tons in morphine equivalent) were sufficient to cover global demand for medical and scientific purposes for those opiates for about 17 months. On the basis of data reported by Governments, total stocks of both opiates and opiate raw materials are sufficient to cover demand for medical and scientific purpose for morphine-based opiates. Global stocks of opiates based on thebaine-rich raw material (oxycodone, thebaine and a small quantity of oxymorphone) decreased to 225 tons in thebaine equivalent at the end of 2014 and were sufficient to cover global demand for medical and scientific purposes for thebaine-based opiates for about 17 months.

97.   In 2014, global demand by manufacturers for opiate raw materials rich in morphine increased to 471 tons in morphine equivalent, but it is expected to decrease slightly in 2015, owing to the decrease in demand for opium, and then to increase again in 2016; it is anticipated to be about 460 tons in 2015 and about 480 tons in 2016. Global demand by manufacturers for opiate raw materials rich in thebaine has been decreasing since 2012, probably owing to restrictions on prescription drugs introduced in the main market (the United States). In 2014, total demand decreased to 202 tons of thebaine equivalent, from 235 tons in 2013. Global demand for raw materials rich in thebaine is expected to rise to about 240 tons of thebaine equivalent in 2015 and reach 260 tons in 2016.

98.   Codeine and hydrocodone are the most consumed opiates manufactured from morphine. Global demand for morphine-based opiates for medical and scientific purposes has increased, with fluctuations since 2010, reaching 416 tons in morphine equivalent in 2014. Demand for thebaine-based opiates is concentrated mainly in the United States and has increased sharply since the late 1990s. Similar to morphine-based opiates, the global demand for thebaine-based opiates increased in 2014, to 151 tons. Global demand is anticipated to reach approximately 160 tons of thebaine equivalent in 2015 and 180 tons in 2016.

[10] The analysis is based predominantly on raw materials obtained from opium poppy rich in morphine but includes the morphine alkaloid contained in opium poppy rich in thebaine and in opium poppy rich in codeine whenever appropriate.

[11] The analysis is based predominantly on raw materials obtained from opium poppy rich in thebaine but includes the thebaine alkaloid contained in opium poppy rich in morphine whenever appropriate.

[12] Prior to 2003, INCB measured global demand only by global consumption of major opiates controlled under the 1961 Convention, expressed in morphine equivalent. However, by using that approximation, the following were excluded: (a) demand for less commonly used narcotic drugs; (b) demand for substances not controlled under the 1961 Convention but manufactured from opiate raw materials and for the consumption of which data are not available to INCB; and (c) fluctuations in the utilization of raw materials owing to developments in the market anticipated by the manufacturers, such as expectations of sales of opiates and expected changes in the prices of raw materials or opiates.

99. The global production of opiate raw materials rich in morphine has exceeded the global demand for those raw materials since 2009. As a result, stocks have been increasing, albeit with fluctuations. In 2014, stocks decreased to 495 tons in morphine equivalent and were sufficient to cover the expected global demand for about 13 months. In 2015, global production of opiate raw materials rich in morphine is expected to exceed global demand again, with the result that global stocks of those raw materials will further increase in 2016. Stocks are expected to reach 661 tons by the end of 2015, which is equivalent to about 17 months of expected global demand at the 2016 level of demand (although not all data are available to have a complete forecast). For 2016, producing countries indicated that they plan to increase production. Stocks are anticipated to reach about 920 tons at the end of 2016, sufficient to cover several months in excess of one year of expected global demand. The global supply of opiate raw materials rich in morphine (stocks and production) will remain fully sufficient to cover global demand.

100. In 2014, global production of opiate raw materials rich in thebaine was again higher than demand, leading to an increase in stocks (287 tons) at the end of 2014, equivalent to global demand for 14 months. Production is expected to increase in 2015 and then to decrease in 2016. By the end of 2015, global stocks of opiate raw materials rich in thebaine will likely reach 423 tons, sufficient to cover global demand for about 20 months, and at the end of 2016 may reach 472 tons, sufficient to cover global demand for several months in excess of one year. The global supply of opiate raw materials rich in thebaine (stocks and production) will be more than sufficient to cover global demand in 2015 and 2016.

(b) Consumption of narcotic drugs and psychotropic substances

101. For 2014, a total of 53 Governments (of 50 States and three territories) have submitted information on consumption of some or all psychotropic substances, in accordance with Commission resolution 54/6. That is similar to the number of countries that did so for 2013. The Board is pleased to note that among those Governments are countries that are major manufacturers and consumers of psychotropic substances, such as Belgium, Brazil, China, Denmark, France, Germany, the Netherlands, South Africa, the United Kingdom of Great Britain and Northern Ireland and the United States. That development will enable the Board to more accurately

analyse the consumption levels for psychotropic substances in the countries and territories concerned and to better monitor consumption trends in countries and regions, with a view to identifying unusual or undesirable developments. INCB therefore encourages those Governments that have submitted consumption data on psychotropic substances to continue doing so, and those that have not yet done so to start without further delay. Such information would enable the Board to analyse levels of consumption of psychotropic substances in an accurate manner and to promote their adequate availability in different regions across the globe.

C. Governments' cooperation with the Board

1. Provision of information by Governments to the Board

102. The Board is mandated to publish each year two reports: the annual report and the report of the Board on the implementation of article 12 of the 1988 Convention. It also publishes technical reports that provide Governments with analyses of statistical information on the manufacture, trade, consumption, utilization and stocks of internationally controlled substances, as well as analyses of estimates and assessments of requirements for those substances.

103. The Board's reports and technical publications are based on information that parties to the international drug control treaties are obligated to submit. In addition, and pursuant to resolutions of the Economic and Social Council and the Commission on Narcotic Drugs, Governments voluntarily provide information on drug control in order to facilitate an accurate and comprehensive evaluation of treaty compliance and the overall functioning of the international drug control system.

104. The provision of data by and other information received from Governments allows the Board to monitor licit activities involving narcotic drugs, psychotropic substances and precursor chemicals. On the basis of its analysis, INCB makes recommendations to improve the system with a view to ensuring the availability of narcotic drugs and psychotropic substances for medical and scientific needs, while at the same time preventing their diversion from licit into illicit channels, as well as preventing the diversion of precursors into illicit drug manufacture.

2. Submission of statistical information

105.   Governments have an obligation to furnish to the Board statistical reports containing information required by the international drug control conventions on an annual basis and in a timely manner.

106.   As at 1 November 2015, annual statistical reports on narcotic drugs (form C) for 2014 had been furnished by 135 States and territories (representing 63 per cent of the States and territories requested to submit such reports), although more Governments are expected to submit their reports for 2014 in due course. In total, 178 States and territories provided quarterly statistics on their imports and exports of narcotic drugs for 2014, amounting to 83 per cent of the States and territories required to provide such statistics. A large number of Governments in Africa, the Caribbean and Oceania do not submit their statistics regularly, despite repeated requests by the Board.

107.   As at 1 November 2015, annual statistical reports for 2014 on psychotropic substances (form P), in conformity with the provisions of article 16 of the 1971 Convention, had been submitted to the Board by 131 States and territories, amounting to 60 per cent of the States and territories required to provide such statistics. INCB notes that the rate of submission for 2014 is similar to that for 2013. In addition, 108 Governments voluntarily submitted all four quarterly statistical reports on imports and exports of substances listed in Schedule II of the Convention, in conformity with Economic and Social Council resolution 1981/7, and a further 53 Governments submitted some quarterly reports.

108.   While the majority of Governments regularly submit the mandatory and voluntary statistical reports, the cooperation of some has not been satisfactory. Among the countries that failed to submit form P before the deadline of 30 June 2015 were major manufacturing, importing and exporting countries such as Belgium, Brazil, Canada, China, France, India, Ireland, Italy, Japan, Pakistan, Spain and the United Kingdom. At the same time, the Board notes with satisfaction that the Republic of Korea, a significant importer and exporter of psychotropic substances that did not furnish form P for the years 2011-2013, resumed reporting to INCB for 2014.

109.   The Board notes with concern that the number of countries and territories that have not furnished form P to INCB is again highest in Africa, Oceania and the Caribbean. A total of 38 countries and territories in Africa (68 per cent) failed to furnish form P for 2014 to INCB. Likewise, 50 per cent of the countries and territories in Oceania and 41 per cent in the Caribbean did not furnish form P for 2014. In contrast, form P for 2014 was furnished by all but two countries and one territory in Europe (Greece and Serbia, and Gibraltar) and by all but three countries in North and South America (Canada, Mexico and Paraguay).

110.   Difficulties encountered by Governments in submitting statistical reports to the Board may indicate deficiencies in their national mechanisms for regulating controlled substances. **INCB therefore wishes to invite Governments concerned to take steps to enhance, as necessary, their mechanisms for regulating licit activities involving controlled substances, including national systems for compiling data for the mandatory and voluntary statistical reports on narcotic drugs, psychotropic substances and precursors, and the provision of adequate training to the staff of the national competent authorities, in line with the requirements of the international drug control treaties.**

111.   The Economic and Social Council, in its resolutions 1985/15 and 1987/30, requested Governments to provide the Board with details on trade (data broken down by countries of origin and destination) in substances listed in Schedules III and IV of the 1971 Convention in their annual statistical reports on psychotropic substances. For 2014, complete details on such trade were submitted by 117 Governments (89 per cent of all submissions of form P), which is about the same as for 2013. For the other 14 Governments, there were only some missing trade data for 2014. The Board notes with appreciation that a number of countries have already been in a position to submit consumption data for psychotropic substances on a voluntary basis in accordance with Commission on Narcotic Drugs resolution 54/6. Thus, in 2014, a total of 54 countries and territories submitted data on consumption of some or all psychotropic substances. **INCB appreciates the cooperation of the Governments concerned and calls upon all other Governments to furnish information on the consumption of psychotropic substances, as such data are key to an improved evaluation of the availability of psychotropic substances for medical and scientific purposes.**

112.   With regard to precursor chemicals, pursuant to article 12 of the 1988 Convention, parties are obliged to report information on substances frequently used in the illicit manufacture of narcotic drugs and psychotropic substances. By providing that information annually on form D, Governments help the Board identify emerging trends in precursor trafficking and the illicit manufacture of drugs.

113. As at 1 November 2015, a total of 113 States and territories had submitted form D for 2014. However, 66 countries failed to meet their obligation to submit the form on time by the annual deadline of 30 June 2015.

114. Of the States and territories that provided data for 2014, 54 Governments reported seizures of scheduled substances, and 33 Governments reported seizures of non-scheduled substances, fewer than in the previous year. Many Governments did not provide details on the methods of diversion and illicit manufacture or on stopped shipments. **The Board urges Governments to put the relevant mechanisms in place to ensure that all data submitted to INCB are comprehensive and timely.**

115. On form D, Governments are urged to provide on a voluntary and confidential basis information about their licit trade in precursor chemicals. The Board requests this information in accordance with Economic and Social Council resolution 1995/20. By accessing those data, INCB is able to identify discrepancies in data reported by trading partners and help prevent the diversion of chemicals. As at 1 November 2015, 125 States and territories had provided relevant information on licit trade for the 2014 reporting period, and 98 States and territories had informed INCB about the licit uses of and requirements for some or all of those substances.

116. In 2014, the international community continued to use a variety of innovative tools to reinforce and bolster the precursor control regime. Domestic legislation or new regulatory measures were used by Australia, China, Colombia, the Lao People's Democratic Republic, Poland, Turkey and the European Union to strengthen controls over the manufacture, import, distribution, or sale of precursor chemicals.

117. The INCB Precursors Incident Communication System (PICS) is a secure online tool for worldwide information-sharing between national authorities on precursor incidents, including seizures, shipments stopped in transit, diversions and diversion attempts and illicit laboratories. Registration with PICS is cost-free and simple for Government authorities to access and use. It is now available in four languages: English, French, Russian and Spanish.

118. PICS has seen tremendous growth, both in the number of users and the number of incidents communicated, demonstrating that it is now a key tool of the international precursor control regime. As at 1 November 2015, there were more than 420 registered users of PICS from 94 countries, representing some 200 national agencies and 10 international and regional agencies. Nearly 1,500 incidents have been communicated since the launch of PICS in 2012.

3. Submission of estimates and assessments

119. Pursuant to the 1961 Convention, States parties are obliged to provide the Board each year with estimates of their requirements for narcotic drugs for the following year. As at 1 November 2015, a total of 149 States and territories had submitted estimates of their requirements for narcotic drugs for 2016, representing 70 per cent of the States and territories required to furnish annual estimates for confirmation by the Board. As was the case in previous years, the Board had to establish estimates for those States and territories that had not submitted their estimates on time, in accordance with article 12 of the 1961 Convention.

120. As at 1 November 2015, the Governments of all countries except South Sudan and all territories had submitted to the Board at least one assessment of their annual medical and scientific requirements for psychotropic substances. The assessments of requirements for psychotropic substances for South Sudan were established by INCB in 2011, in accordance with Economic and Social Council resolution 1996/30, in order to allow that country to import such substances for medical purposes without undue delay.

121. Pursuant to Economic and Social Council resolutions 1981/7 and 1991/44, Governments are requested to provide to the Board assessments of their annual medical and scientific requirements for psychotropic substances listed in Schedules II, III and IV of the 1971 Convention. Assessments for psychotropic substances remain in force until Governments modify them to reflect changes in national requirements. In this regard, the Board created a new form, entitled "Supplement to form B/P", designed to facilitate the submission to INCB by competent national authorities of modifications to assessments for psychotropic substances. The form was translated into the six official languages of the United Nations and introduced to all Governments in October 2014. A year after the official release of the form, almost all countries providing modifications to their assessments have already begun using the new form.

122. **INCB recommends that Governments review and update the assessments of their annual medical and scientific requirements for psychotropic substances at least once every three years.**

123.   Since 1 November 2014, a total of 87 countries and 6 territories have submitted fully revised assessments of their requirements for psychotropic substances, and a further 88 Governments submitted modifications to assessments for one or more substances. Governments of 23 countries and 1 territory have not submitted any revision of their legitimate requirements for psychotropic substances for over three years.

124.   **The Board wishes to emphasize the importance of determining accurate initial levels of estimates for narcotic drugs and assessments for psychotropic substances that adequately reflect actual licit needs.** If estimates and assessments are lower than the legitimate requirements, the importation or use of narcotic drugs or psychotropic substances needed for medical or scientific purposes may be delayed or impeded, whereas estimates or assessments that are significantly higher than legitimate requirements might increase the risk that imported narcotic drugs and psychotropic substances are diverted into illicit channels. **INCB reminds all Governments that they have the possibility of submitting to the Board supplementary estimates for narcotic drugs or modifications to assessments for psychotropic substances at any time during the year, whenever they find that their country's current estimates or assessments are not sufficient to cover licit needs. To be able to adequately assess their country's needs, Governments may wish to avail themselves of the** *Guide on Estimating Requirements for Substances under International Control,* **published in February 2012, which was developed by INCB and the World Health Organization for use by competent national authorities and is available on the INCB website (www.incb.org) in the six official languages of the United Nations.**

125.   The Commission on Narcotic Drugs, in its resolution 49/3, requested Member States to provide annual estimates to the Board of their legitimate requirements for substances frequently used in the manufacture of amphetamine-type stimulants, including 3,4-methylenedioxyphenyl-2-propanone (3,4-MDP-2-P), pseudoephedrine, ephedrine and 1-phenyl-2-propanone (P-2-P) and, to the extent possible, for preparations containing those substances. Those data help give the competent authorities of exporting countries indications of the needs of importing countries, thus alerting them to any potential oversupply and preventing diversion attempts. The information is provided each year on form D and can be updated with INCB at any time and is available on the INCB website. Of note in 2015 was the reduction by almost 70 per cent of the annual legitimate requirement for the import of pseudoephedrine raw material to the Islamic Republic of Iran.

126.   As at 1 November 2015, 157 Governments had provided estimates for at least one of the above-mentioned substances. It is noteworthy that the number of estimates provided by individual Governments has increased steadily over the past 10 years. The number of competent authorities of exporting countries that have consulted with the Board about the legitimate requirements of their trading partners has also steadily increased, thus indicating the value of the estimates and the increased awareness and use of this basic tool.

127.   **The Board wishes to remind all Governments that the totals of estimates of annual medical and scientific requirements for narcotic drugs, as well as assessments of requirements for psychotropic substances, are published in yearly and quarterly publications and that monthly updates are available on the Board's website.** Updated information on annual estimates of legitimate requirements for precursors of amphetamine-type stimulants is also available on the website.

4.   Data examination and identified reporting deficiencies

128.   Problems encountered by Governments in furnishing adequate statistics and/or estimates and assessments to the Board are often an indication of deficiencies in the national control mechanisms and/or health-care systems in the countries concerned. Such deficiencies may reflect problems in the implementation of treaty provisions, for instance, gaps in national legislation, shortcomings in administrative regulations or lack of training of staff of competent national authorities. **INCB invites all Governments concerned to find the causes for deficiencies in reporting statistics and/or estimates and assessments to the Board, with a view to resolving those problems and ensuring adequate reporting. To assist Governments, INCB has developed tools and kits for use by competent national authorities that are available on its website free of charge. Governments are invited to make full use of those tools in the execution of their functions under the international drug control treaties. INCB also wishes to encourage Governments to avail themselves of the specific training that is provided by INCB upon request and provide support to the Board in this regard.**

D. Evaluation of overall treaty compliance

1. Evaluation of overall treaty compliance in selected countries

129. The Board regularly reviews the drug control situation in different countries and overall compliance by Governments with the provisions of the international drug control treaties. The Board's analysis covers various aspects of drug control, including the functioning of national drug control administrations, the adequacy of national drug control legislation and policy, measures taken by Governments to combat drug trafficking and abuse and to ensure the adequate availability of narcotic drugs and psychotropic substances for medical purposes, and the fulfilment by Governments of their reporting obligations under the treaties.

130. The findings of the review and the Board's recommendations for remedial action are conveyed to the Governments concerned as part of the ongoing dialogue between the Board and Governments to enhance the implementation of the international drug control treaties.

131. In 2015, the Board reviewed the drug control situation in Ecuador, France, Jamaica, Morocco and the Philippines, as well as measures taken by the Governments of those countries to implement the international drug control treaties. In doing so, the Board took into account all available information, paying particular attention to new developments in drug control in those countries.

(a) Ecuador

132. The Board notes that the National Assembly of Ecuador adopted a comprehensive drug control law in October 2015, which will replace or supersede several legislative provisions and significantly modify the operation of the drug control system in the country. The new law provides, among other things, for the establishment of a new institutional structure for the coordination of drug control efforts in the country through the creation of an inter-institutional committee mandated with formulating and coordinating drug-related public policy. It also provides for the creation of a technical secretariat on drugs mandated with regulating and monitoring the production, manufacturing, import, export and transport of controlled substances. The law will also confer upon the National Health Authority the responsibility to establish thresholds for the possession of narcotic drugs and psychotropic substances for personal use.

133. The Board wishes to reiterate that the 1961 Convention establishes, in its article 4 ("General obligations"), that the parties to the Convention shall take such legislative and administrative measures as may be necessary to give effect to and carry out the provisions of the Convention and to limit exclusively to medical and scientific purposes the production, manufacture, export, import, distribution of, trade in, use and possession of drugs. In addition, article 3, paragraph 2, of the 1988 Convention sets forth the obligation for each State party, subject to its constitutional principles and the basic concepts of its legal system, to adopt such measures as may be necessary to establish as a criminal offence under its domestic law, when committed intentionally, the possession, purchase or cultivation of narcotic drugs or psychotropic substances for personal consumption.

134. The Board also notes that in July 2014 the Government of Ecuador adopted regulations affecting possession of narcotic drugs or psychotropic substances for personal use as published in the official gazette. Current drug control legislation criminalizes the possession of certain controlled narcotic drugs and psychotropic substances in the amounts above the thresholds set out in resolution No. 001 CONSEP-CD-2013, while possession of narcotic and psychotropic substances for personal use in quantities below those thresholds is not punishable pursuant to constitutional principles. Those principles include the supremacy of the Constitution, the right to personal development and the principle of proportionality of sanctions. In addition, the Constitution defines addiction as a public health problem and establishes the State's responsibility for the prevention of drug abuse and provides that the drug use shall not be criminalized. The Board is engaged in an active dialogue with the Government of Ecuador regarding the conformity of its legal framework on possession with its international obligations under the drug control treaties.

135. The Board notes the commitment, expressed by the Government of Ecuador, to adopting an integrated approach to ensure that controlled substances are handled effectively and that their diversion from licit distribution channels is countered through effective control measures, and urges the Government to continue to strengthen its efforts to address illicit drug manufacture, trafficking and abuse in the country.

(b) France

136. In April 2015, the French National Assembly adopted a draft bill on the modernization of the national health system at first reading. The bill was transmitted to

the Senate, examined by the Commission of Social Affairs and returned to the National Assembly for further consideration.

137.   One of the measures provided for in the draft bill is the establishment of so-called "low-risk consumption rooms" on a six-year trial basis which would begin as of the date of the opening of the first of those establishments. The Government of France has mandated the French National Institute for Health and Medical Research to conduct, at the end of the six-year trial, the preparation of a comprehensive scientific review of the impact of drug-consumption rooms on the target population.

138.   According to the French authorities, the establishment of drug consumption rooms is part of the country's "harm reduction" policy and has three main objectives: to forge links with drug users who constitute a marginalized group often having little or no contact with the formal health-care system and to bring them back into the system; to reduce the transmission of blood-borne diseases among individuals who abuse drugs by injection and reduce drug overdose cases; and to reduce the nuisance and disturbance to public order of drug abuse by injection.

139.   In the past, the Board has expressed its concern that the establishment of drug consumption rooms may not be consistent with the provisions of the international drug control conventions. INCB reminds all States that the ultimate goal of drug treatment measures should be cessation of drug use through treatment of addiction, which should be accompanied by the provision of rehabilitation and social reintegration measures. As such, any form of assistance offered to persons suffering from drug dependence should be delivered within a framework that provides for the active referral of that person to treatment services.

140.   As it does with other Governments on similar issues, the Board has actively engaged with the French authorities in an ongoing dialogue on this matter. The Board looks forward to continuing its dialogue with the Government of France to ensure that the drug control measures taken in that country continue to comply with the provisions of the international conventions.

(c)   Jamaica

141.   The Board takes note of the amendments to the Dangerous Drugs Act approved by the Jamaican Parliament in March 2015. The newly approved measures modify the country's drug control legislation to the effect that possession of up to two ounces of cannabis (56.7 grams) by an adult, including use for religious purposes, is reclassified as a non-criminal offence and will be subject to a fine. The Board notes that following the adoption of the Act, possession of cannabis in amounts greater than the defined threshold remains a penal crime and that the Government of Jamaica has stated that it is not promoting or approving the use of cannabis for recreational purposes. The Board also notes the commitment made by the Government of Jamaica to refer individuals caught in possession of less than two ounces of cannabis but who appear to be drug-dependent to a drug treatment and rehabilitation programme, as well as its planned national education campaign on drug abuse prevention.

142.   The Board underlines that the 1961 Convention establishes, in its article 4 ("General obligations"), that the parties to the Convention shall take such legislative and administrative measures as may be necessary to give effect to and carry out the provisions of the Convention and to limit exclusively to medical and scientific purposes the production, manufacture, export, import, distribution of, trade in, use and possession of drugs.

143.   The Board stresses the importance of universal implementation of the international drug control treaties by all States parties and urges the Government of Jamaica to review implementation of its obligations under international drug control treaties and ensure that implementation of domestic legislation does not contravene the provisions of the international conventions to which Jamaica is a party. The Board will continue to monitor developments in Jamaica and looks forward to continuing its dialogue with the Jamaican authorities on matters related to the implementation of the drug control conventions.

(d)   Morocco

144.   The Board notes that since its high-level mission to Morocco in 2009, there has been a heightened level of cooperation between the Government of Morocco and the Board.

145.   Morocco remains one of the world's largest producers of cannabis resin and continues to be a major source country for cannabis resin trafficked to Europe. Over the past decade, Morocco has been one of the three countries most frequently cited as source or transit countries for cannabis resin seized worldwide.

146.   Morocco has made significant efforts to counter illicit cannabis cultivation, leading to a decrease in

reported cannabis cultivation in 2014 in comparison with 2012. The Board also notes that progress has been made in addressing drug-related problems particularly with regard to the prevention and treatment and reduction of illicit cultivation and trafficking of cannabis in the country. While seizures of cannabis resin reported by the Moroccan authorities have declined significantly since 2012, the country is witnessing the emergence of the trafficking of cocaine, which is being smuggled on commercial flights from Brazil and transits through West Africa and Morocco en route to Europe.

147. The National Commission on Narcotic Drugs of Morocco has continued to adopt measures for the implementation of the international drug control treaties. Over the past two years, Morocco has extended its national action plan on drug use, creating more treatment centres throughout the country. Morocco has implemented its national action plan on harm reduction, launching new opiate substitution treatment programmes and initiating the first such programme in a prison setting. The country has released the first report of the National Observatory on Drugs and Addictions and has carried out its second national study on drug use among high-school students.

148. Morocco is currently developing a sectoral cooperation strategy for the period 2016-2021 with WHO. At a meeting of the steering committee for the development of that strategy held in June 2015, representatives of the Government and WHO discussed the modalities of the proposed strategy.

149. Despite the progress made by Morocco in its drug control efforts, several important challenges remain. The Board notes that illicit drug production in Morocco continues to pose a significant challenge to the Government's efforts to address the drug problem. The Board encourages the Government of Morocco to pursue its drug control efforts, in particular those taking aim at illicit cannabis cultivation and trafficking in the country and stands ready to assist in whatever manner it can.

(e) Philippines

150. The Board continues to engage in a constructive dialogue with the Government of the Philippines on drug-related developments in the country, with a view to promoting compliance by the Government and assisting it with meeting the requirements of the international drug control treaties.

151. The Board welcomes the adoption by the Philippines of an integrated approach to combating drug

abuse and trafficking through its national anti-drug plan of action for the period 2015-2020 and its implementation plan which covers five strategic concepts: supply reduction, demand reduction, alternative development, civic awareness and response, and regional and international strategies. This updated framework redefines the mandates of all stakeholders involved and outlines the national priority areas related to drug abuse and control.

152. In accordance with the national anti-drug plan, the Dangerous Drugs Board, which formulates the national drug-control policy, plays a significant role in realizing the objectives set forth in the Philippine Development Plan, particularly in the areas of peace and security and social development, and in international and regional agreements and declarations. The Dangerous Drugs Board provides the applicable measures for coordination, as well as monitoring and evaluation.

153. The Board acknowledges the legislative and administrative changes introduced by the Government of the Philippines to improve the effectiveness of law enforcement and expand the scope of drug control. There were significant cannabis seizures in 2014 (164 kilograms of cannabis herb and 576 kilograms of dried cannabis); 718.5 kilograms of methamphetamine were also seized. The volume of tablets of 3,4-methylenedioxymethamphetamine (MDMA, commonly known as "ecstasy") seized in 2014 was the largest total amount recorded in the country since 2002.

154. The Board notes with concern that there was also a reported increase in the abuse of amphetamine-type stimulants, in particular methamphetamine, and a high rate of HIV prevalence among people who inject drugs (46.1 per cent).

155. The Board notes that there remain challenges to be addressed, including illicit cannabis cultivation in high-altitude areas of the country that are of difficult access and are often not reached by the eradication efforts of the law enforcement authorities. The Board encourages the Government of the Philippines to take further action in this regard.

2. Country missions

156. In the context of its responsibility to promote compliance by Governments with the international drug control conventions and to monitor the functioning of the international drug control system, the Board undertakes missions to selected countries every year in order to

maintain direct dialogue with Governments on matters relating to the implementation of the provisions of those conventions.

157.   The purpose of the missions is to obtain detailed, first-hand information on the drug control policies in place in the countries visited and to discuss with competent national authorities their practical experience in implementing the conventions, including problems encountered, good practices identified and additional measures to be considered in order to optimize treaty compliance.

158.   The Board's missions are aimed at appraising the prevailing situation in the countries visited on a wide variety of drug control matters within the ambit of the drug control conventions, including national drug control legislation; the supply reduction measures in place; regulatory aspects related to the provision of estimates, assessments, statistics and trade data to the Board; the availability of narcotic drugs and psychotropic substances for medical needs; precursor chemical control; and structures in place for the prevention of drug abuse and the treatment, rehabilitation and social integration of persons suffering from drug dependency and related health conditions.

159.   In order to gain as comprehensive an overview as possible, the Board meets with senior officials from various institutional stakeholders at the political and regulatory levels within the country. In addition, the Board requests that the mission programme include visits to drug treatment facilities and social reintegration initiatives. Recognizing the important role played by nongovernmental organizations and other civil society groups, the Board carries out meetings with such entities, identified in consultation with the Vienna NGO Committee on Drugs, within the context of its country missions.

160.   Based on the outcome of meetings held and information collected, the Board issues a series of confidential recommendations on possible measures to bolster the implementation by the Governments concerned of their treaty obligations under the drug control conventions. The Board encourages all Governments to respond promptly and effectively to requests to conduct country missions, which constitute a pillar of treaty implementation monitoring.

161.   During the period under review, the Board undertook missions to Bahrain, Ghana, Honduras, Iran (Islamic Republic of), Italy, the Republic of Moldova, Timor-Leste and Venezuela (Bolivarian Republic of).

(a) Bahrain

162.   A mission of the Board visited Bahrain in December 2014 to discuss the implementation of the three drug control conventions including the legislative and institutional measures taken by the Government to control narcotic drugs, psychotropic substances and precursor chemicals.

163.   Bahrain is a party to the three international drug control treaties, and the country's primary drug legislation is Law No. 15 of 2007 concerning narcotic drugs and psychotropic substances.

164.   The national anti-drug strategy for the period 2010-2015 covers two major sectors of activity: drug supply reduction and demand reduction. The substantive areas covered in discussions with the authorities of Bahrain included the implementation of a coordination mechanism established under the chairmanship of the Ministry of the Interior at the policymaking/ministerial level to develop national drug-related policies and ensure coordination among the relevant government stakeholders.

165.   The country is also facing the emergence of new psychoactive substances. Although it has introduced some changes to its consumer safety regulations to control new psychoactive substances, none of those emerging substances are currently scheduled under the national drug control law.

166.   Challenges persist in the implementation of the drug control treaties in Bahrain, including the need for more data on drug use prevalence to inform drug control policy, and the limited availability of narcotic drugs and psychotropic substances for medical treatment.

(b) Ghana

167.   A mission of the Board visited Ghana in April 2015. Ghana is a party to all three international drug control conventions. The mission discussed with the authorities the Board's concern about the high level of imports of diazepam into the country over the past few years, inquired about the availability of opioid medications for pain alleviation and palliative care, informed the Government about INCB tools to counter trafficking in precursors and assessed the progress made by the country since the Board's last mission in 2005.

168.   In the past several years, Ghana has made significant progress in drug-related enforcement measures, as evidenced by the sound internal coordination among

different government agencies and cooperation with the international community.

169.   Diazepam consumption in recent years has remained high. The substance is controlled under the 1971 Convention and is the only anxiolytic available for medical use in Ghana. A number of control measures have been enforced by the Government to monitor the utilization of diazepam at the wholesale level.

170.   Data on drug use prevalence in Ghana continue to be limited, which may impact the adoption of evidence-based drug control policy as such information could serve as a basis for the development of pertinent demand reduction strategies and interventions.

(c)   Honduras

171.   A mission of the Board visited Honduras in February 2015. Honduras is a party to the three international drug control conventions. The mission examined recent developments in drug abuse and trafficking in Honduras, the Government's cooperation with INCB, measures taken by the Government to control narcotic drugs, psychotropic substances and the chemicals used in their illicit manufacture, and policies to reduce demand for illicit drugs and treat and rehabilitate drug users. Drug-related violence in Honduras was also discussed. The number of homicides in the country, of which a significant part are drug-related, has declined over the past two years.

172.   The most recent available data on drug use prevalence were from 2005. An up-to-date and objective assessment of the current drug abuse situation is essential to developing policies and appropriate programmes for the prevention of drug abuse and treatment and rehabilitation of those affected by drug abuse and for ensuring the efficient use of limited resources.

173.   The consumption of narcotic drugs and psychotropic substances for medical purposes in Honduras continues to be very low, which may impede access to necessary medical treatment.

(d)   Islamic Republic of Iran

174.   In May 2015, a mission of the Board visited the Islamic Republic of Iran in order to discuss the implementation by the Iranian Government of the three international drug control conventions, to which the country is a party. In particular, the mission discussed with

authorities the country's overall approach to addressing drug abuse and trafficking; the legislative and practical measures it has adopted to curb the supply of illicit drugs, reduce illicit demand and rehabilitate drug users; and its efforts to make available controlled substances for medical and scientific purposes.

175.   The Islamic Republic of Iran has adopted an integrated approach to combating drug abuse and trafficking through its national anti-drug strategy for the period 2011-2015, which covers five pillars of work: combating drug trafficking, treatment and rehabilitation of drug addicts, "harm reduction", development of alternative livelihoods, and the promotion of regional and international cooperation on issues of drug trafficking and abuse.

176.   The Islamic Republic of Iran has adopted drug control legislation, the most significant law being the Anti-Narcotics Law of 1988. The reform of the law in 2011 provided for the treatment and rehabilitation of drug addicts. The Government is currently working on new drug control legislation that would consolidate all the schedules of controlled substances.

177.   The Islamic Republic of Iran is among the countries with the greatest drug addiction problems, and there may be a need to collect up-to-date information on the prevalence of drug abuse in the country. Substantially fewer treatment and rehabilitation services are available to women compared to those available for men.

178.   The availability of narcotic drugs, in particular opioids, and psychotropic substances for medical purposes continues to be low.

179.   The Government of the Islamic Republic of Iran continues to apply corporal punishment and the death penalty for drug-related offences.

(e)   Italy

180.   A mission of the Board visited Italy in February 2015. Italy is a party to the three international drug control conventions. The objective of the mission was to review the drug control situation in Italy and the Government's compliance with the three international drug control conventions.

181.   Cannabis is cultivated in Italy within the framework of a pilot project to generate a reliable source of supply of cannabis for persons authorized to use cannabis for medical reasons. The Board encourages the

Government to proceed with the establishment of a national cannabis agency, which is required pursuant to the provisions of the 1961 Convention, as well as all other obligations related to the cultivation of cannabis, including reporting requirements.

182.   Italy has an extensive network of activities to reduce the demand for illicit drugs, with many drug prevention activities targeting selected population groups that are deemed to be vulnerable to drug abuse. Services to treat and rehabilitate drug users are available all over the country, although the level of care provided varies.

183.   Action against illicit trafficking in drugs is well coordinated, and several significant seizures of drugs have been made over the past years. Italy has also adopted a national action plan on new psychoactive substances and has established a national early warning system to be able to respond to the emergence of those substances in a timely manner.

(f)   Republic of Moldova

184.   A mission of the Board visited the Republic of Moldova in May 2015. The objective of the mission was to review the drug control situation in the country and the Government's compliance with the three international drug control conventions to which the Republic of Moldova is a party.

185.   Since the last INCB mission to the country in 1996, the Government has made significant progress in some areas of drug control. The Permanent Committee on Drug Control and the Republican Narcology Dispensary have taken measures to fully implement the provisions of the international drug control treaties. In particular, the Government has taken noticeable steps to address the emerging problems generated by increasing levels of drug abuse and the need to provide the affected population with adequate treatment, including opioid substitution therapy. In order to ensure the adoption of targeted and effective drug control policies, regular national surveys on drug abuse, particularly among youth, may be of benefit.

186.   Despite the progress achieved, significant challenges remain. The Republic of Moldova continues to be used as a transit country for illicit drug shipments and precursor chemicals trafficked through its territory to markets in Europe. The Republic of Moldova is

continuing to strengthen law enforcement, border protection, regional cooperation and information-sharing to prevent drug trafficking within and through the country.

187.   The availability of narcotic drugs and psychotropic substances used for medical purposes in the country is very low. The Government may need to assess the requirements for those substances, identify possible impediments to their availability and ensure that narcotic drugs and psychotropic substances are available to those in need in adequate quantities.

(g)   Timor-Leste

188.   The Board's mission to Timor-Leste in February 2015 was the Board's first since the country became a State Member of the United Nations in 2002. Timor-Leste acceded to the 1988 Convention in 2014 but is not yet party to the 1961 Convention or the 1971 Convention. The objective of the mission was to obtain detailed information on the Government's policy, national legislation and practical experience in the area of drug control, and to discuss obstacles to the accession of Timor-Leste to the international drug control treaties.

189.   Timor-Leste does not have a national drug control strategy in place and the country's main drug control legislation is only at the draft stage. Timor-Leste lacks an institutionalized mechanism to implement the provisions of the international drug control conventions, notably in the area of precursor control. Progress needs to be made in several areas of drug control, including ensuring availability of opioid medications; promoting rational use of opioids for palliative care and pain management; drug demand reduction, especially drug use prevention; raising awareness on precursor control; and training and capacity-building for law enforcement.

190.   The Board recognizes the efforts of and the progress achieved by the Government of Timor-Leste in building a State with functioning institutions. The Board urges the Government of Timor-Leste to accede to the 1961 Convention and the 1971 Convention and implement their provisions. Furthermore, the Board encourages the Government of Timor-Leste to take steps to draw up a national strategy for drug control and proceed with setting up a dedicated national coordinating body as envisaged in the draft drug control law. The Board also encourages the Government of Timor-Leste to adopt a balanced approach to the drug problem, to recognize the

need for demand reduction efforts and to increase awareness within its institutions, as well as civil society, about illicit drugs.

(h)   Bolivarian Republic of Venezuela

191.   INCB carried out a mission to the Bolivarian Republic of Venezuela in December 2014. The country is a party to all three drug control conventions. The objective of the mission was to review the progress made by the Bolivarian Republic of Venezuela in the implementation of the three international drug control conventions since its last mission in 2001.

192.   The Board discussed with the relevant government agencies the national drug control strategy, which is well defined and embraces the call for a comprehensive and balanced approach to drug control by devoting resources to supply reduction and by investing considerable resources in drug demand reduction.

193.   The Government's cooperation with INCB has been good, as has its compliance with the international drug control conventions. A new national drug control plan is in development. The Board notes that the Government remains committed to combating the trafficking of drugs from neighbouring countries and to continuing to effectively fund the activities of the various governmental agencies involved in drug control and prevention.

194.   The Bolivarian Republic of Venezuela aims to strengthen its regional and cross-border cooperation in tackling drug trafficking by engaging with subregional organizations and the relevant agencies of other Governments in the region. The Board trusts that the Government will continue to implement its air control and interception programme in full respect of the relevant international protocols and conventions.

195.   Several prevention activities are being implemented in the country, and the Government is taking steps to evaluate the quality and effectiveness of those interventions. The Government may also wish to take into consideration the International Standards on Drug Use Prevention prepared by UNODC in an effort to further refine the prevention strategy and approaches. The Board is encouraged by the fact that the overall level of consumption of narcotic drugs and psychotropic substances for medical use in the Bolivarian Republic of Venezuela has improved in recent years and trusts that the Government will continue its effort to ensure the adequate availability of those substances for rational medical use.

3.   Evaluation of the implementation by Governments of recommendations made by the Board following its country missions

196.   As part of its ongoing dialogue with Governments, the Board also conducts on a yearly basis an evaluation of Governments' implementation of the Board's recommendations pursuant to its country missions. In 2015, the Board invited the Governments of the following six countries, to which it had sent missions in 2012, to provide information on progress made in the implementation of its recommendations: Brazil, Cambodia, Cuba, Nigeria, Pakistan and Peru.

197.   The Board wishes to express its appreciation to the Governments of Brazil, Cuba, Nigeria, Pakistan and Peru for submitting the requested information. Their cooperation facilitated the Board's assessment of the drug control situation in those countries and the Governments' compliance with the international drug control treaties. Information from the Government of Cambodia, once received, will be reviewed by the Board and the outcome of its review will be included in the annual report for 2016.

198.   In 2015, the Board also reviewed the implementation of the Board's recommendations following its 2011 mission to Serbia, for which the information was not received in time for review in 2014. The Board wishes to express its appreciation to the Government of Serbia for the information provided.

(a)   Brazil

199.   The Board notes that, following its mission to Brazil in 2012, the Government of that country has taken substantial measures to implement the Board's recommendations in a number of areas. In order to streamline and optimize the drug control efforts of stakeholders at the federal, state and municipal levels, Brazil has created both formal and ad hoc mechanisms for increased communication and cooperation. In this regard, the Board welcomes the planned establishment of a permanent forum for the exchange of information and focal points to enhance inter-institutional dialogue between the Brazilian National Health Surveillance Agency (ANVISA) and the Federal Police. In addition, the Board commends Brazil for its efforts to engage State authorities in order to promote cooperation between them and between the various levels of government on drug control matters. Brazil has also actively initiated and participated in regional and interregional cooperation initiatives, in

particular under the framework provided by the Southern Common Market (MERCOSUR) and the Community of Portuguese-speaking Countries. In addition, Brazil has also taken steps to improve its reporting to the Board, in particular by increasing the resources of the Office of Controlled Substances.

200.   The Board commends the Government of Brazil for its efforts in the field of primary prevention, in particular for its adoption of a comprehensive drug abuse prevention programme prepared by the Ministry of Health. In order to further complement that initiative, the Board wishes to recommend that the prevention materials be supplemented with references to the dangers of psychoactive substances available through Internet pharmacies and social networking sites and with references to the dangers associated with the abuse of traditional herbal substances and new psychoactive substances. Brazil has also invested significant resources in the prevention of "crack" cocaine abuse and the study of measures for the treatment of "crack" cocaine abuse and dependence. The Board encourages the Government of Brazil to disseminate its findings with respect to treatment of "crack" cocaine addiction to the international community.

201.   The Board notes those positive developments and encourages the Government of Brazil to continue to pursue the establishment of comprehensive treatment and rehabilitation services to be offered in Brazilian prisons to inmates with drug abuse problems. The Board notes that a research programme has been launched and is jointly carried out with the National Prison Department and the Ministry of Health, in order to provide the same health services to inmates as those available to the general public. The Board welcomes that positive initiative and wishes to underline the importance of the establishment of treatment and rehabilitation programmes, tailored to the prison setting, and recalls the importance of ensuring that treatment and rehabilitation programmes are offered to inmates with drug abuse problems in all penitentiaries.

202.   The Board also notes that the Government of Brazil has reported making progress regarding guidelines for travellers under treatment with internationally controlled drugs, in particular the updating of the country's guidelines for travellers to bring it in line with the new national legislation adopted in February 2015. However, the Board underlines the importance of training law enforcement officers on the guidelines for international travellers and ensuring that those guidelines are accessible to all international travellers, especially given Brazil's status as a major tourist destination and as host country of the 2016 Olympic Games.

203.   The Board also reiterates its request to the Government of Brazil to take steps to ensure the adequate availability of controlled substances for medical and scientific purposes in the light of the actual demand of the population. For that purpose, the Board recommends that the Government of Brazil take measures to ensure the rational use of narcotic drugs and psychotropic substances for medical purposes, including the use of opioids for the treatment of pain, in accordance with the *Guide on Estimating Requirements for Substances under International Control* prepared by INCB and WHO.

(b)   Cuba

204.   The Government of Cuba has acted on the Board's recommendations following its mission to the country in 2012, and progress has been made in a number of areas of drug control.

205.   The Board notes the measures taken to consolidate the organizational structure of the Directorate of Medicines and Medical Technology and its Section for the Control of Narcotic Drugs, Psychotropic Substances and Substances with Similar Effects under the Ministry of Health, with the aim of improving availability of narcotic drugs and psychotropic substances for medical purposes. The Board notes that, based on the legislative framework established in 2014, the Analysis and Planning Department of the Ministry of Health has adopted a new system to identify the requirements of health-care establishments and pharmacies of narcotic drugs and psychotropic substances at various levels of the national health system. The Board encourages the Government to take further measures, in conjunction with the National Anaesthesia and Pain Management Group to update the range of treatment options available for acute and chronic pain and ensure the necessary availability of narcotic drugs and psychotropic substances for pain management and other medical purposes.

206.   The Board notes the measures taken to ensure security at locations where narcotic drugs, psychotropic substances and substances with similar effects are stored, produced or handled. The Board welcomes the measures taken by the Government to systematically monitor compliance with established requirements for the storage of controlled substances and redress eventual shortcomings to ensure full compliance with the established security standards.

207.   While acknowledging the country's technological limitations affecting the systematic collection, processing and analysis of drug control data, the Board invites the

Government to examine the process of reporting to the Board and ensure that information reported continues to be of good quality. Furthermore, the Board encourages the Government of Cuba to strengthen its cooperation with the Board for the control of precursors, in particular by using PEN Online for pre-export notification for shipments of precursor chemicals, pursuant to article 12, paragraph 10 *(a)*, of the 1988 Convention. The Board encourages the Government to continue its efforts in the area of drug control and to keep the Board informed of the drug control situation in Cuba and further measures taken against drug trafficking and abuse in the country.

(c)   Nigeria

208.   The Government of Nigeria has acted on the Board's recommendations following its mission to the country in 2012, and progress has been made in a number of areas of drug control. The Board notes with appreciation that the Government has initiated the development of a new National Drug Control Master Plan for the period 2015-2019, under the leadership of the Inter-ministerial Committee on Drug Control, as recommended by the Board.

209.   The Board welcomes the measures taken against illegal cultivation of cannabis plant and against drug trafficking. The drug control division of the federal police has stepped up its eradication efforts in collaboration with authorities at the state level and local communities in the areas most affected. Drug interdiction capacities at the Lagos international airport have been significantly strengthened, and operations to detect and destroy "cannabis farms" have been conducted jointly by the National Drug Law Enforcement Agency and other law enforcement agencies. Measures taken include the establishment of an inter-agency coordination team to improve operational cooperation at the airport among the relevant drug law enforcement entities, as well as capacity-building training sessions for law enforcement personnel such as police staff, airport administration personnel, regional police supervisors and customs officials.

210.   While welcoming those measures, the Board notes that continued efforts need to be made in the area of drug abuse prevention and availability of treatment, under the leadership of the National Agency for Food and Drug Administration and Control. The Board notes the plans supported by the Government to conduct a national survey on drug abuse in Nigeria, which will assist the Government in developing a drug prevention and treatment policy that reflects the needs of the Nigerian population. The Board encourages the Government to increase its efforts in the prevention of drug use, particularly among young people and to ensure that activities in this area address all commonly abused controlled substances, including pharmaceutical preparations containing such substances.

211.   The Board notes that little progress has been made in ensuring the availability of narcotic drugs and psychotropic substances for medical purposes in Nigeria. The availability of opioids for the treatment of pain in medical institutions continues to be inadequate. The Board notes that efforts are under way for the decentralization of the distribution of opioid-based medicines, in order to increase access to those substances in each of the six geopolitical zones of Nigeria, a key activity stipulated in the National Drug Control Master Plan for the period 2015-2019. The Board further notes that the Government is currently working on developing estimation guidelines to improve accessibility and rational use of controlled substances for medical purposes and at the same time prevent their diversion into illicit channels. The Board requests that the Government examine the current situation and take the steps necessary to ensure that narcotic drugs and psychotropic substances, particularly opioids, are made available for medical purposes to the entire population in need, and, in this pursuit, the Board encourages the Government to make use of the *Guide on Estimating Requirements for Substances under International Control*.

(d)   Pakistan

212.   The Board notes that some progress has been made by the Government of Pakistan in drug control since the mission of the Board to that country in 2012. The Government has introduced a number of measures to strengthen coordination among the relevant government agencies under the Drug Regulatory Authority of Pakistan, established in 2012. The Government has also strengthened its cooperation in the exchange of information on precursor chemicals with the neighbouring countries participating in several international initiatives. Pakistan has invoked article 12, paragraph 10 *(a)*, of the 1988 Convention and is actively using PEN Online to clear import and export shipments of precursors from and into the country. The Board remains concerned that information on trafficking and seizures of precursor chemicals in Pakistan continues to be limited.

213.   While drugs are widely abused in Pakistan, the extent of drug abuse in the country is not known to the authorities, as there has never been a systematic assessment of the nature, extent and patterns of drug abuse.

The Board calls on the Government to carry out an assessment of drug abuse, including the collection and analysis of data on the incidence, prevalence and other characteristics of drug abuse. Such an objective assessment is indispensable for the design of programmes for the prevention of drug abuse and the treatment and rehabilitation of drug abusers.

214.   In addition, the Board notes that little progress has been made in ensuring the availability of narcotic drugs for medical purposes in Pakistan. Allocation of opioids (morphine, pethidine and fentanyl) is made by the Narcotics Control Division of the Ministry of Interior and Narcotics Control of Pakistan based on recommendations received from provincial governments. The availability of narcotic drugs and psychotropic substances, particularly opioids for the treatment of pain in medical institutions, continues to be inadequate. The Board requests the Government to examine the current situation and take the steps necessary to ensure that narcotic drugs and psychotropic substances, particularly opioids, are made available for medical purposes and encourages the Government of Pakistan to make use of the *Guide on Estimating Requirements for Substances under International Control* in its efforts to do so.

(e)   Peru

215.   The Board notes that efforts have been made by the Government of Peru in the implementation of the Board's recommendations following the INCB mission to that country in 2012. The Board notes that the National Coca Company has adopted its institutional strategic plan for the period 2013-2017, which seeks to improve the management of the collection, processing and sale of coca leaf for legal purposes.

216.   The Board notes that increased efforts have been made in Peru to limit the cultivation of coca bush. In 2013, the area of coca bush cultivation decreased for the second consecutive year, to 49,800 hectares—a decrease of 17.5 per cent compared with the 60,400 hectares of cultivation in 2012. That decline is the most successful outcome in the past 14 years and is due to the sustained eradication and post-eradication measures carried out within the framework of the Peruvian Government's integral and sustainable alternative development programme.

217.   The Board calls on the Government of Peru to establish a system for controlling precursors and other chemicals used in the illicit manufacture of drugs. That is particularly important as Peru has already been used

by traffickers for the diversion of those substances. The Board invites the Government to further strengthen cooperation with it in the control of precursors and to provide prompt responses to the Board's inquiries on the legitimacy of orders for export of precursors to Peru, in particular by using the PEN Online system.

218.   The Board notes that further efforts need to be made to ensure the availability of narcotic drugs and psychotropic substances for medical purposes in Peru. The availability of opioids for the treatment of pain in medical institutions continues to be particularly inadequate. The Board requests the Government to examine the current situation and take the steps necessary to ensure that narcotic drugs and psychotropic substances, particularly opioids, are made available for medical purposes.

219.   Although Peru has improved its system for the treatment and rehabilitation of drug abuse, further development of the system is required to fully respond to actual demand for those services. The Board encourages the Government to increase its efforts to ensure that sufficient treatment facilities are available to cover the needs of the population. The Board also encourages the Government to take measures to increase programmes addressing prevention of drug abuse, particularly among youth, and to ensure that activities in this area address all commonly abused controlled substances.

(f)   Serbia

220.   The Board notes that since its mission to Serbia in 2011, the Government has taken steps to implement the Board's recommendations in a number of areas.

221.   The Board welcomes the adoption by the Government of Serbia of a new national drug strategy and action plan for the period 2014-2021. Moreover, the Board notes the efforts that have been undertaken to strengthen Serbia's drug addiction prevention and treatment frameworks, by including the development of rehabilitation programmes in the national drug strategy.

222.   The Board also commends the Government of Serbia for its adoption in July 2014 of the decree for the establishment of the Office for Combating Drugs to improve the coordination of governmental drug control measures and improve inter-agency cooperation. During its mission, the Board underscored the importance of the Government ensuring the adequate availability and rational use of opioids for the treatment of pain. The Board encourages the Government of Serbia to take

further action on this matter and recommends that the Government review its framework for the elaboration of estimates and assessments of controlled substances for medical and scientific purposes, taking into account the *Guide on Estimating Requirements for Substances under International Control.*

223.   The Board also continues to emphasize the importance of greater regional and international cooperation in the area of drug control and invites the Government of Serbia to continue to strengthen its efforts in this area.

E.   Action taken by the Board to ensure the implementation of the international drug control treaties

224.   The period under review in Afghanistan was characterized by the formation of a National Unity Government and the introduction of several interim measures to ensure continuity in governance, increased regional engagement and improved bilateral relations with neighbouring countries.

225.   Challenges for the implementation of the drug control treaties remain, including an increase in security-related incidents, weak border control enforcement, stunted economic development and limited human and material resources.

226.   During the period under review, drug crop eradication efforts in various Afghan provinces contributed to a 19 per cent decrease in the area under opium poppy cultivation in the country, with the total area of eradication of opium poppy cultivation increasing by 40 per cent. However, a significant amount of illicit cultivation of cannabis continued, posing a further challenge to Afghan drug control efforts.[13]

227.   Afghan law enforcement authorities continue to conduct counter-narcotics operations, resulting in the seizure of large amounts of heroin, opium and cannabis resin.

_____
[13] See also the section on West Asia in chapter III, below.

1.   Action taken by the Board pursuant to article 14 of the 1961 Convention as amended by the 1972 Protocol and article 19 of the 1971 Convention

228.   Article 14 of the 1961 Convention as amended by the 1972 Protocol, and article 19 of the 1971 Convention set out measures that the Board may take to ensure the execution of the provisions of those Conventions. Such measures, which consist of increasingly severe steps, are considered by the Board when it has objective reason to believe that the aims of the Conventions are being seriously endangered by the failure of a party, country or territory to comply with the treaty obligations contained therein.

229.   Since its establishment, INCB has invoked those provisions with respect to a limited number of States. The Board's objective in doing so has been to encourage compliance with the Conventions when other means have failed. The names of the States concerned are not publicly disclosed until the Board has decided to bring the situation to the attention of the parties, the Economic and Social Council and the Commission on Narcotic Drugs. Following extensive dialogue with INCB, according to the process set out in the above-mentioned articles, most of the States concerned have taken remedial measures, resulting in a decision by INCB to discontinue action taken under the relevant articles with respect to those States.

230.   As at 1 November 2015, Afghanistan was the only State regarding which action was being taken pursuant to article 14 of the 1961 Convention as amended by the 1972 Protocol.

2.   Consultation with the Government of Afghanistan pursuant to article 14 of the 1961 Convention as amended by the 1972 Protocol

231.   Consultations between the Board and the Government of Afghanistan pursuant to article 14 of the 1961 Convention as amended by the 1972 Protocol have continued in 2015.

232.   On the margins of the fifty-eighth session of the Commission on Narcotic Drugs, held in Vienna from 9 to 17 March 2015, the President of the Board met with the delegation of Afghanistan, which was headed by the Minister of Counter Narcotics. The Minister provided the Board with information on measures taken by the

Government of Afghanistan to address the drug control situation in the country, including the planned establishment of a new faculty of drug education; the development of alternative livelihood programmes; the continued action aimed at countering opium poppy cultivation and trafficking; the strengthening of regional cooperation and enforcement measures to address the trafficking of precursors; and the establishment of good governance principles. The Government representatives acknowledged the need for greater investment in drug treatment and rehabilitation and the importance of breaking the cycle of poverty and political instability affecting Afghanistan. Furthermore, they highlighted the need for greater resources to reduce cannabis cultivation, the need to enhance regional cooperation to address drug abuse in the country and the need for technical assistance to enhance capacity-building.

233.   In June 2015, an Afghan delegation headed by the Minister of Counter Narcotics briefed the Board on recent developments with respect to drug control in Afghanistan. Among the issues discussed were the development and implementation of a new counter-narcotics strategy, progress made in the Government's opium poppy eradication efforts, legislative amendments to the country's drug control legal framework and the further implementation of demand reduction activities. The Minister also briefed the Board on the Government's continued efforts to stem the cultivation of opium poppy through assistance to farmers in the form of alternative development and through improving security, good governance and community mobilization.

234.   INCB has continued to engage the Government of Afghanistan in the planning of its high-level mission to the country, scheduled to take place in 2016, during which consultations under article 14 of the 1961 Convention as amended by the 1972 Protocol will be continued. The Board has also continued its dialogue with the Government of Afghanistan through regular contact between its secretariat and representatives of the Permanent Mission of Afghanistan to the United Nations (Vienna) to follow up on the Government's implementation of the international drug control treaties and the upcoming high-level mission to the country.

Cooperation with the Board

235.   In recent years, there has been continued cooperation on the implementation of the international drug control treaties between the Government of Afghanistan and the Board.

236.   The Government has substantially improved its reporting performance since 2010, submitting data to INCB regularly, as required under the international drug control treaties.

237.   In February 2015, Afghanistan acceded to the 1972 Protocol amending the 1961 Convention, a development welcomed by the Board.

238.   In June 2015, the Government submitted its 2014 report to the Board, reflecting the Government's efforts to comply with their reporting requirements with regard to the implementation of the international drug control treaties and relating to its efforts to facilitate the delivery of the required technical assistance.

239.   INCB notes an increase in the counter-narcotics operations led by Afghan law enforcement authorities. However, the lack of budgetary allocation for addressing the cultivation of cannabis plant in the country remains a challenge.

Cooperation with the international community

240.   The Government of Afghanistan has continued to take steps to enhance regional and international cooperation to address the drug-related threats affecting the country. Afghanistan pursued its engagement with Afghan national ethnic groups and regional interlocutors to promote national reconciliation.

241.   In terms of interregional cooperation, successful global and interregional activities undertaken in the past few years continued, including the Paris Pact Initiative, a well-established key international partnership to counter the trafficking in and consumption of opiates originating in Afghanistan. In addition, the United Nations Office on Drugs and Crime (UNODC) Global Programme against Money-Laundering, Proceeds of Crime and the Financing of Terrorism continued to assist the national authorities of Afghanistan and neighbouring countries in collecting information on illicit financial flows linked to Afghan opiates.

242.   Contact was made several times at a high level between Afghanistan and Pakistan, in particular between officials from both countries responsible for implementing the relevant provisions of international treaties, in order to strengthen their bilateral relationship and demonstrate the will of both countries to enhance cooperation. This cooperation is particularly important, as large-scale cross-border population movements continue as a result of military operations in the North Waziristan Region of Pakistan.

243. At the fifty-eighth session of the Commission on Narcotic Drugs, the Executive Director of UNODC presented a report entitled "Strengthening international cooperation in combating illicit opiates originating in Afghanistan through continuous and reinforced support to the Paris Pact initiative" (E/CN.7/2015/12). The report describes steps taken by UNODC, as a technical assistance provider, towards the implementation of resolution 56/3 throughout the first year of the fourth phase of the initiative, entitled "Reducing drug abuse and dependence through a comprehensive approach".

244. In March 2015, the President of Afghanistan and the President of the United States released a joint statement announcing a new development partnership, through which up to $800 million in bilateral economic assistance would be earmarked for Afghan development and reform priorities. The parties also announced that the United States would maintain a military presence of 9,800 troops in Afghanistan until the end of 2017.

245. Ministers for foreign affairs discussed the situation in Afghanistan during meetings of the Collective Security Treaty Organization and of the Commonwealth of Independent States, both held in April 2015. Also in April 2015, experts from Afghanistan, Pakistan and Tajikistan met in Dushanbe, where they finalized the draft Trilateral Transit Trade Agreement. In the same month, the President of Afghanistan visited the Islamic Republic of Iran. The two countries pledged to increase cooperation in the area of counter-narcotics.

246. During the first quarter of the year, several initiatives were implemented involving the participation of international bodies such as the Organization for Security and Cooperation in Europe, the United Nations Regional Centre for Preventive Diplomacy in Central Asia and the United Nations Counter-Terrorism Implementation Task Force. Other examples of initiatives to combat money-laundering are the Criminal Assets Southern Hub (CASH), which is aimed at countering illicit money flows and confiscating the assets of drug trafficking networks in Afghanistan and neighbouring countries, and the Southern Trafficking Operational Plan (STOP), which is focused on interdiction efforts within the Triangular Initiative, involving Afghanistan, Iran (Islamic Republic of) and Pakistan.

247. In September 2015, the Minister of Counter-Narcotics of Afghanistan gave a briefing at UNODC headquarters in Vienna on the current drug control situation in Afghanistan and on the measures taken and progress made under article 14 of the 1961 Convention as amended, as well as the main challenges and trends that the country faces. The Minister also presented an overview of the Afghan counter-narcotics strategy, a cornerstone of the national development agenda. The strategy acknowledges the links between counter-narcotics and the need to address the financing of terrorism and the challenges related to border management. The Minister announced that her country's action plan would be released shortly and reiterated Afghanistan's commitment to implementing drug control measures through a multidimensional approach incorporating development considerations and international cooperation.

248. Improved coordination of regional bodies was fostered through the initiatives of the Afghanistan National Disaster Management Authority, supported by Japan under the Heart of Asia-Istanbul Process confidence-building measures. The National Intelligence Working Group on Precursors continued to support inter-agency cooperation in strengthening precursor control and information-sharing in the country.

249. Cooperation by the international community involves all relevant stakeholders in the country, including non-governmental organizations and civil society groups. The civil society-led Afghan People's Dialogue on Peace commenced its third phase of activities, focusing on convening policymakers and civil society organizations to assist in the implementation of national and provincial road maps for peace. Facilitation continues to be provided by the United Nations Mission in Afghanistan.

250. New regional criminal intelligence centres, modelled upon good practices from the International Criminal Police Organization (INTERPOL), the European Police Office (Europol) and the World Customs Organization (WCO), have been established in the Central Asian Regional Information and Coordination Centre and the Criminal Information Centre to Combat Drugs of the Cooperation Council for the Arab States of the Gulf, together with a joint planning cell covering Afghanistan, Iran (Islamic Republic of) and Pakistan.

251. Regional cooperation remains a crucial element in reinforcing the likelihood of success of Afghan-led reconciliation efforts, political stability and sustainable economic development.

Conclusions

252. Afghanistan continued to face major challenges in the period under review despite the decrease in illicit opium poppy cultivation reported in 2015.

253. Other challenges remain, such as the transition of security functions from international military forces to the national army and police, the ongoing national reconciliation process, the impact of conflict and the limited capacity of the Government to give priority attention to the increasing levels of drug trafficking and abuse in the country.

254. Despite those challenges, the Government has invested in an increase in licit crop cultivation, primarily in areas which are relatively poppy-free, and has expressed its commitment to addressing the illicit cultivation of opium poppy and cannabis plant in the country. It has also expressed its commitment to addressing drug trafficking and drug abuse through eradication campaigns, law enforcement measures, alternative livelihood initiatives and international cooperation at the regional and global levels. The Government has been fully cooperative with the Board, including through its readiness to facilitate a high-level mission of INCB to Afghanistan and its submission of a progress report on the drug-related situation in the country. INCB notes the increased engagement of the Government of Afghanistan with neighbouring countries during the reporting period.

255. While noting the progress made in Afghanistan over the last year, the Board remains concerned about the significant challenges surrounding the drug control situation. INCB asks the Government of Afghanistan to continue to keep it informed of developments with regard to the adoption and implementation of new national counter-narcotics policies. The Board recommends that the Government of Afghanistan continue strengthening its counter-narcotics capacity by drawing on specialized international technical assistance to address the drug problem and to strengthen its cooperation at the regional and international levels.

256. The Board encourages the Government of Afghanistan to strengthen its efforts to address widespread drug abuse in the country through the adoption of measures aimed at prevention, treatment, rehabilitation and aftercare for affected individuals. INCB notes the fundamental role played by alternative development initiatives in curbing opium poppy cultivation and providing farmers with legitimate means for supporting themselves and their families. INCB calls upon members of the international community to continue to support the Government of Afghanistan in its drug control and development efforts. INCB will continue to closely monitor the drug control situation in Afghanistan in cooperation with the authorities, as well as measures taken and progress made by the Government of Afghanistan in all

areas of drug control. To that end, the Board looks forward to its mission to Afghanistan in 2016.

F. Special topics

1. Precursor control: new developments, challenges and the way forward

257. Measures to monitor trade in precursor chemicals and prevent their diversion into illicit channels are key components of all strategies to prevent or curb illicit manufacture of and trafficking in narcotic drugs and psychotropic substances.

258. The mechanism for the monitoring of licit trade and the prevention of diversion is laid down in article 12 of the 1988 Convention, which has been complemented over the years by a series of resolutions at various levels of the international drug control system. The fundamental assumption underlying the system of international precursor control is that chemicals that can be used as drug precursors are licit commodities and that any transaction involving them is therefore presumed to be legitimate unless there is suspicion or evidence that the chemical concerned is to be used for illicit purposes. As such, "the procurement of chemicals necessary to manufacture drugs is one of the few points ... where drug trafficking intersects with legitimate commerce. Regulation of legitimate commerce to deny traffickers the chemicals they need is one of our most valuable tools in the battle against drug criminals."[14]

259. INCB has reviewed the achievements, progress and challenges of international precursor control in its annual reports on precursors.[15] Over the past 25 years, since the entry into force of the 1988 Convention on 11 November 1990, States have succeeded, through the Convention and the oversight work undertaken by INCB, in substantially reducing the diversion of substances listed in Tables I and II of the 1988 Convention from international trade into illicit drug manufacture. After a quarter of a century, the 1988 Convention enjoys near universal adherence by States worldwide. Through its provisions and requirements, the Convention has served to establish, in

---

[14] Chemical Action Task Force, *Status Report for the 1992 Economic Summit* (Washington, D.C., June 1992), p. 11.

[15] See E/INCB/2011/4, E/INCB/2012/4, E/INCB/2013/4 and E/INCB/2014/4.

partnership with industry, the infrastructure for the control of precursor chemicals. To support the monitoring of the licit trade in precursor chemicals and to prevent their diversion into illicit channels, INCB has developed electronic tools such as PEN Online and PICS, which are available to all States upon request at no cost. These tools have served the international community well in preventing illicit drug manufacture and the diversion of controlled chemicals.

New developments and challenges

260.   In reviewing the effectiveness of international precursor control, INCB has also identified remaining gaps and has concluded that the key challenges facing precursor control today are a result of the following:

(a)   The lack of comprehensive and systematic implementation of the provisions of the 1988 Convention and related resolutions of the General Assembly, the Economic and Social Council and the Commission on Narcotic Drugs;

(b)   The emergence of new challenges not comprehensively addressed in the existing legal framework.

261.   That the implementation of existing treaty provisions could be further improved is reflected in the fact that 150 Governments have registered for use of PEN Online, the automated global online system for the exchange of pre-export notifications, but only 109 Governments have requested to be pre-notified of some or all planned shipments to their territories.[16] Considering that the international precursor control system focuses on the monitoring of international trade, it is now evident that in the past, insufficient attention had been placed on national controls and on the monitoring of domestic movements and the end use of precursor chemicals. INCB estimates that, depending on the specific precursor or group of precursors, between 30 and 95 per cent of all seizures reported are of substances originating within the country of seizure; in other words, those diversions are occurring outside the international precursor trade monitoring system. While serving as a reminder of the need for further action at the national level, those statistics are at the same time a reflection of the successes in preventing diversion at the international level.

262.   One of the largest new challenges today is the emergence of non-scheduled substitute chemicals, including "designer precursors", to circumvent controls. In recent years, an increasing variety of such "designer" chemicals has emerged, typically manufactured on a made-to-order (demand) basis. The manufacture of those non-scheduled chemicals is, in itself, legal according to the existing international legal framework, although those chemicals are sourced with no other purpose than for use in illicit drug manufacture. Many of the chemicals are derivatives or common intermediates in regular drug synthesis that can be easily converted into a controlled precursor; many have no regular legitimate commerce or use, thus creating a challenge for the existing control system due to the sheer number of possible chemical starting materials and because the sourcing of those chemicals further blurs the area where drug trafficking intersects with legitimate commerce.

263.   A second, related challenge identified by INCB is that posed by the great increase in the sophistication, diversification and scale of illicit synthetic drug manufacturing operations. As a result, there are virtually no limitations to the range of chemicals and manufacturing methods that can potentially be employed in illicit manufacture, including chemicals and methods that had previously been considered to be impracticable in illicit settings. Sophisticated, industrial-scale illicit manufacturing operations have been dismantled in all regions with the exception of Africa and most parts of Oceania. Such laboratories are the source of a significant portion of the illicit worldwide supply of synthetic drugs, while small-scale manufacture continues to supply markets of a more local nature.

264.   The emergence of what are known as synthetic new psychoactive substances[17] adds a potentially unlimited number of chemicals to those already being monitored in connection with the illicit manufacture of drugs under international control. However, the concepts and approaches developed in connection with monitoring non-scheduled chemicals could also be directly applied to address precursors of new psychoactive substances.[18]

---

[17] Although there is no universally accepted definition of new psychoactive substances, broadly they are referred to as substances of abuse, in either a pure form or a preparation, that are not controlled under the 1961 Convention or the 1971 Convention but which may pose a public health threat. New psychoactive substances can be man-made, synthetic substances or natural materials.

[18] They could also possibly apply to new psychoactive substances end products which are—from a chemical and control point of view—another set of non-scheduled substances, often with no known legitimate use other than in small amounts for research and laboratory analysis purposes.

---

[16] Importing countries can make it mandatory for exporting countries to inform them prior to a planned export by invoking article 12, paragraph 10 (a), of the 1988 Convention.

265. Challenges are also evident in relation to heroin and cocaine manufacture. Especially in the case of cocaine manufacture, the chemicals and processes now being used increase manufacturing efficiency and reduce the amount of chemicals required. With regard to the sources of the chemicals used, there are still significant information gaps. What seems to be clear, however, is that the majority of those chemicals are either sourced from within the country of drug manufacture or are sourced from another country within the same region and then smuggled to the country of manufacture. For example, more than 80 per cent of potassium permanganate, the key oxidizer used in illicit cocaine manufacture, and more than 90 per cent of solvents originate within the country of seizure.[19] For acetic anhydride, the key chemical for heroin manufacture, available data suggest that more than 80 per cent of the substance can be traced to other countries within the same region.[20] Further, there have been no reports of the diversion of potassium permanganate or acetic anhydride from international trade in more than five years.

266. Other developments posing a challenge for precursor control efforts at the national, regional and international levels are a consequence of the improvements in global communication, transportation and trade facilitation. An area of increasing concern is the growth of free trade zones and free ports, which often lack sufficient transparency. Another fact of modern life is the increase in the number and geographic extent of trade and customs unions.

The way forward: areas for action

267. In view of these developments, INCB has identified a set of priority actions for Governments,[21] including the following:

(a) *Public-private partnerships.* All national authorities should adopt the concept of making industry a critical partner in the prevention of chemical diversion and formalize their commitment to such partnerships; industries and industry associations should incorporate the principles of chemical diversion prevention as integral components of corporate industry responsibility, accountability and credibility;

(b) *National regulatory controls.* Governments should review the effectiveness of their national chemical control systems and work to close any gaps in those domestic systems and make them fit their purpose;

(c) *Law enforcement.* Governments should provide their law enforcement authorities with the legal framework enabling them to take appropriate law enforcement action, where required. (The 1988 Convention provides guidance to develop national legislation to that effect for substances in Tables I and II and, in combination with article 13, for non-scheduled chemicals.) Law enforcement authorities should pay more attention to precursor chemicals used in illicit manufacture by investigating seizures, stopped shipments and attempted diversions in order to identify the sources of diversion and the criminal organizations behind those activities, and share their findings globally to prevent future diversions using similar modi operandi.

268. The special session of the General Assembly on the world drug problem to be held in 2016 provides an opportunity to recall the fundamental basis of precursor control, namely, international cooperation to prevent chemicals from being used in the manufacture of substances of abuse. The special session also provides an opportunity to acknowledge that the existing control system, which is based on the monitoring of licit trade, has a limited ability to deal and keep pace with large numbers of emerging chemicals, including series of related chemicals and "designer" chemicals, largely as most of these chemicals are without legitimate use and/or trade.

269. On the basis of those insights, INCB hopes that Governments will make use of the special session of the General Assembly in 2016 to reconfirm the importance of precursor control as a preventive component in a balanced drug control strategy. The Board also hopes that Governments will demonstrate the political will to accept a shared responsibility for precursor control, as there is virtually no country in which chemicals are not either manufactured, domestically distributed, used, imported, exported or re-exported or through which they transit. Finally, the special session in 2016 will provide the opportunity to lay the bases for a forward-looking strategy that addresses the limitations of the existing system, mainly in relation to non-scheduled chemicals, including "designer precursors" and precursors of new psychoactive substances. Concepts are available, such as those known as "immediate precursors" and the reversal of the burden of proof, which bring to life the spirit of article 12 of the 1988 Convention without overburdening authorities and industry.

---

[19] E/INCB/2014/4, figure V.

[20] E/INCB/2014/4, figure XVI.

[21] Technical details are contained in the 2015 report on precursors (E/INCB/2015/4) and the reports of previous years.

2. The use of benzodiazepines among older adults

270. According to the WHO Global Health Observatory, global life expectancy at birth has increased by six years since 1990. In 2013, the global population aged 60 years could expect to live another 20 years on average, 2 years longer than in the 1990s. Life expectancy at age 60 in high-income countries was six years longer than that in low-income and lower-middle-income countries. Furthermore, according to the Population Division of the Department of Economic and Social Affairs of the Secretariat, the percentage of the global population aged 60 and over increased from 8.5 per cent in 1980 to 12.3 per cent in 2015. This upward trend is expected to continue (see figure 1).

Figure 1. Percentage of the population aged 60 and over, estimated for 1980-2015 and projected to 2050

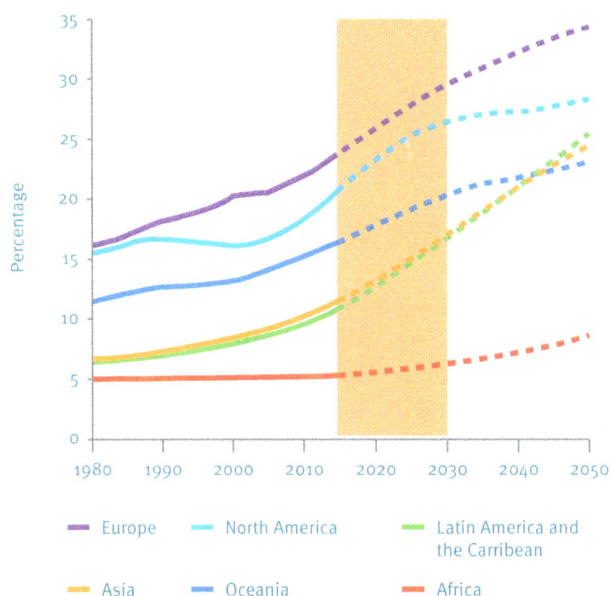

Ageing is not a disease

271. Ageing is by no means an illness. However, old age is often accompanied by illness. Illness affects older people more because it comes on top of changes in their health resulting from normal ageing. In older people, the distinction between healthy and sick is much more difficult to make, which increases the likelihood that they are overmedicated, undermedicated or medicated unnecessarily.

272. Older people often face isolation and loneliness. They often suffer from chronic illness and certain conditions associated with ageing such as Alzheimer's disease, anxiety, insomnia, depression and dementia, and co-morbidity is common. Their sleeping patterns are different from those of younger people, and insomnia seems common among otherwise healthy individuals aged 65 and older, making them an attractive target group for manufacturers of sleeping pills. There are concerns that insomnia is being treated excessively as a result. This could be dangerous, as the elderly generally have more medical problems, and many of them take medications for more than one condition.

273. In most cases, the treatment of insomnia in older patients involves psychosomatic therapy and requires prescription drugs, in particular anxiolytics and hypnotics. Furthermore, given the demographic changes and the ageing of the population worldwide, the proportion of older patients undergoing surgery and therefore anaesthesia is increasing.

274. Pharmaceutical preparations containing benzodiazepines have been proved effective. Hypnotics, sedatives and anxiolytics are an essential part of health care, and they are prescribed worldwide to patients of all ages. Benzodiazepines have a wide range of indications; they are prescribed as hypnotics, sedatives, muscle relaxants and anxiolytics, as well as for pre-medication (prior to surgical procedures) and the induction of general anaesthesia. There are currently 35 benzodiazepines under international control, almost all of which are listed in Schedule IV of the 1971 Convention.

275. When they are well prescribed, benzodiazepines are considered relatively safe, as they are effective, fast-acting, have low toxicity and can be prescribed to patients of all ages. However, as with any medicine, their use also carries the risk of side effects and toxic reactions, particularly among the elderly. The elderly are more prone to adverse reactions because they tend to eliminate medication more slowly and for that reason often need lower doses.

Overuse and unwarranted use

276. In the United States of America, people aged 65 and over make up about 10 per cent of the total population, yet they account for 30 per cent of medical prescriptions. The discrepancy is wider than the figures suggest, because the elderly are more sensitive to medication and therefore need less of it.

277. According to the information available to the Board, the overall manufacture of benzodiazepine-type sedative hypnotics and anxiolytics and their global calculated consumption in absolute terms have been stable in recent years. Since 2000, manufacture of these substances has stood at around 30 billion defined daily doses for statistical purposes (S-DDD) with consumption rates at similar levels, despite an increasing number of older patients (see figure 2).

278. Europe has traditionally been the region with the highest calculated average national consumption rates for benzodiazepine-type anxiolytics. In 2014, the United States, Brazil, Spain, Japan, France, Italy, Argentina, Germany and the United Kingdom (in descending order) were the largest consumers of benzodiazepine-type anxiolytics in absolute terms. Recently there have been reports from the United States about widespread overuse, under medical supervision, of psychoactive drugs among elderly people suffering from dementia.

Figure 2.   Global manufacture and calculated consumption of benzodiazepines (anxiolytics and sedative-hypnotics)

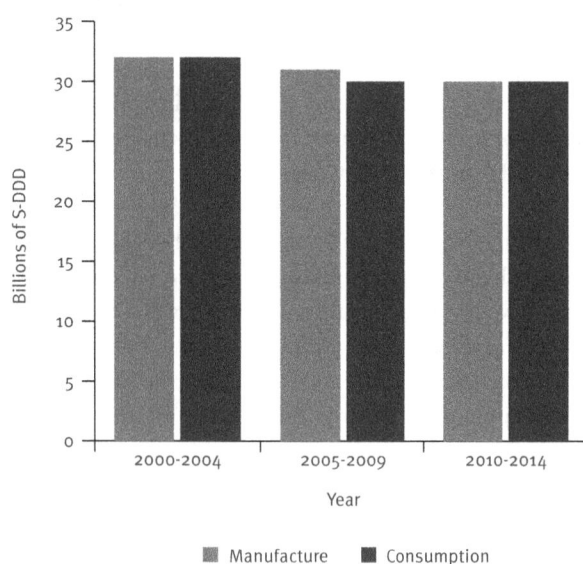

Hazardous use

279. The debate about the use of benzodiazepines among older people is not new. Numerous studies on the consequences of unwarranted and chronic use among older adults have highlighted the risk of drug dependence.

280. A recent Japanese study showed that the prevalence of prescriptions for hypnotics and anxiolytics is disproportionately high among elderly patients. The study also showed that the simultaneous prescription of anxiolytics and hypnotics in high doses is common among patients suffering from sleep and/or anxiety disorders, that more than half of the prescriptions in question are issued by physicians, and that the long-term prescription of benzodiazepines is still widespread in spite of international clinical guidelines recommending benzodiazepine treatment to be limited to only a few weeks (two to four weeks).

281. The unwarranted prescribing and use of benzodiazepines by older patients is not harmless. A French study suggests that benzodiazepines are associated with an increased risk of dementia. The study found that patients over the age of 65 who start taking benzodiazepines had a 50 per cent higher chance of developing dementia within 15 years, compared to people who had never used them.

282. With an increased sensitivity to benzodiazepines and a slower metabolism, older patients are at high risk of developing delirium and cognitive impairment, and are more susceptible to falls and fractures. Moreover, long-term use of benzodiazepines is commonly associated with withdrawal syndrome.

Sensible use for better care

283. In its 2012 update of the Beers criteria for potentially inappropriate medication use in older adults, the American Geriatrics Association recommended avoiding all benzodiazepines in the treatment of insomnia, agitation or delirium. Furthermore, successful treatment discontinuation may result in improvement of cognitive and psychomotor function, particularly in older people.

284. As already noted, the Board fully recognizes that hypnotics, sedatives and anxiolytics containing controlled benzodiazepines have been proved to be effective and are essential in medical practice and health care. **However, the Board calls on all Governments to be alert to adverse reactions and problems resulting from the misuse and overuse of benzodiazepines, particularly among older adults. INCB calls on the Governments concerned to adopt, where necessary, measures to prevent the over-prescription and misuse of sedative-hypnotics and anxiolytics containing benzodiazepines among older patient groups.**

285. To avoid the harmful side effects of benzodiazepines, Governments must ensure that health-care

providers carefully consider the risk-benefit ratio, safety, adverse drug reactions and the simultaneous use of other drugs before prescribing any medications containing benzodiazepines to older patients. Guidelines for clinical care and training should be made available to health-care providers, in particular in nursing homes and geriatric care facilitates. Other measures may involve raising awareness of the risks associated with inappropriate use of benzodiazepines, targeting, in particular, family members of elderly patients, their caregivers, nursing staff and employees at residential facilities for the elderly.

3. New psychoactive substances

286.   New psychoactive substances are a very heterogeneous group of substances that, in different forms, continues to grow in every region of the world. As at October 2015, the UNODC early warning advisory on new psychoactive substances, which monitors the emergence of new psychoactive substances as reported by Member States, had identified 602 unique substances, a 55 per cent increase from the 388 substances reported in October 2014.

287.   As in the past, the most reported substances continued to be synthetic cannabinoids, which accounted for nearly 40 per cent of all the substances reported, and phenethylamines and synthetic cathinones, which together accounted for about one third of all substances. While the number of new psychoactive substances continues to grow, not all those substances become established substances of abuse. In fact, many may be encountered only once.

288.   The definition of "new psychoactive substances" used for the purposes of the early warning advisory encompasses both synthetic and plant-based substances (such as khat (*Catha edulis*), kratom (*Mitragyna speciosa*) and *Salvia divinorum*), as well as substances with established medical uses (e.g., ketamine). What all new psychoactive substances have in common is not necessarily that they have recently been invented but that they have recently emerged on the market and have not been scheduled under the international drug control conventions.

289.   INCB uses the same definition, except that it focuses on synthetic substances of abuse with little or no known medical or industrial use. The Board believes that these substances pose particular challenges, given the various possible modifications that can be made to them to circumvent existing legislation and the lack of knowledge about their health effects.

290.   In the light of the number and transient nature of many of the new psychoactive substances, as has been previously noted,[22] INCB is providing Member States with the infrastructure, known as Project Ion (international operations on new psychoactive substances) for real-time information-sharing on incidents involving new psychoactive substances (e.g., suspicious shipments, trafficking, or manufacture or production, for any new psychoactive substance), as well as follow-up between authorities of the countries concerned with a view to assisting investigations and devising practical solutions aimed at preventing those substances from reaching consumer markets. The task force on new psychoactive substances, which steers Project Ion activities, held two meetings in 2015.

291.   Since the Board's annual report for 2014, the global focal point network on new psychoactive substances for Project Ion expanded to 120 countries, in every region of the world. A special operation, Operation Postman, conducted in March and April 2015, focused on postal and express courier shipments containing non-scheduled synthetic new psychoactive substances. Forty-one countries worldwide participated, resulting in the communication of nearly 200 individual incidents involving some 70 different new psychoactive substances.

292.   In December 2014, the Project Ion Incident Communication System (IONICS) was launched, a secure platform dedicated to the real-time communication of incidents involving suspicious shipments, trafficking, manufacture or production of new psychoactive substances. After just under one year of operation, in November 2015, the system had more than 170 users from 60 countries in all regions of the world (see map below). There have been more than 500 incidents communicated in as little as two days after the incident occurred. The majority of incidents involved synthetic cathinones (e.g., methylone, mephedrone, MDPV, 3-methylmethcathinone (3-MMC)), synthetic cannabinoids (e.g., APINACA), and phenethylamines (e.g., 2C-I-NBOMe).[23] Information communicated through IONICS has triggered follow-up investigations in countries of destination that led to significant additional seizures of new psychoactive substances, seizures of money and arrests of distributors.

---

[22] E/INCB/2014/1, paras. 248-256.

[23] The difference in order of classes of new psychoactive substances compared with the early warning advisory on new psychoactive substances is due to differences in the user bases and the purposes of the two systems, focusing on, respectively, unique substances (reported to early warning advisory) and individual new psychoactive substance incidents (communicated through IONICS).

Map of Project Ion focal point network, as at 1 November 2015

The boundaries and names shown and the designations used on this map do not imply official endorsement or acceptance by the United Nations. The final boundary between the Sudan and South Sudan has not yet been determined. The dotted line represents approximately the Line of Control in Jammu and Kashmir agreed upon by India and Pakistan. The final status of Jammu and Kashmir has not yet been agreed upon by the parties. A dispute exists between the Governments of Argentina and the United Kingdom of Great Britain and Northern Ireland concerning sovereignty over the Falkland Islands (Malvinas).

293. Other important developments since the last annual report of the Board were the decisions of the Commission on Narcotic Drugs, at its fifty-eighth session, upon the recommendations of the WHO Expert Committee on Drug Dependence, placing 10 new psychoactive substances under international control, as follows: AH-7921, a synthetic opioid, was added to Schedule I of the 1961 Convention; 25B-NBOMe (2C-B-NBOMe), 25C-NBOMe (2C-C-NBOMe) and 25I-NBOMe (2C-I-NBOMe) were added to Schedule I of the 1971 Convention; and BZP, JWH-018, AM-2201, MDPV, mephedrone (4-methylmethcathinone) and methylone (*beta*-keto-MDMA) were added to Schedule II of the 1971 Convention. Decision 58/3, scheduling AH-7921 under the 1961 Convention, became effective on 8 May 2015, and the other nine decisions, all for substances scheduled under the 1971 Convention, became effective on 4 November 2015.

294. At its thirty-seventh meeting in November 2015, the WHO Expert Committee on Drug Dependence reviewed, among other substances, MT-45, acetylfentanyl, *alpha*-pyrrolidinovalerophenone (α-PVP), 4-fluoroamphetamine (4-FA), *para*-methyl-4-methylaminorex (4,4'-DMAR), *para*-methoxymethylamphetamine (PMMA) and methoxetamine (MXE). The Expert Committee's recommendations will be transmitted to the Commission on

Narcotic Drugs, which will decide at its next session on the international scheduling of all or some of those substances. In that connection, the Board acknowledges the cooperation between WHO and UNODC to establish criteria for the prioritization of substances for the Expert Committee's review.

295. In addition to scheduling at the international level, countries also continue to bring new psychoactive substances under national controls. India, often cited as a source of new psychoactive substances, took the important step of controlling mephedrone and its salts and preparations under the Narcotic Drugs and Psychotropic Substances Act, 1985, effective 5 February 2015. China had already taken steps to control several new psychoactive substances in January 2014; effective 1 October 2015, 116 substances were placed in a new list of "non-medical narcotic drugs and psychotropic substances". Additionally, since the Board's last report, Project Ion has received information on national controls of various new psychoactive substances in several countries, including Argentina, Armenia, Chile, Egypt, Mexico, Sweden, Turkey and Ukraine. The information was communicated to the Project Ion focal point network with a view to enabling operational cooperation in cases of shipments of a controlled new psychoactive substance known to have

originated in, or be destined for, one of the countries with newly enacted national legislation.

296. New psychoactive substances have also been the subject of an increasing number of meetings, conferences and symposiums in almost all regions of the world; however, effective strategies are still forthcoming. At the same time, the challenges posed by new psychoactive substances and the diversification of the market continue to grow, with a rising number of reports about the role of such substances in hospital emergencies and deaths, and other worrying developments such as the use of new psychoactive substances by injection.

297. At its fifty-eighth session, the Commission on Narcotic Drugs adopted a resolution on promoting the protection of children and young people, with particular reference to the illicit sale and purchase of, among other substances, new psychoactive substances via the Internet (Commission resolution 58/3) and a resolution on

promoting international cooperation in responding to new psychoactive substances (Commission resolution 58/11). At a joint INCB/UNODC international conference on precursor chemicals and new psychoactive substances held in Bangkok on 21-24 April 2015, some 200 experts from 37 countries and 9 international organizations adopted an outcome document entitled "Proposed measures against the misuse of scheduled and non-scheduled precursors and new psychoactive substances".

298. INCB encourages all Governments to build on those and previous resolutions and recommendations, regional experiences and the experiences of individual Member States, and use the upcoming sessions of the Commission on Narcotic Drugs and the special session of the General Assembly on the world drug problem to devise practical and realistic solutions to protect individuals and the public at large from the adverse consequences of using harmful new psychoactive substances belonging to a wide range of substance classes.

Chapter III.

Analysis of the world situation

HIGHLIGHTS

- The increasing prominence of East Africa as a transit area for Afghan heroin has led to the increased abuse of opiates in the subregion. West Africa has been identified as a source of the amphetamine-type stimulants reaching Asia.

- The region of Central America and the Caribbean remains a significant supplier of cannabis and a transit route for cocaine to North America and Europe. The region continues to be affected by drug trafficking and drug-related violence and has homicide rates that are among the highest in the world.

- North America had the highest rates of drug-related mortality in the world, including a growing number of accidental overdose deaths, and was affected by the growing public security and health consequences of widespread cannabis abuse in the United States and Canada.

- Coca bush cultivation in Colombia increased by 44 per cent in 2014, reversing the decreases of recent years, while Bolivia (Plurinational State of) and Peru once again registered decreases.

- Amphetamine-type stimulants, in particular methamphetamine, continue to be the largest drug threat for East and South-East Asia. The rapid emergence of new psychoactive substances remains an additional major concern.

- In South Asia, the rise in the illicit manufacturing, trafficking and abuse of methamphetamine and the diversion and abuse of pharmaceutical preparations containing narcotic drugs and psychotropic substances remain major drug-related challenges.

- The security and conflict situation in some countries in West Asia and the resultant mass movement of people within the region and beyond provide significant opportunities for organized criminal groups to traffic drugs and increased drug abuse.

- The number of new psychoactive substances identified and distributed in Western and Central Europe continued to grow in 2014.

- In Eastern and South-Eastern Europe, rates of drug abuse by injection are nearly five times the world average.

- Oceania is actively engaged in enhancing joint operations and improving border control, particularly given the region's vulnerability to the abuse and trafficking of drugs, including amphetamine-type stimulants.

A.   Africa

1.   Major developments

299.   Africa continues to be one of the main transit areas for drug trafficking. West Africa is regularly used by traffickers to smuggle cocaine and other drugs into Europe. Furthermore, North Africa remains a primary source of drugs entering Europe, while East Africa is increasingly being used as a trafficking hub for Afghan heroin destined for Europe. The latter development is evidenced by the fact that East African countries and certain European countries have reported annual growth in seizures of heroin of African origin. This may be a reason for the increased abuse of heroin in East Africa.

300.   Traffickers in search of new illicit markets for cocaine and heroin have targeted the nascent middle class in certain African countries, such as Benin, which has been used as a transit country for many decades, and Namibia, a transit country that is becoming a consumer country. Drug trafficking in West Africa may have an impact on the abuse of certain types of drugs, such as cannabis, cocaine, heroin and amphetamine-type stimulants, in the subregion.

301.   The increase in drug trafficking has been accompanied not only by growing illicit drug use, especially among younger people, but also by increasing activities of organized criminal groups. In West and Central Africa, organized crime continues to contribute to social and economic costs by increasing drug trafficking and addiction and by concentrating wealth and power in the hands of comparatively few well-armed criminals.

302.   Although the Economic Community of West African States (ECOWAS) has made efforts to counter the impact of drug trafficking and abuse in West Africa, there has been an overall increase in drug trafficking between Latin America and Europe using Africa as a transit area. The increase in illicit drug use in West Africa has resulted in challenges related to security, treatment and negative health and social consequences of that drug use.

303.   According to South African law enforcement authorities, drug trafficking organizations from China and the Balkans have established a significant presence in Southern Africa. In addition to importing drugs directly into Southern Africa, drug trafficking organizations ship drugs to Maputo, and from there the drugs are transported by truck to South Africa.

2.   Regional cooperation

304.   A five-year strategic framework on drug control, focusing on drug abuse prevention and treatment standards, as well as the establishment of national and regional drug observatories, was discussed at the first meeting of the African Union Specialized Technical Committee on Health, Population and Drug Control, held in Addis Ababa in April 2015. During that meeting, African ministers of health, population and drug control held a meeting to discuss linkages between health and drug control. The recommendations contained in the final report of the ministers' meeting include: *(a)* the establishment of a regional drug control focal point by the regional economic community secretariats to develop and implement regional drug control strategies and to support individual States; and *(b)* the development of regional and national centres of excellence for the treatment and care of drug dependence. The ministers also recommended that the member States of the African Union, in partnership with WHO and UNODC, should develop model laws to provide a basis for legislative review at the member State level to address new and emerging drug control challenges.

305.   An ECOWAS action plan for the period 2016-2020 establishes the following priorities for combating drug trafficking and transnational organized crime in West Africa: *(a)* improvement in the effectiveness of national and subregional cooperation in the detection and suppression of drug trafficking and organized crime; *(b)* the establishment of appropriate, adequate and effective criminal justice systems; *(c)* effective and sustainable demand reduction through the prevention of drug abuse, the treatment of drug addiction and the rehabilitation of drug-dependent persons; and *(d)* the establishment of a viable system for the collection of valid and reliable data for monitoring drug trafficking, organized crime and drug abuse.

306.   Officials from 13 African countries attended the fourth International Annual Meeting of the Airport Communication Project (AIRCOP), held in Panama City from 21 to 23 April 2015. The meeting was organized jointly by UNODC, INTERPOL and WCO, with the support of the National Security Council of Panama, with the aim of creating a link between countries participating in AIRCOP, the interregional initiative aimed at facilitating the exchange of experiences and good practices in countering drug trafficking by air, to strengthen the coordination of their activities and share information between the joint airport interdiction task forces. In May 2015, joint airport interdiction task forces were operational in Benin, Cabo Verde, Côte d'Ivoire, the Gambia, Ghana, Mali, the Niger, Nigeria, Senegal and Togo.

307. A technical level meeting on heroin trafficking in the maritime domain was held on Mahé, in Seychelles, from 30 March to 1 April 2015. The meeting was aimed at enhancing drug control cooperation among littoral and island States of the Indian Ocean. The interregional initiative, supported by the UNODC Maritime Crime Programme, was attended by high-ranking officers from drug law enforcement agencies and state prosecutors, who proposed recommendations to counter drug trafficking in the area of the Indian Ocean.

3. National legislation, policy and action

308. In 2014, Egypt, Ghana and Nigeria took steps towards strengthening their national legislation and capacities to counter trafficking in drugs, including new psychoactive substances.

309. In November 2014, the Egyptian authorities scheduled five synthetic cannabinoids. The Ministry of Health added the following substances to the list of controlled substances included in the law of 1960: JWH-018, JWH-073, JWH-200, CP 47,497 and the C8 homologue of CP 47,497. According to the new law, the import, export, production, possession, handling, buying and selling of these substances are banned.

310. In Ghana, the authorities broadened the scope of their surveillance operations to include the monitoring of websites through which psychoactive substances are sold. The Parliament of Ghana is considering amendments to the Provisional National Defence Council law to strengthen sanctions related to synthetic psychotropic substances such as methamphetamine and its derivatives; and in order to introduce legislation to transform the Narcotics Control Board, under the Ministry of the Interior, into a drug control commission, under the President, with prosecutorial powers.

311. The Government of Nigeria approved its third national drug control master plan, covering the period 2015-2019. The new master plan, which was launched on 26 June 2015, provides a framework for reducing harm caused by drugs and for suppressing illicit drug production, supply and trafficking, as well as a platform for strengthening drug control responses. The master plan, developed by the interministerial committee on drug control, has four pillars: *(a)* law enforcement; *(b)* drug demand reduction; *(c)* access and control of narcotic drugs and psychotropic substances used for medical and scientific purposes; and *(d)* coordination of implementation.

312. In April 2015, the authorities of South Africa convened a conference to examine, among other issues, the potential use of cannabis for medical purposes. The round-table discussions focused on how to address the problems of cannabis use, abuse and dependence in the country.

4. Cultivation, production, manufacture and trafficking

(a) Narcotic drugs

313. Illicit cannabis cultivation, production, trafficking and use continue to represent major challenges to countries in Africa. While the illicit production of cannabis resin is concentrated in a few countries in North Africa, cannabis herb is produced throughout the continent.

314. Production of cannabis herb continues to be an issue of concern in Nigeria, where 158 tons of packaged cannabis herb were seized in 2014. Nigeria reported that over 53 million kg of cannabis illicitly cultivated on a total of 4,529 hectares (ha) of farmland were seized and destroyed in 2014, the highest level reported in 10 years. That also represents a dramatic increase over the level reported in 2013 (the eradication of cannabis covering a total area of 847 ha).

315. Nigeria was confirmed as a source country for cannabis destined for China, through the analysis of seizures made at the international airport near Lagos, where a total of 94.3 kg of cannabis were seized in 2014. At the same airport, 90.9 kg of cannabis destined for China also, as well as 64.5 kg destined for the United Arab Emirates, were seized between January and July 2015. In Ghana, 98 kg of cannabis destined for the United Kingdom were seized at Kotoka International Airport in Accra in 2014.

316. Morocco remains one of the world's largest producers of cannabis resin and continues to supply cannabis resin to Europe. Seizures of cannabis resin reported by the Moroccan authorities have declined significantly since 2012 (from 137 tons in 2012 to 107 tons in 2013 and to about 70 tons in 2014), whereas there was an increase in seizures of cannabis resin in other countries in North Africa. The Moroccan authorities made significant efforts to counter illicit cannabis cultivation. In 2013, the Moroccan authorities reported 47,196 ha of cannabis cultivation, 9.2 per cent less than in 2012. The authorities expect the total area under cannabis cultivation to

decline further, to 34,000 ha, in the next few years. It has been reported that the concentration of tetrahydrocannabinol (THC) in cannabis cultivated in Morocco has increased.

317. Other countries in North Africa continue to report large amounts of seized cannabis resin. Seizures of cannabis resin increased in North Africa by 31 per cent in 2013. The increase was mainly attributed to large quantities of cannabis resin reported seized in Algeria and Egypt. In 2014, however, the seizures of cannabis resin reported by Algeria declined by nearly 14 per cent (from 211 tons in 2013 to 182 tons in 2014), and seizures reported by Egypt declined by 35 per cent (from 84 tons in 2013 to 55 tons in 2014). Most of the cannabis resin seized in Algeria was reportedly seized in a province in the north-western part of the country, on its border with Morocco. Other African countries also reported substantial seizures of the substance in 2014. For example, Tunisian authorities intercepted consignments of cannabis resin totalling 11 tons.

318. In 2014, Egyptian authorities resumed eradication campaigns targeting cannabis and opium poppy cultivation sites, eradicating cannabis plants covering a total area of 344.7 ha and opium poppy covering a total area of 306.5 ha. In 2014, Egyptian authorities seized over 395 tons of cannabis herb, compared with 212 tons seized during the previous year.

319. For West Africa, cocaine trafficking remains a major concern. Cocaine arriving from South America transits in particular countries in West Africa on its way to Europe. One of the main modes of transport used for such trafficking is commercial aircraft; it is likely that that development is related to the increased number of commercial flights between Brazil and West Africa. Data provided by the National Drug Law Enforcement Agency of Nigeria on drug interceptions at the international airport near Lagos indicate that a total of about 120 kg of cocaine were seized at the airport in 2014.

320. Togolese authorities seized about 268 kg of cocaine in 2014. Since December 2013, when direct flights to Brazil from the international airport at Lomé first began, the volume of cocaine seized at the airport has increased, reaching 221 kg in 2014. In 2014, 32 cocaine consignments were seized at the international airport at Lomé from flights originating in Brazil; of those consignments, 25 per cent had been destined for Nigeria, 22 per cent for Benin, 16 per cent for Togo and 13 per cent for Guinea-Bissau. Morocco also witnessed the emergence of cocaine trafficking using commercial flights from Brazil. In 2014, 570 kg of cocaine were seized in Morocco.

321. Cabo Verde continues to be used as a hub for organized criminal groups trafficking in cocaine. Cabo Verdean authorities reported in November 2014 the seizure of 521 kg of cocaine, and the interception by the Spanish navy of a consignment of 1,500 kg of cocaine in the Atlantic, 129 km west of Cabo Verde, was reported in January 2015.

322. Seizures of cocaine continue to be reported by countries in East Africa, but to a lesser extent than in previous years. Countries in the subregion had reported the seizure of large quantities of cocaine between 2010 and 2012; the quantities reported in 2014 were smaller. That may indicate a shift in the concealment methods used, from sending large amounts of cocaine in fewer consignments to sending smaller amounts packed in small consignments to avoid detection by law enforcement authorities. In 2014, the Kenyan authorities seized 11 kg of cocaine, 30 per cent of which had arrived by air. Because of the high price of cocaine, estimated at $35,000-$36,000 per kilogram, most of the cocaine is reportedly intended for illicit markets in European and other countries and only a small portion of it is kept for local consumption.

323. Africa's importance as a transit area for Afghan heroin destined for Europe and other regions has grown, as suggested by increasing seizures of heroin reported in recent years by some African countries, particularly in East Africa. In 2014, Kenyan authorities reported the seizure of 387 kg of heroin, 3,200 litres of water mixed with heroin and 2,400 litres of diesel mixed with heroin; 377 kg of the 387 kg of heroin had been seized on a single ship in the port of Mombasa.

324. Kenyan authorities reported that heroin is transported to the country in large ships that anchor in the high seas and are then offloaded onto small vessels, including dhows, fishing boats and speedboats. The main countries of destination were Italy, the Netherlands, the United Kingdom and the United States. As a result of the heroin being trafficked through Kenya, heroin has become one of the most commonly abused drugs in the country, second only to cannabis. Most of the cases involving heroin abuse in Kenya have been reported in Mombasa.

325. Seizure data indicate that the smuggling of heroin to and through the United Republic of Tanzania has also increased. Of all the substances seized by Tanzanian authorities, cannabis, khat (*Catha edulis*) and heroin (in that order) accounted for the highest amounts seized. During the first eight months of 2014, Tanzanian authorities intercepted consignments containing over 321 kg of

heroin, more than in any previous year. The seized heroin originated in Afghanistan, India, Iran (Islamic Republic of) and Pakistan and had been destined for China, Japan, South Africa, Turkey and the United States, as well as countries in Europe.

326. Egyptian authorities reported that seizures of heroin increased significantly from 260 kg in 2013 to 613 kg in 2014. Algerian and Moroccan authorities also reported seizures of heroin; however, the quantities seized were smaller, totalling less than 10 kg in 2014.

(b) Psychotropic substances

327. The South African Police Service reported an increase in the number of clandestine drug manufacturing laboratories producing synthetic drugs such as methamphetamine (known locally as "tick"), largely intended for the illicit market in South Africa.

328. West Africa appears to have become an established source of the methamphetamine that is smuggled into East and South-East Asia via South Africa or Europe. According to information provided by UNODC, the significant volume of amphetamine-type stimulants seized in West Africa over the past year may indicate an increase in the illicit manufacturing of and trafficking in amphetamine-type stimulants, in particular methamphetamine. A total of 10 clandestine methamphetamine laboratories were dismantled in Nigeria between 2011 and July 2015.

329. In May 2015, Nigerian authorities dismantled two facilities used for the illicit manufacture of methamphetamine in Anambra State. Between January and July 2015, Nigerian authorities effected four seizures of methamphetamine, totalling approximately 92 kg, at the international airport near Lagos. Three of the seizures were of minimal amounts; however, the fourth seizure is noteworthy for its size—about 91 kg. In addition, Nigerian authorities also reported the detection of 2.6 kg of liquid methamphetamine and 250 g of crystalline methamphetamine and some laboratory equipment used for the illicit manufacture of methamphetamine.

330. Senegalese authorities have reported major seizures of amphetamine-type stimulants, including the seizure of 30 kg of methamphetamine at Kidira, near the Malian border, in January 2015, followed by the seizure of an additional 82 kg of methamphetamine in Koumpetoum in February 2015. In both cases, the drugs had originated in Mali and had been smuggled out of Bamako.

331. In 2014, the smuggling of amphetamine-type stimulants through East Africa to illicit markets in Asian countries continued. Kenya reported the illicit manufacture of crystalline methamphetamine using ephedrine and pseudoephedrine, precursors that are legally imported into the country and then diverted. The methamphetamine is then smuggled predominantly to Asian countries and South Africa, the biggest illicit markets for the substance being Japan, Malaysia, the Republic of Korea and Thailand. The abuse of methamphetamine is also increasing in Kenya.

332. West Africa did not play a key role in the synthetic drug market until recent years. The reasons behind the change, part of an overall increase in global illicit demand for amphetamine-type stimulants, may be explained by weak controls on legal imports of their precursors and the socioeconomic situation in the subregion.

(c) Precursors

333. Countries in Africa continue to be vulnerable to trafficking in precursor chemicals, in particular as countries of destination and/or transit countries. The main precursor chemicals involved are ephedrine and pseudoephedrine, which are used in the illicit manufacture of amphetamine-type stimulants. According to information provided through PICS, the following African countries have been identified as having been involved in incidents reported between November 2014 and November 2015: Democratic Republic of the Congo, Ethiopia, Malawi, Mozambique, Nigeria, Seychelles, South Africa and Zimbabwe. The seizures communicated through PICS, however, involved relatively small amounts of ephedrine (totalling over 500 kg) and pseudoephedrine (totalling about 70 kg).

334. The data on seizures of substances listed in Tables I and II of the 1988 Convention and seizures of internationally non-scheduled substances remain limited. Information on methods of diversion and illicit manufacture, stopped shipments and thefts involving those substances, which is provided annually by Governments to the Board, has also been insufficient. As at 1 November 2015, the Governments of 16 African countries[24] provided form D for 2014 to the Board. Only 4 of the 16 countries (Namibia, Senegal, Zambia and Zimbabwe) reported the seizure of moderate amounts of ephedrine (in bulk form and in the form of

[24] Algeria, Benin, Côte d'Ivoire, Democratic Republic of the Congo, Egypt, Ghana, Morocco, Mozambique, Namibia, Senegal, Sudan, Tunisia, Uganda, United Republic of Tanzania, Zambia and Zimbabwe.

pharmaceutical preparations), ergometrine, isosafrole and potassium permanganate. Most of the ephedrine seized (82 kg) was reported by Senegal.

335.   As noted by the Board in its report for 2014,[25] by 1 November 2014, the Governments of only a few African countries had invoked article 12, paragraph 10 *(a)*, of the 1988 Convention, requiring them to be informed of shipments of substances in Table I of the Convention prior to their departure from the exporting country. Effective May 2015, the Government of the Sudan requires pre-export notification for imports of all substances in Tables I and II.

336.   In May 2015, Nigerian authorities dismantled at least three clandestine laboratories in south-east Nigeria, where toluene, a substance in Table II of the 1988 Convention that is commonly used as a solvent, had been found. There are indications that the precursors were obtained locally, from domestic distribution channels, after they had been legally imported.

337.   In February 2015, 133 kg of ephedrine were seized at the international airport near Lagos. The consignment had been sent as cargo and had been destined for Mozambique and South Africa.

338.   An additional challenge has emerged in Africa: online sales of controlled drugs (web-based marketplace sales via the Internet). The increase in online trafficking has made it difficult for law enforcement authorities to identify website owners and users involved in trafficking in precursor chemicals.

339.   A comprehensive review of the situation with respect to the control of precursors and chemicals frequently used in the illicit manufacture of narcotic drugs and psychotropic substances in the region can be found in the 2015 report of the Board on the implementation of article 12 of the 1988 Convention.

(d)   Substances not under international control

340.   Some African countries continue to raise their concerns over the abuse of substances not under international control, namely ketamine and tramadol. Nigeria, where ketamine is widely used in human and veterinary practice as an anaesthetic, brought tramadol and ketamine under national control in 2010.

341.   The abuse of and trafficking in tramadol, a synthetic opioid not under international control, continues to represent challenges to a number of countries in Africa, notably in North Africa and West Africa. In 2014, more than 43,578 kg of tramadol were seized by the joint port control units of Cotonou, Benin, and Tema, Ghana. In February 2015, the joint port control unit of Cotonou seized 13,612 kg of tramadol, which had arrived from India and had been destined for the Niger. Seizures of tramadol in Egypt declined significantly, from 435 million tablets in 2012 to 157 million tablets in 2014. According to the Egyptian authorities, the decrease could be attributed to the fact that tramadol had been brought under national control in 2013.

342.   There continues to be only limited information about the African continent regarding the emergence of new psychoactive substances, the extent of their abuse and their seizures. However, according to information provided to the Board, incidents with new psychoactive substances in 2015 involved the following African countries, particularly as countries of origin or as transit countries: Ethiopia, Kenya, South Africa and United Republic of Tanzania. The majority of the incidents concerned khat; the amounts of khat involved were in the range of 6-166 kg. Other seizures communicated during the reporting period included 27 kg of methylone, a synthetic cathinone included in Schedule II of the 1971 Convention by the Commission on Narcotic Drugs at its fifty-eighth session, in 2015.

5.   Abuse and treatment

343.   Although the prevention and treatment of drug abuse are part of the main provisions of the international drug control treaties, it is estimated that in Africa only 1 out of 18 people suffering from drug use disorders or drug dependence receive treatment each year and that a large proportion of drug users may not be dependent but may still require intervention.

344.   The fact that almost half of the problem drug users who inject drugs follow unsafe injecting practices contributes to the rise in the incidence of HIV. In Southern Africa, for example, evidence indicates that high-risk injecting practices, such as the reuse and sharing of needles and syringes and the ineffective cleaning of injecting equipment, contribute to HIV transmission among people who inject drugs. This is also the case in sub-Saharan countries such as Kenya, Senegal, Uganda and the United Republic of Tanzania, where people who inject drugs often use non-sterile injecting equipment.

---

[25] E/INCB/2014/1, para. 295.

345.   Despite the paucity of data on drug abuse in Africa, it is estimated that the annual prevalence of cannabis use in the region remains high (7.5 per cent of the population aged 15-64), almost double the global annual average (3.9 per cent), and it is particularly high in West and Central Africa (12.4 per cent). Cannabis is reported to be the primary substance for which people in Africa receive treatment for substance abuse.

346.   According to information on demand for treatment, heroin remains the second most abused drug (after cannabis), in Africa. The annual prevalence of opiate abuse in the region is estimated at 0.3 per cent of the population aged 15-64 (or about 1.88 million individuals).

347.   The annual prevalence of cocaine use in Africa, estimated at 0.4 per cent, remains comparable with the global estimate.

348.   In West Africa, the growing availability of cocaine, heroin and amphetamine-type stimulants may have led to increased drug abuse and dependence. This increase is attributable to the emergence of illicit production and distribution centres for synthetic drugs in Côte d'Ivoire, Guinea and Nigeria.

349.   The Government of Senegal has increased the availability and accessibility of services for the evidence-based treatment and care of drug dependence by setting up in December 2014 the Dakar integrated treatment centre for persons with addictions. The centre, located at the University Hospital of Dakar, also provides a methadone maintenance programme, drug dependence treatment services, outreach programmes and programmes for the treatment of HIV infection and hepatitis infection for drug users.

350.   Cabo Verde is piloting a "one-stop shop" for drug abusers, a centre offering multiple drug abuse treatment services in a vulnerable neighbourhood in the capital city of Praia, promoting the implementation of a community-based treatment approach.

351.   In Kenya, after an opioid substitution treatment facility (known locally as a medically assisted therapy clinic) was opened in Nairobi in December 2014, a second facility was opened in Malindi in February 2015 and two others were opened in Mombasa in September 2015. The national medically assisted therapy programme, launched on 18 August 2015, has been made available to people who inject drugs. In 2014, there were approximately 18,327 injecting drug users in Kenya, about 18 per cent of whom were HIV-positive, which is significantly higher than the HIV prevalence in the general population (5.6 per cent).

352.   Several countries in Africa, namely Burundi, Comoros, Eritrea, Madagascar and the United Republic of Tanzania, have improved national systems for the treatment of drug dependence, mainly as a result of skill development and capacity-building initiatives. According to UNODC, Kenya and the United Republic of Tanzania have enhanced their capacity to prevent HIV infection and hepatitis infection among people who inject drugs. Mauritius and Seychelles have received technical support in this area.

353.   In South Africa, the government of Gauteng province opened a centre for the treatment of substance abuse in Soweto in May 2015. The centre offers free assistance to alcohol- and drug-dependent persons.

B.   Americas

Central America and the Caribbean

1.   Major developments

354.   The region of Central America and the Caribbean continues to be used as a major trans-shipment area for consignments of drugs originating in South America and destined for North America and Europe. In the Caribbean, countries have begun playing an increasing role as secondary distribution points for cocaine shipments to Europe.[26] Impunity, corruption and weak institutions undermine drug control efforts and the rule of law in the region, despite attempts to reform law enforcement and judicial systems. Drug trafficking activities are often carried out under the protection of local gangs (*maras*) operating in border areas, especially in El Salvador, Guatemala and Honduras.

355.   There are indications that links have been established between drug cartels and criminal organizations operating in the region. Law enforcement authorities have reported a significant change in trafficking patterns, with drug traffickers cancelling confirmed flights at the last minute, only to make bookings immediately thereafter on the same flight, in an attempt to avoid detection during the process of screening the passenger list.[27]

356.   Drug trafficking has become a major security threat and is contributing to an increase in drug abuse in the sub-region. The number of homicides linked to organized

---

[26] *World Drug Report 2015.*

[27] Ibid.

crime has risen in areas where criminal groups fight to gain control of local drug distribution. The increase in criminal acts may be linked to the struggle to control local markets and the increasing availability of drugs, which in turn may be attributable to the fact that drug traffickers are frequently paid in drugs rather than cash.

357.   The drug problem has also led to drug-related corruption, which has increasingly weakened the criminal justice systems in Central America and the Caribbean. Corruption, including among police and other law enforcement officials, has interfered with the ability of Governments in the region to promote development, blocking the delivery of services and distorting public spending. Drug money and corruption have become entrenched in the security services in Central America, paving the way for other forms of organized crime, including trafficking in firearms. Limited law enforcement capacity, corruption and weak governability in Central America and the Caribbean have facilitated the use of smuggling channels and drug trafficking activities. INCB encourages the Governments of countries in Central America and the Caribbean to consider regional strategies for countering the drug problem that involve concerted action in the area of crime prevention and criminal justice reform, together with regional approaches to reducing drug trafficking and controlling firearms.

358.   In February 2015, Jamaican legislators passed an amendment to the Dangerous Drugs Act to the effect that possession of two ounces or less of cannabis (56.6 g) is no longer a criminal offence and will no longer result in a criminal record. The use of cannabis for personal consumption has also been authorized for members of the Rastafari community, in the context of their religious activities. The amendment entered into force on 1 April 2015.

359.   The Board continues to closely follow drug policy developments in the region, including the adoption of amendments to the legal frameworks regulating substances under international control in Costa Rica, Guatemala and Jamaica. INCB underscores that Governments, whenever considering potential changes to their national drug legislation and policies, should take steps to ensure that those changes are consistent with their obligations under the three international drug control conventions.

2.   Regional cooperation

360.   A regional seminar on the role of research in the development of effective policy in the field of drug abuse prevention was held in Port of Spain from 29 to 31 October 2014. The seminar was organized by the

Inter-American Drug Abuse Control Commission, through its Inter-American Observatory on Drugs, and the Government of Trinidad and Tobago, with the participation of representatives of 30 Caribbean States members of the Organization of American States (OAS). Participants emphasized the need to strengthen State institutions and their capacity to gather, analyse and report drug-related information to guide the drug-related policy of the participating countries.

361.   On 12 February 2015, the Montevideo Declaration was adopted by the seventeenth high-level meeting of the Coordination and Cooperation Mechanism on Drugs between the European Union and the Community of Latin American and Caribbean States (CELAC). In the declaration, States committed to continuing to provide support to projects in the region, in both demand and supply reduction areas, and emphasized the need to address the world drug problem using a comprehensive, multidisciplinary, intersectoral and balanced approach.

362.   The Seventh Summit of the Americas was held in Panama City on 10 and 11 April 2015. Participants emphasized the need for a comprehensive and effective strategy against the world drug problem in the Americas. In its final "Mandates for action" document, the Summit decided to continue with the dialogue in preparation for the special session of the General Assembly on the world drug problem to be held in 2016.

363.   A workshop on drug trafficking over the Internet was held in San José on 19 May 2015. It was organized by the Inter-American Drug Abuse Control Commission (CICAD) of OAS and the Costa Rican Drug Institute. The objective of the seminar was to develop mechanisms to control and prevent the diversion and abuse of pharmaceutical products over the Internet.

364.   The Twenty-fifth Meeting of Heads of National Drug Law Enforcement Agencies, Latin America and the Caribbean, was held in San Pedro Sula, Honduras, from 5 to 9 October 2015. Among the major issues discussed were: (a) prevention, investigation and prosecution of microtrafficking and its links to transnational criminal networks; (b) border management; (c) ways to address current trends in trafficking in cocaine; and (d) curbing access to the supply of precursor chemicals.

3.   National legislation, policy and action

365.   In February 2015, Jamaican legislators passed an amendment to the Dangerous Drugs Act to the effect that

possession of two ounces or less of cannabis (56.6 g) is no longer a criminal offence and will no longer result in a criminal record. Possession for personal use will be treated as an administrative offence, similar to a traffic violation, with a 30-day period to pay the administrative fine. The amendment also allows each household to cultivate up to five cannabis plants. The amendment provides for a cannabis licensing authority to be established to monitor the distribution of cannabis for scientific and medical purposes. The use of cannabis for personal consumption has also been authorized for members of the Rastafari community in the context of their religious activities. The amendment entered into force on 1 April 2015.

366.   In June 2015, the Ministry of Health of Costa Rica released an expert opinion that included details of implementation of a pending bill to promote cannabis for medical and industrial purposes. Among the conditions specified by the Ministry are that medical cannabis may be prescribed only as the last-resort medical alternative, while recreational use of cannabis remains illegal. Medical cannabis may be distributed through conventional pharmacies, exclusively on prescription. The bill, pending since late 2014, contains a proposal on the legalization of the growing, processing and sale of cannabis for medical and industrial use. The pending bill is expected to be debated by the Parliament by the end of 2015.

367.   In Guatemala, the National Commission for the Reform of Drug Policy was established in 2014. The Commission aims to conduct a comprehensive review of the current policy on drugs and to propose reforms. It also aims to guide Government drug policy reform in the context of a broad and informed dialogue worldwide.

4. Cultivation, production, manufacture and trafficking

368.   In Central America and the Caribbean, circumstances such as poverty, social inequality and a lack of economic opportunities for young people have contributed to an increase in drug trafficking. The migration situation in Central American countries is one of the most complex in the world, with many thousands of migrants arriving, transiting and departing every year. The easily accessible coasts of Jamaica have been used increasingly by various criminal networks to use the country as a transit and destination country for smuggling drugs, firearms, ammunition and migrants.

369.   Cocaine continues to be trafficked from the border area between Colombia and Venezuela (Bolivarian Republic of) to airstrips in Central America and the Caribbean, in addition to the use of the more established sea routes via Haiti and the Dominican Republic. In terms of maritime trafficking, remote coastal areas of Honduras and parts of northern Nicaragua are also used. Once offloaded, shipments are moved further north by air.[28] In Nicaragua, most cocaine is seized in remote, underpopulated and isolated areas along the Atlantic coast.

370.   Drug trafficking by sea remains a major problem in Central America and the Caribbean. In addition, light aircraft operating from clandestine airstrips in remote areas of South America are increasingly being used to transport cocaine. More and more often, drug traffickers use stolen or falsified aircraft registration numbers when transporting illicit consignments by air. INCB encourages Governments to monitor the sale and movement of light aircraft more closely, step up airspace security and strengthen control over privately owned landing fields.

(a) Narcotic drugs

371.   Significant levels of cannabis herb are produced in most countries in Central America and the Caribbean. Jamaica remains the largest producer of cannabis in the Caribbean, with total cultivation of cannabis plant estimated by local authorities at about 15,000 ha. Jamaican law permits only manual eradication. Eradication of cannabis increased in 2014, with the destruction of 588 ha, compared with 247 ha in 2013. In the Dominican Republic, the cannabis cultivated is mainly for local consumption, and seizures are concentrated in the north-western and south-western provinces that border Haiti. In 2014, seizures of more than 1 ton of cannabis were reported by the Dominican Republic.

372.   In the eastern Caribbean countries (Antigua and Barbuda, Barbados, Dominica, Saint Kitts and Nevis, Saint Lucia, and Saint Vincent and the Grenadines), South American drug cartels use the many uninhabited islands for trafficking and temporarily storing cocaine shipments for onward trafficking to North America and Europe. Cannabis plant cultivation is present in the mountainous regions of Dominica, Grenada and Saint Vincent and the Grenadines. Law enforcement authorities in Barbados have reported an increased number of shipments of cannabis and cocaine originating in Trinidad and Tobago. Antigua and Barbuda reported an increased flow of cannabis and cocaine from Jamaica via Sint Maarten.

---

[28] United Nations Office on Drugs and Crime, *Transnational Organized Crime in Central America and the Caribbean: A Threat Assessment* (Vienna, September 2012).

373.   In 2014, according to official statistics, drug seizures in the Caribbean totalled about 1.7 tons of cocaine
and more than 376 tons of cannabis. Those seizures led
to a total of 277 drug-related arrests, 234 drug-related
prosecutions and 218 convictions during that year.

374.   Saint Vincent and the Grenadines continues to be
an important source of cannabis in the Caribbean.
Another important source of cannabis in the region is
Costa Rica, a regional leader in the eradication of cannabis plants and the seizure of cannabis. In Costa Rica,
locally grown cannabis is primarily for domestic use; only
a small fraction is exported. Seizures of cannabis from
Colombia and Jamaica are also fairly common in Costa
Rica; most of it is intended for the domestic market.

375.   Cocaine and synthetic drugs are not produced in
Jamaica. Drugs are trafficked from and through Jamaica
by maritime vessels, air freight, human couriers and, to
a limited degree, private aircraft. Factors contributing to
drug trafficking include the country's strategic geographic
position, its lengthy and largely unprotected coastline and
the large numbers of tourists visiting the country and the
corresponding airline traffic. Cannabis and cocaine are
trafficked from and through Jamaica mainly to markets
in Belgium, Canada, Germany, the Netherlands, the
United Kingdom and the United States, as well as other
Caribbean countries. Reports indicate that Jamaica is
emerging as a transit point for cocaine, in addition to
cannabis leaving Central America and destined for the
United States.

376.   According to UNODC, cocaine trafficking patterns
in Central America in 2013 remained the same as those
in previous years. Costa Rica reported significant changes:
from being primarily a transit country, it has become a
secondary distribution point and a country of temporary
storage of cocaine for onward trafficking.

377.   Central America and the Caribbean was the only
region worldwide where cocaine seizures increased in
2013, to 162 tons, compared with 78 tons in 2012. The
largest quantities of cocaine seized in 2013 were in
Panama (41 tons) and Costa Rica (20 tons). That, however, was significantly lower than the 26 tons of cocaine
seized in Costa Rica in 2014. In 2013, Trinidad and
Tobago reported seizures of cocaine totalling 2.3 tons.[29]
In 2014, authorities in the Dominican Republic seized
more than 5 tons of cocaine, down from the approximately 8 tons seized in 2013, a decline owing partially to
disruptions to trafficking organizations. The drug squad
of Saint Vincent and the Grenadines reported a surge in

the trans-shipment of cocaine, and authorities indicated
that trafficking in drugs to and from nearby Guadeloupe
had increased manifold over the previous few years.

378.   Panama reported seizing more than 35 tons of
cocaine in 2014. Several local drug trafficking organizations in Panama continued to provide logistical support
to international trafficking organizations smuggling
cocaine into Panama for further distribution northward
into Central America. These organizations, based along
the Caribbean coast of Panama, coordinate the receipt of
"go-fast" vessels from several organizations in Colombia.
Once in Panama, these vessels are refuelled and the illicit
drugs stored in remote locations along the coastline, from
where they are trafficked further north.

(b)   Psychotropic substances

379.   There are reports indicating that methamphetamine laboratories are being increasingly established in
Central America. Over the past few years, clandestine laboratories used for manufacturing amphetamine-type
stimulants have been dismantled in Belize, Jamaica,
Guatemala, Honduras and Nicaragua.

380.   The Board has noted the scarcity of data reported
on manufacture and trafficking of psychotropic substances and on the nature and extent of drug abuse of
such substances in most countries in the region. INCB
once again urges Governments to take additional measures to increase national capacity to collect data and conduct national assessments to determine the true extent
and nature of problems caused by availability of psychotropic substances in the region.

(c)   Precursors

381.   The Central American subregion has also reportedly witnessed an increase in imports of chemicals that
are not subject to international control but are suspected
of being illicitly used in the manufacture of drugs.
Following the adoption of legislation regulating the use
of such chemicals in many countries in the subregion, the
number of reported attempts to divert chemicals has
declined.

382.   In Central American and Caribbean countries,
additional measures are being taken to address the
increasing diversion of precursors used in illicit drug
manufacture; some countries, such as Antigua and
Barbuda, Barbados, Costa Rica and Grenada, have established mechanisms for regulating the use and distribution

_____

[29] World Drug Report 2015.

of controlled chemicals. In the region as a whole, however, the movement of precursors is poorly monitored and regulated owing to weak infrastructure and the inadequate level of resources allocated by Governments. INCB encourages the Governments of countries in Central America and the Caribbean to adopt and strengthen legislation and to establish a regional cooperation mechanism for preventing trafficking in and diversion of precursors.

383.   A comprehensive review of the situation with respect to the control of precursors and chemicals frequently used in the illicit manufacture of narcotic drugs and psychotropic substances in the region can be found in the report of the Board for 2015 on the implementation of article 12 of the 1988 Convention.

(d)   Substances not under international control

384.   New psychoactive substances also continue to be reported by countries of Central America and the Caribbean, in particular Costa Rica. According to the UNODC early warning advisory, Costa Rica continued to report substances in the groups of phenethylamines, piperazines and other substances in 2015. Use of those substances may have serious health consequences, as the effects of such substances on the human body are not fully understood or known. In addition, the trafficking of those substances creates additional challenges for the regulatory and enforcement authorities.

5.   Abuse and treatment

385.   Cannabis abuse patterns and trends in the region have remained fairly stable. The prevalence of cocaine abuse in Central America and the Caribbean remains higher than the global average,[30] with an estimated average annual prevalence of 0.6 per cent for both subregions. As regards the use of opioids in Central America, UNODC has estimated annual prevalence at 0.2 per cent, which is below the global average.

386.   According to the *Report on Drug Use in the Americas, 2015*,[31] annual cannabis prevalence among secondary school students in Central America was reported to be highest in Belize, at 15.8 per cent, and lowest in Honduras, with a little more than 1 per cent. In the

Caribbean, Saint Lucia reported the highest annual prevalence rates, of more than 15 per cent. Prevalence rates of less than 5 per cent were reported in Antigua and Barbuda, Barbados, Dominica, the Dominican Republic, El Salvador, Guyana, Haiti, Honduras, Panama, Saint Kitts and Nevis, and Saint Vincent and the Grenadines.

387.   According to the *Report on Drug Use in the Americas, 2015*, the annual prevalence of cocaine abuse among high-school students in the Caribbean ranges from 0.5 per cent to slightly more than 2 per cent. In six countries (Antigua and Barbuda, Grenada, Haiti, Saint Kitts and Nevis, Saint Lucia and Trinidad and Tobago) reported prevalence is about 1.5 per cent and three countries in Central America have prevalence rates of about 1 per cent (Belize, El Salvador and Panama). Approximately 50 per cent of all demand for treatment for drug abuse in the region is reportedly related to cocaine abuse. Cocaine is also ranked as the main substance causing drug-induced or drug-related deaths.

388.   Cocaine abuse among secondary school students is higher among male students in all countries, regardless of the prevalence rate reported. The exception is Saint Vincent and the Grenadines, where the estimated prevalence among males is 0.58 per cent, while for women it is 0.69 per cent. In Grenada, the country with the highest level of cocaine use in the Caribbean, the ratio of male to female use is 32 to 1, followed by Saint Lucia with 7 to 1, and Haiti and Jamaica, with about 3 to 1. In Honduras and Costa Rica, cocaine abuse by male students is three and four times higher than females, respectively.[32]

389.   The highest prevalence rates of "crack" cocaine in the Caribbean, ranging between 1.5 per cent and 2.2 per cent, are found in Antigua and Barbuda, Barbados, Grenada, Haiti, Saint Kitts and Nevis, and Saint Lucia. Guyana, Jamaica, Panama, and Trinidad and Tobago reported prevalence rates of around 1 per cent. The lowest prevalence rates (under 0.5 per cent) in Central America are found in Costa Rica and Honduras. The lowest prevalence rates in the Caribbean are found in the Dominican Republic.

390.   The Board notes with concern the increase in the abuse of MDMA ("ecstasy") in countries in Central America and the Caribbean, particularly in Antigua and Barbuda, and Belize. Abuse of "ecstasy"-type substances is also increasing in Jamaica, especially in the tourist areas of Negril and Montego Bay. The "ecstasy" found in the

[30] *World Drug Report 2015*.

[31] Inter-American Drug Abuse Control Commission of the Organization of American States, *Report on Drug Use in the Americas, 2015*.

[32] *World Drug Report 2015*.

region continues to be smuggled from European countries or, more recently, from Canada.[33]

391.   "Ecstasy" use among high-school students in the Caribbean remains high, with the highest annual prevalence rate (3.7 per cent) reported in Antigua and Barbuda. In Central America, the highest rate was found in Belize, with 2.4 per cent. In terms of lifetime prevalence of "ecstasy" among the general population, Belize reported the highest rate in Central America (0.5 per cent).[34]

392.   Inhalant abuse is particularly high in the Caribbean. Of the 12 Caribbean countries that have provided information on abuse of those substances, 8 have prevalence rates of over 5.9 per cent, which are higher than the rates in all other countries of the western hemisphere, with the exception of the Dominican Republic. In Central America, there are considerable differences between the country with the highest rate of inhalant use (Belize, at 5.5 per cent), and that with the lowest (Honduras, with 0.6 per cent).[35]

393.   The development and successful implementation of programmes for the prevention and treatment of drug abuse in Central America and the Caribbean are largely restricted by the limited resources and institutional capacity of countries in the region. INCB recognizes that a central problem in the design of effective prevention and treatment programmes is that, throughout Central America and the Caribbean, there is a lack of capacity for the collection of drug-related data and a lack of centralized agencies mandated to assess that information. In addition, Governments have to strike a balance between competing developmental priorities and the need to adopt drug abuse prevention and treatment measures. INCB reiterates the importance of Governments in the region taking tangible steps to improve frameworks for the collection and analysis of drug-related data to be used to implement adequate programmes for prevention and treatment that are available to the entire population of the region.

North America

1.   Major developments

394.   Opioid abuse has remained one of the major challenges facing North America (Canada, Mexico and the

United States), with a regional annual prevalence rate of 3.8 per cent in 2013, significantly higher than the global average of 0.7 per cent. However, patterns of abuse and trafficking have continued to shift, requiring Governments in the region to adapt their drug control policies accordingly.

395.   Abuse of prescription drugs continues to be the single biggest challenge to drug control efforts in the region. In the United States, federal authorities have reported that deaths involving controlled prescription drugs outnumber those involving heroin and cocaine combined. The lucrative nature of illicit trade in prescription drugs in North America has led to the growing involvement of organized transnational criminal groups in trafficking, which had previously been controlled by small-scale dealers and street gangs.

396.   Prescription drug abuse continues to exact a heavy human and economic toll on the region; it is one of the leading causes of accidental death and costs Governments in the region billions of dollars annually. In the United States, drug overdose deaths, primarily related to prescription drug abuse, continue to outnumber those caused by motor vehicle accidents, thus constituting the single leading cause of "injury deaths" in the country. The Drug Enforcement Administration of the United States estimates that the costs of the non-medical use of prescription drugs alone total more than $53 billion annually.

397.   The growth of the illegal market in prescription drugs has been spurred in part by the imposition of stricter controls on the prescription and dispensing of those drugs in various jurisdictions in the region, including through the establishment of programmes for prescription drug monitoring, increased controls on pharmacies and greater cooperation between law enforcement agencies, although there remain significant gaps in that system, in part because they are state-level rather than national-level control systems.

398.   Stricter controls on the availability of prescription opioids have also contributed to the continued resurgence of heroin as a major substance of abuse in North America, reversing years of decline in prevalence. The increase in heroin abuse has been particularly pronounced in the United States, where it has affected urban centres and—increasingly—rural regions where historically large-scale abuse of the drug had not been an issue. United States law enforcement officials have reported that Mexican drug cartels have been increasing their share of the United States illicit heroin market using established distribution channels for other drugs. There has also been an increased incidence of drug overdose deaths caused by fentanyl-laced heroin.

[33] World Drug Report 2014.

[34] Report on Drug Use in the Americas, 2015, chap. 6.

[35] Ibid., chap. 4.

399. Cannabis remains the most commonly abused drug in the region, in part due to its high level of availability. The drug is illicitly cultivated in all three countries for domestic abuse and, to a lesser extent, trafficked between countries. In the United States, the high supply of cannabis is due to extensive illegal production within the country, large-scale smuggling from Mexico and large-scale production and diversion from states within the United States that allow cannabis production for non-medical purposes and for medical cannabis programmes. Authorities of some states have complained of a spillover effect created in their territory by the diversion for trafficking purposes of cannabis from neighbouring states that have legalized the drug for non-medical purposes. United States authorities have also reported a 62 per cent increase in the number of cannabis-related emergency department visits between 2004 and 2011. In 2011, the number of medical emergency visits for illicit drug use-related causes that were cannabis-related were second only to those for cocaine.

400. In Mexico, drug syndicates continue to constitute a major source of criminal activity, including murders, abductions and corruption, posing a sustained threat to public order and security in many parts of the country. In addition, there are signs that the illicit manufacture of methamphetamine destined for the United States illicit market has been on the increase. The number of methamphetamine laboratories detected in Mexico has increased significantly since 2008, and seizures of the drug at the United States border have increased by a factor of three since 2009.

2. Regional cooperation

401. Regional cooperation between the three countries in the region is extensive and generally considered to be effective. It includes high-level political summits, joint action plans, intelligence-sharing, joint law enforcement activities and border control initiatives.

3. National legislation, policy and action

402. In late 2014, the United States Justice Department sent a "policy statement regarding marijuana issues in Indian country" to all United States attorneys. The document was intended to provide additional guidance on the enforcement by United States attorneys of the Controlled Substances Act on tribal lands on cannabis-related matters. It reiterated the eight enforcement priorities set by the Department of Justice in its 2013

memorandum[36] to United States attorneys and established their applicability to reservations and tribal lands, many of which traverse state borders and federal districts.

403. In December 2014, Oklahoma and Nebraska, two states bordering Colorado, filed a lawsuit against the State of Colorado before the United States Supreme Court urging the Court to prohibit the establishment of a regulatory regime for the cannabis industry. Oklahoma and Nebraska argue that because of the federal Government's prohibition of cannabis under the Controlled Substances Act, states cannot act in contradiction of that ban by creating a regulatory framework for legalization. The suit argues that Colorado's official efforts to regulate the legal cannabis industry bring the state into conflict with federal and international drug laws. In addition, both states argue that Colorado's official regulation of recreational cannabis imposes a nuisance burden on surrounding states due to an increase in drug trafficking. The Supreme Court has not yet decided whether it will accept the case.

404. The Board reiterates its view that measures taken in various states of the United States to legalize the production, sale and distribution of cannabis for non-medical and non-scientific purposes are inconsistent with the provisions of the international drug control treaties. INCB wishes once again to draw attention to the fact that the 1961 Convention as amended establishes that the parties to the Convention should take such legislative and administrative measures as may be necessary "to limit exclusively to medical and scientific purposes the production, manufacture, export, import, distribution of, trade in, use and possession of drugs". The limitation of the use of controlled substances to medical and scientific purposes is a fundamental principle which lies at the heart of the international drug control legal framework which cannot be derogated from. Regardless of whether they are federal or unitary States, all parties to the conventions have a legal obligation to give effect to and carry out the provisions of the convention within their own territories.

405. In February 2015, the United States Government announced that the President's 2016 budget submission to Congress would request historic levels of public funding for "health responses to illicit drug use" totalling more than $25 billion. Of that amount, $12 billion in federal funds are to be earmarked to fund initiatives for demand reduction, representing an increase of more than $760 million over the President's 2015 budget submission. Of that funding for 2016, $133 million has been earmarked to intensify efforts to reduce opioid abuse. The initiatives

36 See E/INCB/2014/1, para. 141.

to be funded include prevention measures such as the strengthening and increased interoperability of State prescription drug monitoring programmes and the expansion of mechanisms for the disposal of prescription drugs. Additional funding will be provided to the Centers for Disease Control and Prevention to study measures to curb heroin overdose deaths and provide naloxone, which is used to rapidly counteract the effects of opioid overdose, to first responders and train them in its use. Part of the earmarked funds will also be used to offer substance abuse treatment to all eligible federal prison inmates through the Department of Justice's Federal Bureau of Prisons.

406.   In July 2015, Health Canada announced that it was reviewing the prescription requirement for naloxone. That initiative comes at a time when opioid overdoses continue to increase across the country. As a first step towards facilitating access to the medicine, the federal Government was undertaking consultations with provincial and territorial health authorities to collect information about the use of naloxone, in particular with respect to the possibility of allowing a wider range of professionals, including first responders, to inject patients with naloxone.

407.   In August 2015, the United States Administration announced $13.4 million in funding for the high-intensity drug trafficking areas (HIDTA) programme, which is intended to ensure coordination among federal, state, local and tribal law enforcement agencies operating in areas identified as critical drug trafficking areas of the country. Of the total investment, $5 million will be earmarked to fund efforts to reduce heroin trafficking and abuse, including $2.5 million to fund the Heroin Response Strategy, a partnership among five regional HIDTA programmes to address the severe heroin threat facing those communities through public health-public safety partnerships across 15 states. In addition, $1.3 million in HIDTA funds will be directed to the five regional HIDTA programmes along the United States-Mexico border to enhance investigations of large-scale transnational criminal organizations, reduce the flow of dangerous drugs, including heroin and methamphetamine, across the border, and prevent illicit drug use in border communities. Finally, nearly $500,000 will be used to address challenges posed by illicit drug use on tribal lands in six states through the investigation and dismantling of organizations that exploit tribal communities to traffic and distribute dangerous drugs.

408.   In Mexico, health authorities continue to take measures to increase access to controlled substances for medical purposes. In June 2015, the head of the Federal Commission for Protection against Health Risks (COFEPRIS), announced the establishment of an electronic prescription system to facilitate access to morphine for patients suffering from severe pain. Under the previous system, doctors wishing to prescribe morphine needed to go to COFEPRIS offices in order to secure a bar code that validated morphine prescriptions, with the result that very few prescriptions were ever actually issued. The Mexican Secretariat of Health expressed its confidence that the new system in place would help to reduce barriers to availability of morphine for the treatment of severe pain.

409.   In August 2015, the Minister of Health of Canada announced regulatory changes to make *Salvia divinorum* and its preparations and derivatives controlled substances under schedule IV of the Controlled Drugs and Substances Act. All activities beyond simple possession will be illegal unless authorized by regulation or by an exemption. The scheduling of *Salvia divinorum* will also enable law enforcement agencies to take action against suspected illegal activities involving those substances.

410.   In June 2015, the Respect for Communities Act came into effect in Canada. The legislation, which amends the Controlled Drugs and Substances Act, establishes specific criteria that must be met by applicants seeking an exemption for activities involving illicit substances at a "supervised consumption site" in order for the exemption request to be considered by the Ministry of Health. Canada currently has one supervised consumption site, but additional applications for the establishment of drug consumption rooms have been received by Health Canada and are currently under consideration.

411.   In June 2015, the Supreme Court of Canada issued its judgement in the *R. v. Smith* case relating to the definition of "marihuana" in the country's medical cannabis programme which, until then, limited the lawful use of cannabis to "dried herb". Pursuant to the judgement, individuals licensed to possess and consume cannabis under the Marihuana for Medical Purposes Regulations may now possess cannabis derivatives for their own personal use, in addition to or instead of dried cannabis herb.

412.   Also in June 2015, Health Canada announced amendments to the Narcotic Control Regulations and the Marihuana for Medical Purposes Regulations to further strengthen public health and safety. The new measures respond to requests from medical licensing bodies for increased information on how doctors are authorizing cannabis use. The regulations require licensed producers of cannabis for medical purposes to provide quarterly reports to health-care licensing bodies on how health-care

practitioners are authorizing the use of cannabis, which will be provided to provincial and territorial medical and nurse licensing bodies upon request, allowing them to more effectively monitor the professional practice of their members.

413. In May 2015, the Government of Canada announced that it was providing the Canadian Institute for Health Information with over 4 million Canadian dollars over five years to develop a coordinated national approach for the monitoring and surveillance of prescription drug abuse in cooperation with provinces, territories and other stakeholders in order to develop and enhance data collection and dissemination and contribute to a national report on surveillance.

414. In response to the persistent public health threat posed by prescription drug abuse, authorities in Canada and the United States have continued to stage "prescription drug take-back days". In November 2014, the United States Drug Enforcement Administration reported that it had collected over 2,400 tons of unwanted prescription drugs in the previous four years of take-back initiatives.

4. Cultivation, production, manufacture and trafficking

(a) Narcotic drugs

415. There continue to be various source countries of the heroin trafficked and abused in North America. Afghan heroin, mostly smuggled through India, Iran (Islamic Republic of) and Pakistan, accounts for approximately 90 per cent of the heroin abused in Canada, while most of the heroin abused in the United States is sourced from Mexico and South America and smuggled across the United States-Mexico border. However, according to UNODC, the market share of Afghan-manufactured heroin abused in the United States may be increasing.

416. According to the Drug Enforcement Administration, the threat posed by heroin is increasing in all parts of the United States, particularly in the north-east and north-central regions. Based on reports from law enforcement agencies, the availability of heroin appears to be increasing. Heroin seizures in the United States have increased by 81 per cent over five years, from just over 2,763 kilograms (kg) in 2010 to over 5,000 kg in 2014. Over the same period, the average size of heroin seizures grew from 0.86 kg to 1.74 kg. Heroin-related arrests doubled between 2007 and 2014, and, in 2014, surpassed cannabis-related arrests for the first time.

417. Heroin seizures reported by authorities in Mexico amounted to over 386 kg in 2014. Mexican drug cartels have also increased their market share of the illicit heroin market in the United States and are now the most prominent wholesale-level heroin traffickers in several large cities in the country. The number of heroin seizures and the quantities seized at the border with Mexico have also risen sharply, from 846 kg seized in 295 incidents in 2009 to 2,196 kg seized in 580 incidents in 2013. The increased smuggling of Mexican and Colombian heroin into the United States through the Mexican border has led to a change in heroin trafficking patterns, as western states in the United States are becoming major transit areas for the drug.

418. In Mexico, opium poppy eradication efforts have continued. According to UNODC, Mexico eradicated 14,662 hectares of opium poppy cultivation in 2013, a decrease of 7 per cent since 2012.

419. Most of the cocaine available in the United States continues to be produced in Colombia and smuggled across the Mexican border and, to a lesser extent, through the Caribbean. Despite the fact that cocaine continues to be widely available throughout the country, its availability has decreased continually since 2007, with the biggest markets for the drug concentrated along the east coast of the United States. Mexico, for instance, reportedly seized 2.8 tons of cocaine in 2014, a decrease of 11 per cent compared with 2013.

420. Law enforcement officials in the region attribute the decrease in availability of cocaine to less coca bush cultivation in producing countries in South America, successful law enforcement efforts, changing patterns of abuse and conflicts between transnational criminal groups.

421. Despite declining seizures of cannabis herb in Mexico and the United States, cannabis has maintained its status as the most widely available and most widely abused illicit drug in North America.

422. In all three countries, domestic production of cannabis has continued, particularly in indoor growth operations and on private land. In addition, large quantities of the drug are also smuggled into the United States from Mexico, with seizures remaining at 1.3 million kg to 1.4 million kg per year. Smuggling methods include subterranean tunnels, shipment containers and hidden compartments in private vehicles. Mexican authorities estimate that of the 868 tons of cannabis seized in the country in 2014, just over 84 per cent was intended for domestic consumption, while over 15 per cent was intended to be trafficked to the United States.

423. According to the Drug Enforcement Administration, states neighbouring those in which cannabis has been legalized for non-medical purposes have reported a spillover effect as the drug is trafficked into their jurisdictions. The Drug Enforcement Administration has also found that the legalization of cannabis in some states has not eliminated the illicit market for the drug in those states due to high taxes and other state-imposed restrictions on the legal cannabis.

424. The THC content of cannabis seized in the region has also reportedly continued to increase. In its "2014 National drug threat assessment summary", the Drug Enforcement Administration reported an increase in potency, with THC levels rising from 3.96 per cent in 1995 to an average potency of 12.55 per cent in 2013. Another growing trend has been the production and abuse of cannabis concentrates through THC extraction from cannabis plant materials, which can yield THC levels of up to 80 per cent.

425. Trafficking of fentanyl-laced drugs has continued to emerge as a major threat to public health in the region, particularly in Canada and the United States. In Canada, the Royal Canadian Mounted Police has identified two primary ways the drug is infiltrating the illicit drug market. The first is the diversion of pharmaceutical fentanyl products (primarily transdermal patches) from domestic supply and distribution channels into illicit trade. The second is the smuggling into Canada of pharmaceutical-grade fentanyl and fentanyl analogues. Law enforcement authorities in western Canada, which is particularly affected by fentanyl trafficking, have indicated that the main source region is Asia (in particular China), with fentanyl being smuggled into British Columbia by organized criminal groups and, from there, further eastward to other provinces, particularly the province of Alberta.

426. Fentanyl is typically smuggled in powder form and is often combined with illicit drugs (primarily heroin) and illicit synthetic drug tablets manufactured in domestic clandestine laboratories which is often sold as counterfeit oxycodone tablets. According to data from Health Canada's Drug Analysis Service, the number of seizures of fentanyl in Canada increased by a factor of more than 30 in five years, from 29 seizures in 2009 to 894 seizures in 2014. In the United States, a nationwide alert on fentanyl was issued, identifying trafficking of the substance as a threat to health and public safety. The Drug Enforcement Administration has reported that most fentanyl-induced deaths in the United States are caused by clandestinely manufactured fentanyl and not by diverted pharmaceutical fentanyl. Seizures of the drug continue to increase, and law enforcement authorities have identified

some trends such as the smuggling of the drug in hidden compartments in sport utility vehicles.

(b) Psychotropic substances

427. On the basis of a wide variety of indicators including seizure data, law enforcement reporting and local-level treatment information, the Drug Enforcement Administration has indicated that large-scale methamphetamine trafficking and abuse are continuing to increase in the United States. The Drug Enforcement Administration's "2014 National drug threat assessment summary", notes that almost 32 per cent of responding agencies indicated that methamphetamine was the greatest drug threat in their areas.

428. United States authorities have stated that most of the methamphetamine available in the United States is manufactured in Mexico. While most of the methamphetamine is smuggled into the United States in powder or crystal form, the drug is increasingly being trafficked across the border in liquid form after its dilution in a liquid solvent, making its detection more difficult. Reflecting that trend, methamphetamine seizures reported by Mexico in 2014 amounted to 19.7 tons, an increase of more than 34 per cent over the amount in 2013. The country also reported an increase in the number of methamphetamine laboratories dismantled, with 131 clandestine laboratories dismantled in 2014, primarily in the States of Guerrero, Michoacán and Sinaloa. Mexico has also been identified as a source country for crystalline methamphetamine seized in East and South-East Asia and Oceania.

(c) Precursors

429. Methamphetamine manufacture in the United States continues to be dominated by small-scale laboratories using ephedrine and pseudoephedrine preparations. In 2014, the United States reported a decrease in domestic methamphetamine manufacture, likely attributable to an increase in the supply of methamphetamine manufactured in Mexico.

430. A comprehensive review of the situation with respect to the control of precursors and chemicals frequently used in the illicit manufacture of narcotic drugs and psychotropic substances in the region can be found in the report of the Board for 2015 on the implementation of article 12 of the 1988 Convention.

(d)   Substances not under international control

431.   Despite a slight decline in availability, new psychoactive substances, particularly cathinones and synthetic cannabinoids, continue to pose a significant challenge to drug control efforts in the region, which is one of the largest and most diversified markets in the world for new psychoactive substances. Most manufacture, trafficking and abuse of new psychoactive substances in the region takes place in Canada and the United States, with reports of new psychoactive substances having tripled in those two countries between 2010 and 2013. A major challenge is that those substances continue to be widely available through retail outlets in both countries, as well as through the Internet.

432.   In response to the threat posed by new psychoactive substances, Governments in the region have continued to make use of legislative, administrative and law enforcement mechanisms to remove those substances from the market and to investigate and prosecute individuals responsible for their manufacture and trafficking.

5.   Abuse and treatment

433.   With annual prevalence rates of 11.6 per cent, cannabis continues to be the drug most commonly abused in North America among the population aged 15-64 years. According to UNODC, cannabis abuse in the United States is on the increase, including among high school students, for which annual prevalence rates rose from 24.7 per cent in 2012 to 25.8 per cent in 2013.

434.   North America continues to have the highest rate of drug-related mortality in the world, with 43,300 drug-related deaths in 2013, a rate of 136.8 deaths per million inhabitants compared with an estimated global average range of 40.8-50.5 deaths per million inhabitants. In 2013, there were 40,239 drug-related deaths in the United States alone, accounting for one of every five drug-related deaths worldwide. According to data released by the White House Office of National Drug Control Policy in January 2015, deaths due to drug overdose in the United States have increased overall by 6 per cent since 2012. While deaths related to prescription opioids have remained relatively stable, increasing by 1 per cent from 2012 to 2013, the mortality rate for other drugs has significantly increased. The number of overdose deaths related to cocaine in 2013 saw a 12 per cent increase over 2012. The biggest increase in the number of overdose deaths identified was related to heroin. Drug overdose deaths related

to heroin increased by 39 per cent from 2012 to 2013, the third consecutive annual increase. The United States administration attributes the stability of the number of deaths related to prescription opioids to prevention campaigns and stricter control measures on prescribing and dispensing practices.

435.   According to information provided by the United States Government based on the 2013 National Survey on Drug Use and Health, there were an estimated 7.6 million people in need of drug treatment in the country in 2014.

436.   The public health effects of heroin abuse in the United States have continued to increase, with abuse spreading from its traditional urban base to suburban and rural areas. From 2010 to 2013, the number of recorded heroin-related drug overdose deaths almost tripled, reaching 8,620 deaths in 2013, although public health officials assume the real number of deaths is much higher because heroin rapidly metabolizes into morphine and is difficult to detect. According to United States officials, possible reasons for that increase include an overall increase in the number of heroin users; batches of the drug with greater purity being sold in certain markets; an increase in new and inexperienced heroin users, including those using heroin to supplement or replace prescription opioids; and the presence of toxic substances such as fentanyl in the heroin consumed.

437.   In Canada and the United States, deaths related to fentanyl abuse have continued to increase, with many recreational drug users succumbing to overdoses after ingesting opioids (primarily counterfeit oxycodone) which they were unaware were fentanyl-laced. According to the Drug Enforcement Administration, individuals who have overdosed on fentanyl represent a diverse population from all regions of the United States, all age groups and both sexes and include both new and more experienced users.

438.   While the Canadian Pharmacists Association have identified fentanyl-related overdoses as a public health threat affecting people from all parts of the country, the problem has been particularly acute in the provinces of British Columbia, Alberta and Ontario. According to the British Columbia Coroners Service, of the 300 deaths related to opioid overdose in 2014, approximately 25 per cent involved fentanyl, compared with 5 per cent in 2011. In Alberta, public health authorities have indicated that 120 people died as a result of fentanyl-related overdoses in 2014, compared with 6 overdoses in 2011. In order to address the growing public health risk, British Columbia launched the "Know your source" initiative in March 2015 to make the public aware of the dangers of

consuming fentanyl-laced drugs, suggest ways of minimizing overdose risks and direct the public to public health resources. The province has also increased its distribution of "take-home naloxone kits", which began in 2012. In August 2015, provincial health authorities announced that 250 overdoses in the province had been reversed since the kits first became available in 2012. Similarly, the Government of Alberta began implementing a "take-home naloxone" programme across the province in the summer of 2015 in response to the growing number of fentanyl-related deaths in the province. The take-home project provides naloxone kits to people who are at high risk of overdose so that the drug can be administered immediately should an overdose occur.

439.   In North America, as in many parts of the world, the problem of drug injection is compounded in the correctional setting. According to UNODC, it is estimated that between 24 and 36 per cent of all people using heroin in the United States—more than 200,000 people—pass through the correctional system each year. Drug use in prison settings, including intravenous injection, is commonplace. INCB reminds Governments in the region of the importance of ensuring adequate measures for the prevention and treatment of drug abuse in the prison system in accordance with article 38 of the 1961 Convention as amended.

440.   Drug abuse by injection in North America has led to the increasing transmission of blood-borne diseases in the region. According to estimates submitted to UNODC by the Government of Mexico, drug use by injection in the country has led to hepatitis C prevalence rates of up to 96 per cent among people who abuse drugs by injection. Hepatitis C prevalence rates in Canada and the United States for people who inject drugs also continue to be high: 68 per cent and 73 per cent respectively. In March 2015, the Governor of the State of Indiana declared a public health emergency in a rural southern county of the state that had been heavily affected by an HIV outbreak linked to intravenous drug use. In an executive order, the Governor authorized the county to institute a "targeted short-term needle exchange programme" to contain the outbreak. According to public health authorities, most of the cases of HIV infection were due to abuse of oxymorphone tablets, which were dissolved and then injected.

441.   In states of the United States that have medical cannabis programmes, the diversion of cannabis from the programmes has been reported as a major source for the drug's illicit use, particularly among young people. Prevalence surveys cited by the Drug Enforcement Administration indicate that 34 per cent of the twelfth grade students (aged 17-18 years) who had used cannabis in the past 12 months and who lived in states that have medical cannabis schemes, identified medical cannabis prescribed to another person as one of their sources for the drug.

442.   Authorities in the United States have indicated that the medical consequences of cannabis abuse continue to grow: the percentage of emergency room visits and admissions to treatment reported as cannabis-related increased from 6.9 per cent in 1993 to 17.5 per cent of all drug-related admissions in 2012. At the same time, surveys conducted in the North American region indicate that among young people there is a low perception of risk associated with regular cannabis use. In the United States, the Monitoring the Future Survey showed that 60 per cent of twelfth grade students (aged 17-18 years) do not consider regular cannabis use to be harmful.

443.   In the State of Colorado, which has legalized the sale and distribution of cannabis for non-medical purposes, cannabis prevalence rates are higher and increasing faster than the national average, according to the results of the United States National Survey on Drug Use and Health. According to the United States Government, based on data for the period 2001-2012, the number of primary treatment admissions for cannabis in Colorado is significantly higher than the national average and is rising (160 admissions to treatment per 100,000 people aged 12 or older in Colorado in 2012, compared with less than 120 nationally).

444.   An increasing number of cases of ingestion of cannabis edibles by young children has also been reported in the United States, particularly in states that have legalized the drug for non-medical purposes. The Rocky Mountain Poison Control Center has reported that, since 2009, the Children's Hospital Colorado has seen an increase in the number of children under 5 years of age being treated in emergency rooms due to the ingestion of edible cannabis products such as brownies, cookies and peanut butter, increasing from no cases in the five years prior to medical liberalization to 14 cases between 2009 and 2011.

445.   Public health authorities in the United States have reported a sharp rise in calls to poison centres related to synthetic cannabis. In 2013, poison centres in the country received 2,668 calls about exposure to synthetic cannabis. In 2014, that number increased to 3,680. In 2015, the numbers of reports of exposure to synthetic cannabis had already surpassed 5,300 by mid-August. While calls to poison centres are but one indicator of increased use in the country, that trend is corroborated by other sources such as law enforcement agency records.

446. While annual prevalence rates for methamphetamine use have remained relatively stable in the United States, at 0.5-0.6 per cent of the general population aged 15-64 years, there have been indications that abuse has increased in some pockets of the country. In the Minneapolis-Saint Paul metropolitan area, the number of people treated for methamphetamine use increased by 19 per cent from 2011 to 2012. In Ohio, treatment admissions for the drug increased by 34 per cent from 2009 to 2012. In the county of San Diego, deaths related to methamphetamine increased by 70 per cent from 2008 to 2012.

South America

1. Major developments

447. South America has a relatively strong institutional capacity in the wider context of Latin America and the Caribbean, and countries in the region have been making considerable efforts at the national and international levels to curb the illicit supply of drugs and address the increasing rates of drug abuse.

448. While the region continues to account for virtually all the world's coca bush cultivation and supply of coca paste and cocaine, the efforts made by the Governments of Bolivia (Plurinational State of), Colombia and Peru in 2013 resulted in the lowest total amount of coca bush cultivation since 1990. According to UNODC, that trend may have contributed to a reduction in the global availability of cocaine, which has affected some of the main markets. The trend of a decreasing total area of coca bush cultivation continued in Bolivia (Plurinational State of) and Peru in 2014. Colombia, in contrast, reported an increase of 44 per cent in the area of cultivation compared with 2013, making it once again the country with the largest area of coca bush cultivation in the world. Nonetheless, the area under coca bush cultivation in Colombia is still 30 per cent lower than it was in 2007, and 58 per cent lower than in 2000.

449. Several countries in the region, including Brazil, Chile, Colombia, Ecuador and Uruguay, are debating and enacting new legislation, decisions and resolutions on the use of cannabis. Those range from regulations for the cultivation of cannabis plants and the importation of medicines containing cannabidiol for medical use in some countries, to the further regulation of a market for cannabis for non-medical use, as is the case of Uruguay.

2. Regional cooperation

450. South America continues to be a particularly active region for regional cooperation at the political and technical levels. Several bilateral, intraregional and interregional initiatives took place in the period 2014-2015, including consultations and the exchange of information, joint investigations, extraditions, military and law enforcement operations, capacity-building and the development of standards and guidelines. Cooperation has taken place in diverse and mutually-reinforcing regional initiatives and forums such as the Hemispheric Information Exchange Network for Mutual Assistance in Criminal Matters and Extradition of OAS, the Hemispheric Drug Strategy of CICAD, the Police Community of the Americas, the Ibero-American Network for International Legal Cooperation (IberRed), the South American Council on the World Drug Problem of the Union of South American Nations, the supply control component of the Community of Latin American and Caribbean States, the meetings of Heads of National Drug Law Enforcement Agencies, Latin America and the Caribbean, and the Cooperation Programme on Drug Policies between Latin America and the European Union.

451. Expert cooperation in the region to counter drug trafficking has been particularly active in the area of precursor control, in which States in the region successfully collaborated in the UNODC project "Prevention of the diversion of drug precursors in Latin America and the Caribbean", as well as in the area of countering money-laundering in the context of the Asset Recovery Network of the Financial Action Task Force of Latin America against Money-Laundering. The 15 countries that comprise the Network[37] developed guidelines for international judicial cooperation on asset recovery and approved the Network's action plan for the strengthening of information exchange and the development of guidelines on joint and combined investigations.

452. The growing concern at the increasing levels of drug abuse in the region has led mostly to responses at the national level, but many countries have also engaged in regional cooperation to address drug demand, such as the international network of drug dependence treatment and rehabilitation resource centres (Treatnet) and the "Support project on reduction of demand of illegal drugs in the Andean Community (PREDEM)", both supported by UNODC.

---

[37] Argentina, Brazil, Bolivia (Plurinational State of), Colombia, Costa Rica, Chile, Cuba, Ecuador, Guatemala, Honduras, Mexico, Panama, Paraguay, Peru and Uruguay.

453. The countries of the region are taking action to ensure the availability of narcotic drugs and psychotropic substances for medical purposes. The Inter-American Convention on Protecting the Human Rights of Older Persons, adopted in June 2015 by the General Assembly of OAS, which in its article 19, entitled "Right to health", urges Member States to ensure the availability of controlled medicines for the rehabilitation and palliative care of older persons. Palliative care is required in the treatment of cancer and many other diseases and for end-of-life patients of all ages. Some countries in the region have reported a low level of consumption of narcotic drugs and psychotropic substances for medical use.

454. At its meeting held in Lima in August 2014, the Group of Experts on Chemical Substances and Pharmaceutical Products of CICAD submitted a model administrative system for the control of chemical substances and guidelines on the disposal of used fentanyl transdermal patches and suggestions for establishing designated ports of entry/exit for controlled chemical substances. Those proposals were approved by CICAD at its regular session held in Guatemala City on 19-24 November 2014.

455. Bilateral and trilateral counter-narcotics operations continue to abound in the region. Examples include the implementation by Bolivia (Plurinational State of) and Peru of a joint strategy to eliminate the cocaine trafficking "air bridge" between their territories. A total of 5,170 individual operations resulted in the elimination of 50 clandestine airstrips and the seizure of aircraft and drugs (34.8 tons of cannabis, 7.3 tons of cocaine and 6 tons of coca paste). At a joint ministerial-level meeting held in June 2015, the two countries agreed to further strengthen border control (including control of chemical precursors) and the fight against drug trafficking, money-laundering and smuggling. Operation Trapézio, conducted by Brazil and Peru, led to the dismantling of 28 cocaine-manufacturing laboratories. The joint Operation Bracolper, involving the navies of Brazil, Colombia and Peru, which has taken place for 41 consecutive years, was conducted once again in 2015.

3. National legislation, policy and action

456. The Brazilian National Health Surveillance Agency rescheduled cannabidiol from a "prohibited" to a "controlled" substance, as established in resolution RDC No. 17 of 6 May 2015, effective as of 7 July 2015. The rescheduling follows the receipt by the Agency of several requests

for imports of products containing cannabidiol and other cannabinoids for medical treatment.

457. In 2014, Brazil continued joint operations with Paraguay as part of Operation Aliança, the goal of which is to eradicate cannabis plant cultivation. The operations resulted in the destruction of 2,571 tons of cannabis cultivation. The country is also targeting cultivation fields in north-eastern Brazil, where the Brazilian Federal Police conducts eradication operations.

458. Following the enactment of the legislation on cannabis in December 2013, the Government of Uruguay issued a presidential decree in May 2014 further regulating the import, production, storage, sale and distribution of cannabis for non-medical use. The decree establishes procedures for the registration of producers of cannabis for distribution in pharmacies and of domestic producers, cannabis clubs, consumers and pharmacies, and regulates the production and commercialization of cannabis seeds and cuttings. In addition, the Government enacted decrees regulating aspects of non-psychoactive cannabis for industrial use, and the sale and use of cannabis for medical purposes. Once again, INCB wishes to draw attention to its view that the legislation permitting the non-medical use of cannabis is contrary to the provisions of the international drug control conventions, specifically article 4, paragraph (c), and article 36 of the 1961 Convention as amended by the 1972 Protocol, and article 3, paragraph 1 (a), of the 1988 Convention.

459. In the first half of 2015, the Colombian Congress approved the National Development Plan 2014-2018. The document contains the Government's action plan for the four-year period. In relation to the issue of drug control, the Plan aims to address the drug problem by means of a comprehensive and balanced approach. That objective is to be attained through the following six actions: (a) formulating a comprehensive policy to counter illicit drugs that adopts a human rights-based approach; (b) creating a national intervention plan for the reduction of illicit crops in Colombia; (c) designing and implementing alternatives to imprisonment for the most vulnerable population groups; (d) controlling the microtrafficking phenomenon by adopting a social intervention and territorial control approach; (e) preventing and addressing problematic drug consumption from a health perspective; and (f) containing the entry of illicit drugs into the country, their production within the country, and the illegal diversion of controlled substances.

460. In September 2015, the Ministry of Defence of Colombia announced its new strategy to combat drug trafficking, which focuses on improving the justice

framework and procedures and targets illicit cultivation, including by strengthening manual eradication.

461.   In May 2015, Colombia's National Narcotics Council approved the suspension of aerial spraying of coca bush cultivation with glyphosate. The decision followed a recommendation made by the Colombian Ministry of Health and Social Protection in April 2015 based on the classification of the herbicide glyphosate as "probably carcinogenic to humans" by the International Agency for Research on Cancer of WHO. The National Narcotics Council established a technical commission to explore alternative means of eradication, and the country is now exploring the use of other herbicides that may be used in aerial spraying.

462.   Colombia's Ministry of Justice and Law and the Bogotá Chamber of Commerce are supporting the harmonization of the national legislation in line with the standards for the prevention of money-laundering of the Financial Action Task Force. Additionally, the country has developed risk assessment tools on money-laundering and the financing of terrorism for the non-profit and real estate sectors, aimed at raising awareness and promoting self-regulating business environments to prevent the laundering of the proceeds of drug trafficking and connected crimes. Other countries in South America, including Argentina, Chile and Peru, are also adopting initiatives that are in line with the standards of the Financial Action Task Force and focused on risk assessments for the prevention of money-laundering and the financing of terrorism.

463.   In August 2015, the Government of Peru approved Law No. 30339, on the control, vigilance and defence of the national air space. The law regulates national airspace, including the definition of "hostile acts" and "hostile aircraft". It specifies a number of actions that may lead to declare that an aircraft is "hostile", including acts where there is evidence or reasonable suspicion that the aircraft may be engaged in drug trafficking. In such circumstances, an aircraft may be declared "hostile" and may be subject to interception and other measures. Law No. 30339 provides guidelines for the measures that could be undertaken against a hostile aircraft, including the use of force. Notably, articles 11 and 12 stipulate general guidelines for the interception of a hostile aircraft in the air or on the ground or water. The law further specifies that an aircraft cannot be declared "hostile" if it is carrying passengers who are not participating in the "hostile act". Drug traffickers have increasingly resorted to transporting cocaine shipments by air. UNODC has detected an increasing number of clandestine landing strips since 2011, from 49 clandestine landing strips in 2011 to 77 in

2012 and 80 as of October 2014. Similar to the terrestrial routes, the re-established aerial routes lead to the Plurinational State of Bolivia as an intermediary destination and then to Brazil. INCB urges Peru and other Governments implementing such measures to ensure that these measures are carried out in full respect of relevant international protocols and conventions.

464.   Following a risk assessment, in 2014 Brazil placed various new psychoactive substances under national control, including synthetic cathinones such as methylone, as well as NBOMe derivatives (including 25P-NBOMe, 25T2-NBOMe and 25H-NBOMe) and synthetic cannabinoids (including JWH-122, JWH-073 and AM-2201).

4.   Cultivation, production, manufacture and trafficking

(a)   Narcotic drugs

465.   South America is greatly affected by the illicit cultivation and trafficking of cannabis herb. The proportion of global cannabis herb seizures that are recorded in Latin America and the Caribbean rose from 20 per cent in 2012 to 30 per cent in 2013. There was a sharp increase of almost 60 per cent in cannabis seizures in South America between 2012 and 2013, from 821 tons to 1,308 tons. That increase was largely driven by seizures in, in descending order of seizure amounts, Paraguay, Colombia and Brazil.

466.   While the cannabis seized in Colombia in 2014 was cultivated domestically, the seizures reported by Brazil were of cannabis entering the country from Paraguay. Cannabis is widely consumed in the region, but it is also sometimes trafficked together with cocaine and used as payment for transporting, storage and distribution services along the routes towards North America and Europe.

467.   South America continues to be the main source of all cocaine manufactured worldwide, with the cultivation of coca bush and the manufacturing of cocaine and coca paste taking place mainly in Bolivia (Plurinational State of), Colombia and Peru. However, the seizure of coca leaf and coca paste, as well as the discovery of clandestine laboratories, in neighbouring countries such as Argentina and Chile suggests that refining also takes place elsewhere in the region. Argentina reported the discovery of 15 clandestine laboratories for refining, tableting, cutting or packaging in 2014, 12 of which were for cocaine. In the same year, Chile reported the discovery of 22 clandestine kitchen laboratories, all of them dedicated to cocaine

manufacture. The cocaine manufactured in South America is destined for its largest consumer markets—North America and Western and Central Europe—as well as local markets. To reach North America, cocaine is trafficked by land, air and sea, transiting Central America, Mexico and the Caribbean. The cocaine-trafficking route to Europe involves transit by land, rivers and air, affecting all countries but most notably Argentina, Brazil and Venezuela (Bolivarian Republic of), before crossing the Atlantic Ocean as maritime and air cargo, either directly or by way of the Caribbean or West Africa. Maritime trafficking appears to be the preferred means for large shipments, while trafficking by air is more frequent.

468. For cases of individual drug seizures in the period 2005-2014, Argentina and Brazil were the countries most frequently mentioned as transit hubs on the routes to North America and Western and Central Europe. In 2014, Colombia, the Bolivarian Republic of Venezuela, Brazil, the Dominican Republic, Panama, Peru and Ecuador, in that order, were most frequently mentioned as the countries of origin, departure or transit for cocaine shipments from South America and Central America and the Caribbean to Europe. For cocaine seizures, the most significant countries of departure for shipments to Europe in 2014 were, in descending order of volume seized, Costa Rica, Ecuador, Colombia, Brazil, the Bolivarian Republic of Venezuela and Argentina. For individual cocaine seizure cases reported in Europe in 2014, the list of countries of departure in the greatest number of cases was headed by Brazil, followed by Colombia and Argentina. Trafficked drugs enter Argentina through the country's northern provinces, which are vulnerable due to their remote areas and geographical proximity to the Plurinational State of Bolivia and, to a lesser extent, Peru. The illicit narcotics are mainly transported by land using roads that cross the border but also, to a lesser extent, by air. Argentina is making efforts to counter such threats through Operation North Shield, aimed at combating drug trafficking, trafficking in persons and smuggling in the area. After a sharp increase in the quantities seized in 2012 (when the amount of cocaine seized totalled about 10.5 tons, an increase of 151.4 per cent from the previous year), cocaine seizures have remained fairly stable, amounting to 10.4 tons in 2014. In 2014, seizures of coca leaf amounted to about 118 tons, an increase of 34.8 per cent from 2013.

469. For the fourth consecutive year, the Plurinational State of Bolivia reported a decrease in the area of coca bush cultivation. In 2014, the area of coca bush cultivation fell to 20,400 hectares (ha), which was 11 per cent less than in 2013 and the lowest level since 2001. The main areas of cultivation were Yungas de La Paz,

responsible for about 70 per cent of the cultivated area, followed by Trópico de Cochabamba with about 30 per cent of the cultivated area, and the northern provinces of the department of La Paz with less than 1 per cent. The reported decreases in the cultivated areas in Yungas de La Paz and Trópico de Cochabamba in 2014 were 10 per cent and 14 per cent respectively. Among the factors contributing to that decrease are the efforts of the Government in the area of coca bush eradication through the Strategic Operational Command "Tte. Gironda", under the coordination of the Vice-Ministry of Social Defence and Controlled Substances.

470. Brazil is vulnerable to the transit of cocaine by air, land and rivers (especially in the Amazon area) and is considered to have a strategic role in the trafficking of cocaine. It is a transit country from which cocaine is shipped overseas and is the largest cocaine market in South America. Seizures in the country doubled from 2012 to 2013, before decreasing to around 33.8 tons in 2014, which is still above the 2012 level. According to estimates for 2014, only 30 per cent of the cocaine seized in Brazil was destined for external markets. Brazil is intensifying cooperation with several partners to target transnational criminal organizations operating in the country, as exemplified by Operation Monte, a joint undertaking with the governments of the United Kingdom, Italy and Spain, resulting in the seizure of 1.3 tons of cocaine intended for distribution in Europe.

471. Colombia saw an increase of 44 per cent in the area of estimated coca bush cultivation in 2014, and thus became once again the country with the largest area of coca cultivation in the world. The area of cultivation grew from 48,000 ha in 2013 to 69,000 ha in 2014, and potential cocaine production has seen an even greater increase of 52.7 per cent, rising from 290 tons in 2013 to 442 tons in 2014. Most of the cultivation is located in the southern departments of Nariño, Cauca, Putumayo and Caquetá, as well as in the northern region of Catatumbo, located in the department of Norte de Santander, which, altogether, account for 73 per cent of the area of coca bush cultivation.

472. Among the factors that may be contributing to the increase in coca bush cultivation in Colombia, UNODC has pointed to the expected benefits for coca-growing farmers in the context of the negotiations for a peace agreement with the Revolutionary Armed Forces of Colombia (FARC), as there is a perceived leverage associated with growing coca bushes in the negotiations with the Government. Another factor that may also be contributing to the increase in coca bush cultivation is the increase in the price of coca leaf in strategic regions, such

as the departments of Meta and Guaviare, where prices rose 42 per cent, as well as a perception that there is less risk of eradication. In fact, the extent of eradication, notably aerial spraying, has declined in recent years.

473.   One of the largest increases in cocaine seizures in the past five years has been observed in Ecuador, where the amount of cocaine seized rose by over 242 per cent, amounting to 50 metric tons in 2014. The country's authorities arrested 7,772 individuals on drug trafficking charges in 2014 and 6,404 individuals in 2013. Cocaine and coca paste enter the country from the neighbouring countries Colombia and Peru. According to UNODC, coca bush cultivation in Ecuador continued to be of limited relevance in 2014. Coca paste continues to supply local consumption while the cocaine is destined for external markets. In 2014, authorities mentioned, in descending order of the total amounts of cocaine destined for each country, Spain, Belgium and Guatemala as among the countries of destination.

474.   Peru continued to make progress in the reduction of areas of coca bush cultivation. The estimated area of coca bush cultivation decreased for the third consecutive year, from 49,800 ha in 2013 to 42,900 ha in 2014, a decrease of 13.9 per cent. The production of coca leaf dropped 17 per cent from 2013 to 2014. The results are in most part due to State-led eradication programmes in the context of the national strategy for the fight against drugs for the period 2012-2016. Interventions have focused on areas that are most notably connected to drug trafficking organizations and on intensifying alternative development initiatives in those areas. The most affected areas are concentrated in the Apurímac, Ene and Mantaro river valleys and in the province of La Convención and the Lares district of Calca province, which together contain 68 per cent of the country's coca bush cultivation. The shrinking supply has affected the purity levels of the coca base and cocaine, which showed a slight decrease in prices from 2013 to 2014.

475.   In the Bolivarian Republic of Venezuela, authorities reported that cocaine seizures amounted to about 26 tons in 2014. Seizure totals have been relatively stable since 2010, when about 25 tons of cocaine were seized. Intended countries of destination for the cocaine seized included Australia, Italy and Spain, while Colombia is mentioned as country of origin.

476.   There is evidence that the area of opium poppy cultivation has been increasing and appears to have reached a five-year high in Colombia, which had detected 387 ha of cultivation in 2014. The potential increase from 2013 to 2014 in the production of opium and

manufacture of heroin (13 per cent and 15 per cent, respectively), combined with a decrease in their average prices (decreases of 37 per cent and 19 per cent, respectively) over the same period may indicate an increase in the supply of those drugs.

477.   Heroin manufactured in South America is primarily destined for the United States but is also trafficked for consumption within the region. The United States reported increased trafficking from Mexico and South America, and Mexico reported seizures in 2014 of heroin produced in Colombia and destined for the United States.

(b)   Psychotropic substances

478.   Various countries in South America have reported seizures of amphetamine-type stimulants (ATS) in 2014, including amphetamine, methamphetamine and "ecstasy"-type substances, as well as lysergic acid diethylamide (LSD). The substances seem to originate in Europe, with South America being a growing consumer market. However, some of the psychedelic substances marketed in South America as LSD seem in fact to have been new psychoactive substances, such as 25B-NBOMe, 25C-NBOMe and 25I-NBOMe, that is, substituted phenethylamines which were only scheduled by the Commission on Narcotic Drugs in March 2015.

479.   According to a study published by UNODC and CICAD in 2014 entitled "Amphetamine-type stimulants in Latin America", information on ATS and the use of specific substances in the region is still very limited, and categories used in drug use surveys are usually too broad to differentiate between non-medical use of prescription drugs, ATS and new psychoactive substances. While the use of those substances is increasingly affecting youth in the region, the limited data available prevent the accurate estimation of their market size, sources and trafficking routes.

480.   Seizures of "ecstasy"-type substances increased sharply in Brazil in 2014, with 877,853 tablets seized, an increase from 183,289 in 2013. In Colombia, seizures peaked in 2013, when 117,101 tablets were seized, increasing from 6,664 tablets in 2010, but seizures decreased again, to 39,792 tablets, in 2014. Guyana reported, as a new development, seizures of small quantities of "ecstasy" in the past two years.

481.   In 2014, Colombia reported four separate seizures of 4-bromo-2,5-dimethoxyphenethylamine (2C-B), amounting to 14,068 units in total.

(c) Precursors

482. Seizures reported by coca-producing countries of most of the acids and solvents listed in Table II of the 1988 Convention have decreased over the past decade, partly due to the fact that solvents are increasingly being recycled and reused several times and due to changes in illicit processing practices. Forensic analysis of seized cocaine originating in Colombia in 2013 suggests that more illicit cocaine-manufacturing laboratories are using significantly reduced amounts of the solvents required for processing.

483. A comprehensive review of the situation with respect to the control of precursors and chemicals frequently used in the illicit manufacture of narcotic drugs and psychotropic substances in the region can be found in the report of the Board for 2015 on the implementation of article 12 of the 1988 Convention.

(d) Substances not under international control

484. The Colombian Drug Observatory has created an early warning system for detecting new psychoactive substances. The system was triggered for the second time, when tablets sold as 2C-B, an internationally controlled drug, were found to contain ketamine and small quantities of other unidentified substances.

485. In 2014, Chile seized NBOMe derivatives of a total of 30 milligrams in five different events. The country also reported seizures of 2,5-dimethoxy-4-chloroamphetamine (DOC).

486. Certain South American countries have placed several substances under national control due to their use in the illicit manufacturing of cocaine or as cutting agents, including caffeine and cement.

5. Abuse and treatment

487. UNODC data confirm that the drugs with the greatest annual prevalence among the general adult population aged 15-64 years in South America continue to be cannabis (5.9 per cent) and cocaine (1.2 per cent), followed by amphetamines and prescription stimulants (0.5 per cent) and opioids (0.3 per cent). Annual prevalence of cannabis and cocaine continued to be higher than the global average, which is calculated by UNODC to be 3.9 per cent for the former and 0.4 per cent for the latter.

488. There are gender differences in the prevalence of drug abuse in South America. While cannabis is the drug most abused by both men and women in terms of annual prevalence, cocaine is the second most frequent drug of abuse for men, whereas for women cannabis is followed closely by the misuse of tranquillizers, with cocaine coming a distant third.

489. Experts in South America perceive an increase in cocaine use in the region, which is considered to be driven by increased abuse in Brazil. The rise in abuse of smokable cocaine has been receiving particular attention from national authorities, with the annual prevalence of "crack" cocaine being estimated at 0.7 per cent in 2014. The country is investing in improving the collection of data on drug abuse, and a survey among prisoners is planned to take place in 2015.

490. A national study on drug abuse in Bolivian households in 2013/14, published in March 2015, found that among abused illicit substances, cannabis (1.27 per cent), cocaine (0.32 per cent) and inhalants (0.30 per cent) had the highest rate of annual prevalence. With the exception of tranquillizers, the abuse of all other substances appears to have decreased between 2007 and 2013. The study found that the average age of drug use initiation was 19 years and that abuse is highest among men and youth. Recommendations include the introduction of a selective drug prevention policy focusing on young people at universities and work environments.

491. Increased abuse of synthetic drugs is a concern in South American countries such as Colombia, where they negatively affect local communities. The drugs are distributed in small quantities and may have their quality altered in mixtures that may be particularly harmful. Another trend observed in the country is the decrease in the average age of the users of such drugs.

492. Small-scale trafficking in Colombia, commonly referred to as "microtrafficking", has become a growing problem in several Colombian cities. It has been reported that municipal Colombian authorities have been taking experimental steps to control such trafficking with the aim of reducing social harms, including some types of efforts, such as substituting one controlled substance, such as cocaine, for another, such as cannabis, which may be inconsistent with Colombia's obligations under the Conventions.

493. Reports on substances seized at the level of microtrafficking reflect the fact that drug abuse is a steadily growing problem in Paraguay. The country has reported a change with respect to abuse patterns, the substances abused and the age of first-time abuse. According to the

second national study on persons with problems resulting from the consumption of alcohol and other drugs in treatment centres and self-help groups, conducted in 2012, substances of first-time abuse are primarily alcohol followed by tobacco, cannabis, smokable forms of cocaine, cocaine, solvents, anxiolytics, anti-depressants, amphetamine-type stimulants, opiates and others.

494.   Through an integral drug abuse prevention plan, the Government of the Bolivarian Republic of Venezuela reported reaching over 4.6 million people in 2014 by organizing more than 35,000 activities with a focus on communities, children and adolescents at risk. The plan is based on a strategy of decentralization, the adoption of a people-centred approach and the scaling-up of prevention activities that strengthen life skills and promote healthy lifestyles, also targeting workplaces, prison settings and indigenous communities.

C. Asia

East and South-East Asia

1. Major developments

495.   With an increasing diversification of trafficking routes and a significant increase in the amount of seizures, the manufacturing, trafficking and abuse of amphetamine-type stimulants show no signs of abating. It has been noted that drug trafficking syndicates in other regions, attracted by the size of the markets in East and South-East Asia, have recently become involved in a number of the region's countries. In addition, regional initiatives that facilitate the freer flow of goods and services might be exploited by some criminal groups.

496.   The region continues to face the threats posed by the proliferation of new psychoactive substances and non-scheduled precursor chemicals. Exploiting gaps in legislation and creating the illusion of legality, new psychoactive substances are marketed as "legal highs". Although in recent years some countries have made greater endeavours to place new psychoactive substances under national control, drug trafficking syndicates have responded and adapted by producing substances not yet under control, thus hindering drug control efforts. The abuse of ketamine and its trafficking remain another area of concern for countries in the region.

497.   The illicit cultivation of opium poppy and the manufacture of heroin continue in the countries of the Golden

Triangle (Lao People's Democratic Republic, Myanmar and Thailand). The total area of illicit opium poppy cultivation in the region was estimated to be 63,800 hectares (ha) in 2014, and production of opium estimated to be 762 tons. While the amount of illicit cultivation remains steady, a declining trend in the abuse of heroin in some East and South-East Asian countries has been reported. The scope of cocaine-related activities within the region remains limited compared with other regions and compared with other drug types.

498.   The growing amount of methamphetamine being trafficked into East and South-East Asia from other regions suggests that new trafficking routes have been established connecting previously unrelated markets. In recent years, methamphetamine originating in Africa, West Asia and, more recently, the Americas, has been trafficked into the region. The more timely sharing of intelligence and better collaboration among law enforcement agencies across the region are essential for the early detection of these new trafficking routes and the implementation of measures to address them.

2. Regional cooperation

499.   Multilateral cooperation among the States members of the Association of Southeast Asian Nations (ASEAN) continues, as the regional multilateral body formulates its next approach, subsequent to the prior goal of making the ASEAN region free of illicit drugs by 2015. A ministerial statement adopted at the third ASEAN Ministerial Meeting on Drug Matters, held in Indonesia in December 2014, underscored the political commitment to further strengthening regional cooperation. In September 2014, the ASEAN Narcotics Cooperation Centre was launched in Bangkok as a coordinating platform to further the pursuit of that goal of regional cooperation. The 12th meeting of the ASEAN Inter-Parliamentary Assembly Fact-Finding Committee to Combat the Drug Menace, held in Kuala Lumpur in June 2015, provided an opportunity for the exchange of information on the latest national developments. A resolution adopted at the meeting emphasized the significance of taking a people-centred approach in the delivery of effective demand and supply reduction programmes. Through another platform for multilateral cooperation, the 36th ASEAN Senior Officials Meeting on Drug Matters, held in Singapore in August 2015, various issues related to illicit drugs in the region were discussed.

500.   Faced with the increasing connectivity of drug trafficking organizations across the globe, some regional meetings discussed major region-specific challenges in the

context of the global evolution of such criminal groups. The joint INCB-UNODC international conference on precursor chemicals and new psychoactive substances held in Bangkok in April 2015 highlighted the global challenges posed by precursor chemicals and new psychoactive substances and examined approaches to address those challenges at both the global and regional levels. Bringing together countries of the Asia-Pacific region, the 20th Asia-Pacific Operational Drug Enforcement Conference, held in Tokyo in February 2015, focused on international cooperation in drug law enforcement to counter the threat of amphetamine-type stimulants.

501.   A ministerial meeting, held in May 2015, of the signatories to the 1993 memorandum of understanding on drug control of the Greater Mekong subregion reiterated their continued commitment and stated that the memorandum had proven to be a constructive mechanism for better regional cooperation in law enforcement efforts against drug trafficking in the subregion. The evolving drug situation specific to the countries concerned, such as the greater flow of illicit drugs and precursor chemicals, was highlighted and discussed.

3. National legislation, policy and action

502.   Confronted with the continued and rapid emergence of new psychoactive substances, countries in the region have placed additional substances under temporary listing and/or extended the scope of drug control to defined groups of substances. For instance, the Republic of Korea announced the temporary control of 10 new psychoactive substances (6 synthetic cannabinoids, 2 phenethylamines and 2 other miscellaneous substances) for three years in December 2014, which brought the number of new psychoactive substances currently under temporary control to 86. Under that country's Act on the Control of Narcotics, the possession, management, trade, assistance in the trade, or the giving or receiving of materials that contain a temporary scheduled substance are prohibited. In Macao, China, the anti-drug law (Law 17 of 2009) was amended in 2014 to control five more substance groups: piperazine derivatives, synthetic cannabinoids, derivatives of cathinone (excluding bupropion), *Salvia divinorum* and salvinorin A. In China, the Non-Medical Narcotic Drug and Psychotropic Substance List Regulation, which listed 116 non-medical narcotic drugs and psychotropic substances, entered into force on 1 October 2015.

503.   After the listing of *alpha*-phenylacetoacetonitrile (APAAN) as an internationally controlled precursor in October 2014, several countries have placed it under their national control. On 14 May 2014, the Government of China scheduled APAAN and 2-bromopropiophenone (a known intermediate in the synthetic manufacture of ephedrine and pseudoephedrine from propiophenone) as first-class controlled precursors, requiring import and export permits for its international trade. Similarly, the Government of Thailand listed APAAN and its optical isomers in Schedule 4 (precursor chemicals) of the Narcotics Act. In Hong Kong, China, APAAN has also been controlled under the Control of Chemicals Ordinance (chap. 145). INCB reminds countries that have not yet done so to place APAAN under national control without delay pursuant to the related Commission on Narcotic Drugs decision 57/1 of 19 March 2014.

504.   To improve the effectiveness of law enforcement and expand the scope of drug control, new legislative and administrative changes have been introduced by the Government of the Philippines. In July 2015, amendments were made regarding the custody and disposition of illegal drugs, in particular the requirement to conduct an inventory after seizure operations by law enforcement authorities and the need for witnesses. Under the prior legislation, law enforcement officers had been required to conduct an inventory of the seized illegal drugs and chemicals immediately after confiscation in the presence of the suspects and representatives of the Department of Justice, elected public officials and the media as witnesses. Under the amended law, law enforcement officers can now conduct the inventory at the nearest office of authorities or police station in the case of a warrantless arrest as long as the integrity and evidentiary value of the seized items are properly preserved. A law penalizing driving under the influence of alcohol, dangerous drugs or similar substances was also adopted in 2014.

505.   In the Philippines, a new national anti-drug programme of action for the period 2015-2020 and a timeline for its implementation have been drafted. The action plan outlines strategies in five main areas (demand reduction, supply reduction, alternative development, civic awareness and response, and regional and international strategies) and is intended to guide the country's drug control efforts. Similarly, the Thai Government has developed a national drug control strategic plan for the period 2015-2019 to offer holistic solutions for drug control beyond 2015. The strategic plan contains eight primary strategic focus areas and provides the mechanism for its implementation and the monitoring and review of that implementation. The Government of Myanmar is implementing the last phase of its 20-year drug control plan for the period 1999-2019 for achieving an illicit drug-free status by 2019. While the eradication of opium poppy cultivation was the main priority in the initial phase,

other objectives, such as the rehabilitation of drug abusers, the establishment of further special counter-narcotics task force units and the participation of local communities in the implementation of drug control activities, have now become the current priorities.

4. Cultivation, production, manufacture and trafficking

(a) Narcotic drugs

506. Since the mid-1980s, the illicit cultivation of opium poppy in the region has been concentrated in the Golden Triangle, which was once the main world supplier of heroin. The considerable increases in illicit cultivation in Afghanistan, combined with the eradication efforts of the countries of the Golden Triangle (Lao People's Democratic Republic, Myanmar and Thailand), have significantly reduced the share of illicit opium that is produced in that area. However, illicit cultivation of opium poppy in the Lao People's Democratic Republic and Myanmar has recently started to increase, after reaching its lowest level in recent years, with less than 25,000 ha of illicit cultivation in 2006. In 2014, the total area of illicit opium poppy cultivation reached 63,800 ha, most of it in Myanmar (90 per cent) and a small amount in the Lao People's Democratic Republic (10 per cent). The total amount of opium produced in the region was estimated to be 762 tons.

507. Heroin illicitly manufactured in Myanmar has been trafficked overland into China through Yunnan province. At the same time, precursor chemicals required for the illicit manufacture of heroin have been smuggled into Myanmar from China. There is a risk that two-way trafficking for the manufacture and consumption of heroin may grow as drug trafficking syndicates exploit the easier movement of people and capital resulting from initiatives enhancing regional integration within the ASEAN community. In the light of such challenges, INCB encourages close cooperation and collaboration among the ASEAN member States for the timely exchange of intelligence.

508. Heroin seizures in the region rose each year from 2011 to 2013, reaching 11.8 tons in 2013, with more than 70 per cent being seizures reported by China. With total seizures of 9.5 tons in 2014 (9.4 tons in China, 89 kilograms (kg) in Hong Kong, China, and 3.5 kg in Macao, China), China continues to account for most of the seizures in the region. Reductions in seizures have recently

been reported by other countries such as Cambodia and Thailand. The total amount of heroin seized in Cambodia and Thailand dropped significantly in 2014 (1.8 kg and 371 kg, respectively), back to its longer-term average level.

509. Illicit cannabis cultivation and significant cannabis seizures continue to be reported by Indonesia and the Philippines. To avoid the eradication efforts of the authorities, illicit cannabis cultivation in the Philippines is usually located in high-altitude and mountainous areas of the country that are difficult to access. In 2014, 68 tons of cannabis herb were seized in Indonesia, more than three times the amount seized in 2012. The amount of cannabis seized in transit in Thailand increased from 27 tons in 2013 to 33 tons in 2014, following an upward trend that began in 2012. In 2014, 164 kg of cannabis herb and 576 kg of dried cannabis were seized in the Philippines. Increases in cannabis herb seizures were moderate for Hong Kong, China, and for Singapore.

510. The misuse of cocaine in East and South-East Asia remains limited, as evidenced by a relatively low level of seizures compared with other regions. The latest data point towards a further decline in the amount of cocaine seized within the region. In Hong Kong, China, the quantity of cocaine seized dropped by more than half, from more than 700 kg in 2012 to less than 300 kg in 2014. Similarly, reported seizures in Japan and Macao, China, declined by more than 90 per cent, down to 2 kg and 3 kg respectively in 2014. In Cambodia, cocaine seizures fell from around 13 kg in 2013 to less than 8 kg in 2014. China (excluding Hong Kong and Macao Special Administrative Regions) and the Philippines reported cocaine seizures of 113 kg and 70 kg respectively.

(b) Psychotropic substances

511. Growing availability and the prevalence of amphetamine-type stimulants in the region persist, as demonstrated by the continued upsurge in methamphetamine seizures and the high level of misuse. East and South-East Asia continues to be the region that seizes the largest total amounts of methamphetamine, which is available in two main forms (methamphetamine tablets and crystalline methamphetamine). While the misuse of methamphetamine tablets (usually of lower purity) is more concentrated in the countries of the Mekong river basin, the misuse of crystalline methamphetamine is more widespread geographically. Between 2008 and 2013, seizures of crystalline methamphetamine in the region almost doubled, and seizures of methamphetamine tablets increased eight-fold.

512. Among the countries of the Mekong river basin, Myanmar is considered to be the main country of origin for methamphetamine tablets. Information on seizures of methamphetamine tablets in China and Thailand suggests that more methamphetamine tablets are originating in and being trafficked from Myanmar. In Thailand, a sizeable amount of methamphetamine tablets was seized in 2014 (113 million tablets), while 248 tablets were seized in Singapore.

513. The latest national reports by China reveal that most of the crystalline methamphetamine available in the country is manufactured in the country, with most of the illicit manufacturing base located in the southern part of the country (Guangdong province). More than 80 per cent of the crystalline methamphetamine seized in 2013 had been manufactured in the cities of Shanwei and Jieyang, with the city of Lufeng being the main source of supply of the substances required for manufacture. Some illicit manufacture of crystalline methamphetamine was also found in the western part of the country, in Chengdu and its surrounding cities.

514. Across the region, the growing availability of crystalline methamphetamine remains a worrying trend. In Indonesia, arrests related to crystalline methamphetamine have increased significantly since 2012. In the Republic of Korea, seizures of crystalline methamphetamine increased to about 38 kg in 2013, compared with 21 kg the preceding year. In Cambodia, although the amount of crystalline methamphetamine seized fell in 2014 (29 kg), it remained higher than in 2012 (19 kg). In 2013, the Lao People's Democratic Republic reported its first crystalline methamphetamine seizure since 2005.

515. The most recent methamphetamine seizure data continue to point to a higher volume of trafficking in East Asian countries. In 2014, China reported the highest amount of methamphetamine seizures in the region: close to 28 tons, considerably higher than the amount seized in 2013. In Hong Kong, China, 104 kg of methamphetamine were found in five express cargo consignments in transit from mainland China to Malaysia via Hong Kong, China. Most of the methamphetamine seized in Japan (570 kg) originated in China, followed by Mexico and Thailand. In 2014, totals of 718.5 kg and 12.5 kg of methamphetamine were seized in the Philippines and Singapore respectively.

516. Although the majority of methamphetamine continues to be trafficked within the region, an increasing amount of methamphetamine is being trafficked into the region from other parts of the world. This seems to suggest that new trafficking routes have been established

linking previously unconnected methamphetamine markets of different regions. In recent years, methamphetamine originating in Africa has been seized in Cambodia, China, Indonesia, Japan, Malaysia, the Philippines, Thailand and Viet Nam. While some methamphetamine has also been trafficked from West Asia, quantities originating in Mexico were seized in Japan, the Philippines and the Republic of Korea in the period 2013-2014.

517. In Malaysia, 26 clandestine facilities manufacturing amphetamine-type stimulants were dismantled in 2013: 18 facilities manufacturing crystalline methamphetamine and 8 facilities manufacturing MDMA ("ecstasy") tablets. Also in 2013, two clandestine laboratories manufacturing amphetamine-type stimulants were dismantled in Indonesia, both manufacturing modest amounts of crystalline methamphetamine. In China, 376 clandestine laboratories manufacturing methamphetamine were dismantled in 2014, compared with 397 dismantled laboratories in 2013.

518. The growing abuse and seizure of MDMA ("ecstasy") has been reported by more East and South-East Asian countries. A significant amount of MDMA ("ecstasy") (489,311 tablets) was seized in Indonesia in 2014. In the Philippines, close to 3,600 MDMA ("ecstasy") tablets were seized in 2014—the largest amount seized by the country's authorities since 2002. Similarly, Singapore reported total seizures of more than 3,800 tablets of MDMA ("ecstasy"). Reported seizures of MDMA ("ecstasy") in Cambodia went from none in 2013 to 3.1 kg in 2014.

(c) Precursors

519. A number of countries continued to report the trafficking of pharmaceutical preparations containing ephedrine and pseudoephedrine, which was spurred by the growing illicit demand for amphetamine-type stimulants in the region. Most of the seized quantities reported originated in the region, or, to a lesser extent, in the neighbouring region of South Asia. Myanmar is one of the main destinations for trafficked preparations containing ephedrine and pseudoephedrine, and precursor chemicals seized in Myanmar mainly originated in nearby countries, primarily China, India and, to a lesser degree, Thailand.

520. To circumvent national legislative controls on precursor chemicals, more non-scheduled precursor chemicals and/or pre-precursors are being used. For instance, following the reinforcement of control of *Ephedra* plant in China, 2-bromopropiophenone is being used to

synthesize ephedrine. In 2014, more than half of the crystalline methamphetamine in the country was synthesized using 2-bromopropiophenone. In response, 2-bromopropiophenone was placed under national control in China in May 2014.

521.   Faced with these adaptive diversion attempts, closer cooperation with industry can provide competent national authorities with better intelligence on suspicious orders and transactions involving scheduled and non-scheduled chemicals. For instance, to heighten the awareness of the industry with respect to the potential diversion of chemicals, some authorities have provided chemical companies in the country with the international special surveillance list. Outreach activities for the chemical and pharmaceutical industries, through regular meetings, dialogue sessions, site visits and seminars, would be useful for the more timely detection of changing trends and patterns of diversion attempts.

522.   A comprehensive review of the situation with respect to the control of precursors and chemicals frequently used in the illicit manufacture of narcotic drugs and psychotropic substances in the region can be found in the report of the Board for 2015 on the implementation of article 12 of the 1988 Convention.

(d)   Substances not under international control

523.   From 2008 to 2014, the number of new psychoactive substances identified by countries within the region increased significantly, the majority of them belonging to the synthetic cannabinoid and synthetic cathinone groups. Among countries in the region, the largest number of new psychoactive substances were identified by Singapore (37 substances), Japan (31 substances) and Indonesia. In 2013 and 2014, at least 30 new psychoactive substances were identified by the Government of Indonesia. These include synthetic cannabinoids, synthetic cathinones, phenethylamines, piperazines and plant-based new psychoactive substances. While some of these substances may be imported from countries in the region, some are imported from other regions. Of the 1.8 kg of synthetic cannabinoids seized in the Republic of Korea in 2013, 1.4 kg were imported from the United States. The rapid emergence of substances not yet under control, the limited forensic capability to identify such substances in some countries and the different listing classification for those substances adopted by different countries in the region are factors that create considerable challenges in mitigating the risks posed by new psychoactive substances at the regional level. INCB therefore encourages

all governments to participate in its operational project on new psychoactive substances (Project Ion (international operations on new psychoactive substances)) and make full use of its secure communication platform (IONICS) to prevent non-scheduled new psychoactive substances from reaching consumer markets.

524.   The abuse of ketamine remains a major problem for the region, although the amount of seizures has been decreasing in some countries. While not under international control, ketamine has been brought under national control in a number of countries in the region: China, Democratic People's Republic of Korea, Japan, Malaysia, Myanmar, Philippines, Republic of Korea, Singapore and Thailand. Medical professionals in Brunei Darussalam and China (including Macao Special Administrative Region) indicated an increase in the abuse of the substance. In Hong Kong, China, the annual prevalence rate of ketamine use remained higher than that of amphetamine-type stimulants. The illicit manufacture of ketamine continues to be a problem in China, where the considerable increase in ketamine manufacture has led to a reported change in the main raw material used. Close to 12 tons of ketamine were seized in mainland China in 2014, and more than 80 clandestine laboratories manufacturing ketamine were dismantled. A further half ton of ketamine was seized in Hong Kong, China. Declining quantities of ketamine seizures were reported in Indonesia (declining from 117 kg in 2010 to 4.7 kg in 2013) and Malaysia.

525.   The seizure of the plant-based psychoactive substances kratom and khat and the eradication of their cultivation continues to be reported. The largest total of kratom seizures in the region was reported by Thailand in 2014 (54 tons), up from 45.5 tons in 2013. In Malaysia, kratom-related seizures and arrests have increased recently, with the total amount of kratom seized reaching 9.1 tons in 2013, up more than 74 per cent from the previous year. Considerable seizures of kratom were also reported in Myanmar (219 kg in 2013). More than 6 tons of khat were seized in Hong Kong, China, in 2014. Almost 2 tons of khat leaves imported from Africa were found in the storage facilities of four logistics companies, destined for the United States, Canada and Taiwan Province of China. Recent eradication of illicit kratom cultivation has been reported by Myanmar.

5.   Abuse and treatment

526.   The trend of wider misuse of amphetamine-type stimulants, in particular methamphetamine, continues to be reported by most countries in the region. Increases in

the abuse of amphetamine-type stimulants have been identified in Brunei Darussalam, Japan, the Lao People's Democratic Republic, the Philippines and the Republic of Korea. In the Republic of Korea, crystalline methamphetamine remains the primary drug of concern and accounts for nearly all drug treatment admissions. In the Lao People's Democratic Republic, the abuse of methamphetamine tablets has expanded from urban and land border areas to other parts of the country. Even in countries where other drugs had been the primary drugs of abuse, considerable increases in the abuse of methamphetamine have been reported. In Malaysia, amphetamine-type stimulants constituted the most common drug of abuse among new drug users in 2013. Significant increases in the abuse of methamphetamine and "ecstasy" have been reported in China. In Macao, China, authorities reported that abuse of methamphetamine was linked to the gambling activities in the city. In Myanmar, a more widespread misuse of methamphetamine has been reported since 2005, as evidenced by a rising number of drug treatment admissions related to the substance. A higher prevalence of the misuse of MDMA ("ecstasy") has also been reported by Indonesia and countries in the Mekong region (Cambodia, Thailand and Viet Nam).

527.   UNODC estimated that in the region there were more than 3.3 million opiate users in 2014, with a prevalence rate (0.2 per cent) that was lower than the global average (0.4 per cent). Heroin remains the main drug of concern in China, Malaysia, Myanmar, Singapore and Viet Nam. The largest number of opiate abusers in the region is found in China, where the number of registered opium abusers totalled approximately 1.46 million, almost half of the total number of drug addicts within the country in 2014. According to experts in China and Viet Nam, the substitution of heroin by synthetic drugs has become common among drug addicts. The same trend is reported in Indonesia, where the market for low-purity heroin was large and heroin users comprised a significant portion of persons admitted to drug treatment centres. A declining trend in the abuse of heroin, as reported by experts, has been observed over the last five years, although no regular nationwide surveys of drug-use levels are conducted by countries in the region.

528.   With a prevalence rate of people who inject drugs of 0.2 per cent in East and South-East Asia (compared with the global prevalence rate of 0.26 per cent), the region continues to have the largest number of people who inject drugs. UNODC estimates that there are approximately 3.15 million people who inject drugs in the region, which is one quarter of the worldwide population of people who inject drugs. Around 10.5 per cent of them are living with HIV. Data at the national level, however,

reveal much higher HIV prevalence rates among people who inject drugs in certain countries, including the Philippines (46.1 per cent), Indonesia (36.4 per cent), Cambodia (24.8 per cent) and Thailand (21.9 per cent). As evidence regarding the effectiveness of different services and treatment programmes (needle and syringe programmes, opioid substitution therapy, antiretroviral therapy and the provision of naloxone) becomes more accepted in the countries, it is expected that more targeted service programmes will be implemented in the region.

529.   The provision of psychological treatment services has been expanded in some countries in the region to respond to the demand for treatment for amphetamine-type stimulant use. For instance, the number of persons receiving drug abuse treatment services from state and private centres in Cambodia totalled more than 3,000 people in 2014, the majority of them crystalline methamphetamine users (82 per cent). Similarly, the Lao People's Democratic Republic plans to expand its community-based treatment for abusers of amphetamine-type stimulants and include counselling services in hospitals, health facilities and educational institutions. Despite a growing awareness, the standards of treatment for amphetamine-type stimulants require further enhancement.

530.   Drug abuse among young people continues to be a worrying trend in the region. A survey conducted in schools in Japan revealed that among all types of illicit drug use, solvents and inhalants had the highest life-time prevalence rates among young people in 2014 (0.7 per cent, compared with 0.2 per cent for cannabis, methamphetamine and new psychoactive substances). Male teenagers have a higher prevalence rate than female teenagers for all types of illicit drug use. Given the various concerns of countries in the region, INCB urges all Governments concerned to closely monitor the situation and facilitate the implementation of specific and targeted interventions.

South Asia

1.   Major developments

531.   In 2014, Governments in South Asia continued to cooperate in responding to the threats posed by illicit drugs at the national and regional levels. Those threats were trafficking in Afghan heroin; the emergence of new psychoactive substances; the rise in manufacturing and trafficking in methamphetamine, in both pill and

crystalline forms; the diversion of controlled substances from licit to illicit channels; and the abuse of pharmaceutical preparations containing narcotic drugs and psychotropic substances.

532. There is a relatively low level of availability of and access to opioids for pain relief in all countries in the region. The Government of India continued to take substantial measures to address the situation, including through legislative changes that enabled the introduction of a simple and uniform regulatory regime in respect of opioids for pain relief (Narcotic Drugs and Psychotropic Substances (Third Amendment) Rules, 2015).

2. Regional cooperation

533. The countries of the region have continued their cooperation in drug abuse prevention and control matters under the umbrella of the Colombo Plan for Cooperative Economic and Social Development in Asia and the Pacific. The drug supply and reduction programmes of the Colombo Plan were strengthened through collaboration with other organizations such as the Australian Federal Police and were to focus on precursor chemical control, border protection, abuse of pharmaceutical preparations and trafficking, and forensic drug analysis.

534. The Department of Narcotics of Bangladesh and the Narcotics Control Bureau of India held consultations at the level of directors general in Dhaka, on 22 and 23 March 2015. The two national authorities agreed to implement mechanisms to stop the trafficking in narcotic drugs and to control the illicit use of precursor chemicals; to exchange intelligence on the cross-border trafficking routes; to raise public awareness of illicit drug trafficking; to increase efforts to eradicate the illicit cultivation of opium poppy and cannabis along their common border; and to increase cooperation in capacity-building.

3. National legislation, policy and action

535. The Colombo Plan International Centre for Certification and Education of Addiction Professionals held several training events in the region for national trainers on the universal treatment curriculum for substance use disorders. In May 2015, the universal prevention curriculum was launched as part of the Colombo Plan drug demand reduction programme in Bhutan, and efforts were under way to introduce the universal treatment curriculum in Bhutan as well. The International

Centre was working on the translation and adaptation of the universal treatment curriculum for Bangladesh. Under the Colombo Plan drug advisory programme, the development of a new curriculum on child drug addiction was initiated, since the incidence and prevalence rates of drug addiction among children from infancy to the age of 12 in the region were increasing.

536. In 2014, the Indian Parliament adopted the Narcotic Drugs and Psychotropic Substances (Amendment) Act, 2014. The amending act introduced major changes to national policy and legislation, including the establishment of a new category of drugs referred to as "essential narcotic drugs", through which the central Government could list drugs of medical and scientific use and which would include morphine, fentanyl, methadone, among other drugs. Narcotic drugs identified as essential were made subject to a single set of rules that applied throughout the country, whereas before the amendment, each state used to have its own regulations. The power to amend the rules were vested in the central Government to ensure uniformity. Under the amending act, institutions wishing to use essential narcotic drugs would require a single licence instead of the several licences previously needed. The changes were likely to simplify access to drugs essential for pain relief and palliative care, making them more readily available to the patients who needed them.

537. The amending act included provisions to improve treatment and care for people dependent on drugs. It allowed for the management of drug dependence, and in that context legitimized opioid substitution, maintenance and other tertiary services. The amending act also repealed the mandatory imposition of the death penalty in case of a repeat conviction for trafficking large quantities of drugs. The courts were given the discretion to impose, as an alternative, a 30-year custodial sentence for repeat offences. INCB takes note of this development and again encourages those States which retain and continue to impose the death penalty for drug-related offences to consider abolishing the death penalty for such offences. The amending act further strengthened the forfeiture of the property of persons arraigned on charges of drug trafficking. It opened the way for private sector involvement in the processing of opium and concentrated opium poppy straw.

538. Through notification S.O.376(E) of 5 February 2015 issued by the Ministry of Finance, the Government of India brought mephedrone under the ambit of psychotropic substances by including it in the schedule to the Narcotic Drugs and Psychotropic Substances Act, 1985. The Government issued another notification listing

mephedrone under schedule I of the Narcotic Drugs and Psychotropic Substances Rules, 1985, prohibiting its production, manufacture, possession, sale, purchase, transportation, warehousing, usage, consumption, import, export and transhipment, except for medical and scientific purposes.

539.   India continued to develop a system for the online registration and submission of returns by manufacturers and wholesalers of psychotropic substances. The system opened for registration by users in 2015, and the Government planned to make it mandatory by the end of 2015. Notwithstanding those welcome developments, access to internationally controlled substances for medical purposes in the region remained below the world average, in particular for opiate pain medication. The Board refers to its 2015 report entitled *Availability of Internationally Controlled Drugs: Ensuring Adequate Access for Medical and Scientific Purposes.*

540.   In 2014, Bhutan adopted the Narcotic Drugs, Psychotropic Substance and Substance Abuse Act, 2015, which replaced the Act of 2005 of the same name. The previous law had a number of shortcomings, including inadequate regulatory and procedural requirements for the control and management of controlled drugs and substances (the description and categorization of drug-related offences were not clearly outlined); the absence of penal provisions for drug-related offences; the lack of a basis for determining the magnitude of such offences; and the absence of provisions on the need for and validity of drug test requirements. The new and comprehensive law restored the balance between demand reduction and supply reduction and addresses shortcomings of the Act of 2005.

541.   To improve port security and prevent the illegal use of sea containers in transnational organized criminal activities including drug and precursor trafficking, Bangladesh and Nepal joined the Container Control Programme of UNODC and WCO in 2014. The Programme is operational in the following countries of the region: Bangladesh, India, Maldives, Nepal and Sri Lanka.

4.   Cultivation, production, manufacture and trafficking

542.   South Asia continued to be particularly vulnerable to the trafficking of opiates and heroin. In addition, widespread trafficking of cannabis, synthetic drugs and new psychoactive substances persisted in 2014. The diversion of pharmaceutical preparations containing narcotic drugs and psychotropic substances from the Indian pharmaceutical industry, as well as their trafficking, including through illegal Internet pharmacies, continued over the reporting period.

(a)   Narcotic drugs

543.   In 2014, in India, the number of arrests for drug-related offences increased to become the highest in five years. The number of prosecutions for drug-related offences increased by more than 50 per cent from 2013, and the number of convictions by 127 per cent.

544.   The data reported by the Narcotics Control Bureau of India indicated that most of the seizures made in the country in 2014 pertained to three drugs: cannabis (5,510 cases), heroin (4,467 cases) and cannabis resin (2,247 cases).

545.   The number of cannabis seizures in India increased by 20 per cent, from 4,592 cases reported in 2013 to 5,510 cases in 2014. Indian authorities seized 108,300 kg of cannabis in 2014, up from 91,792 kg in 2013. Seizures peaked in 2010 at 173.1 tons. Substantial quantities of cannabis were trafficked into India from Nepal. An associated trend was the trafficking of cannabis from north-eastern states of India to eastern and other states in the country.

546.   The number of cannabis resin seizures in 2014 decreased by 7.5 per cent (2,247 cases, down from the 2,430 cases reported in 2013). However, in terms of weight there was a decrease of approximately 50 per cent (decreasing from 4,407 kg seized in 2013 to 2,280 kg seized in 2014, the lowest in the past five years). In addition to domestic production, cannabis resin is trafficked into India. A major source is Nepal, with which India shares a long, open border that is readily exploited by drug traffickers. From India, cannabis resin is also trafficked to destinations in Europe and the Americas by means of courier parcels.

547.   The number of heroin seizures and the quantity of heroin seized in India decreased slightly in 2014 (from 4,609 seizures reported in 2013 to 4,467 in 2014, and from 1,450 kg in 2013 to 1,371 kg in 2014). The Indian state of Punjab, which shares a border with Pakistan, accounted for most of the Afghan heroin seized in India. The larger consignments of Afghan heroin are first smuggled into India through Pakistan, and then smuggled out in smaller quantities to major drug consumer markets in Australia, Canada and Europe. Reports from neighbouring countries also indicated the seizure of low-quality heroin manufactured in India, but there are no reports of such locally manufactured heroin being seized in India itself.

548.   Cocaine trafficking has historically been very limited in South Asia, but the rise in annual seizures seen in India over the past few years suggests an increase in trafficking in cocaine. The quantity of cocaine seized in India in 2014 was 15 kg.

549.   In India, the quantities of opium seized in 2014 decreased by 24.3 per cent to 1,766 kg, compared with 2,333 kg the previous year. The number of seizures of opium had been decreasing since 2012 and was at its lowest since 2010. It was suspected that the opium seized in India originated inside the country, both from licitly and illicitly cultivated opium poppy. In 2014, 25 kg of morphine were seized, compared with 7 kg in 2013, which was still significantly less than in 2012, when 263 kg were seized. The Narcotics Control Bureau continued to use satellite imagery, field surveys and intelligence-gathering to track and eradicate illicit poppy cultivation. Eradication operations were undertaken by law enforcement authorities. In 2014, approximately 2,470 ha of illicit poppy were identified and eradicated. Concerted efforts to eradicate illicit opium poppy cultivation yielded encouraging results, and the area needing to be cleared had been declining since 2011. Another illicit crop targeted by eradication efforts was cannabis. In 2014, over 3,198 ha of cannabis were eradicated, the highest amount since 2010.

550.   The Department of Narcotics Control of Bangladesh reported that in 2014, the country had tried 2,689 persons for offences related to drugs. The police of Bangladesh reported handling 42,501 cases related to narcotics. The long borders that Bangladesh shares with India and Myanmar make it vulnerable to drug trafficking. Moreover, Bangladesh has a long history of cannabis production and consumption, and cannabis is the most common drug of abuse in the country. Although it is smuggled into the country from India and Nepal, there were also reports of illicit cannabis cultivation in remote areas of the country. Seizures increased slightly from 35 tons in 2013 to 36.48 tons in 2014.

551.   In June 2015, the Bangladesh Customs Intelligence and Investigation Directorate reported a seizure of so-called "liquid cocaine" at the port of Chittagong. The cocaine was found diluted in drums of sunflower oil believed to have originated in the Plurinational State of Bolivia. The seizure seems to confirm the existence of new routes and markets for cocaine, which recently seem to be finding its way into countries in South Asia.

552.   Seizures of heroin decreased by 32.1 per cent, from 123.73 kg in 2013 to 84 kg in 2014, the lowest amount since 2009. The heroin abused in Bangladesh was mostly crude and impure, with the estimated purity of heroin

sold on the street not exceeding 5 per cent. According to experts, most of the heroin seized in Bangladesh was either manufactured in India, or originated in Afghanistan and smuggled through India. At the same time, heroin of high purity from the Golden Triangle (Lao People's Democratic Republic, Myanmar and Thailand) sometimes entered the country from the south-east. There were some reports of seizures in China of heroin trafficked through sea ports in Bangladesh. Dhaka airport continued to be a transit point for heroin being trafficked to China, Europe and the Middle East.

553.   In 2013, 11.62 kg of opium were seized in Bangladesh, but no seizures were reported in 2014.

554.   Trafficking of codeine-based cough syrups, such as phensedyl, from India to Bangladesh continued to be reported. Although Bangladesh banned codeine-based cough syrups, its medical use is allowed in India. In 2014, 748,730 bottles of codeine-based preparations were seized in Bangladesh, a decrease from the 987,661 bottles seized in 2013. Seizures of phensedyl had been declining consistently since 2012, and the seizures recorded in 2014 were the smallest since 2009. Synthetic opiates such as buprenorphine and pethidine (chemical name meperidine) in injectable form continued to be trafficked into Bangladesh. Seizures of buprenorphine decreased to 99,509 ampoules in 2013.

555.   In 2014, Bhutan witnessed the highest number of drug cases ever registered by the authorities (644 cases). The great majority (90 per cent) were related to the possession of controlled substances. Cannabis, which in addition to being cultivated also grew in the wild, was the most common drug of abuse. Cannabis, along with small quantities of low-quality heroin, was also being smuggled into the country from India.

556.   In 2014, in Nepal, both the illicit cultivation and the wild growth of cannabis were reported in the districts bordering India and in the interior. Although the Government carries out cannabis eradication campaigns every year, illicit cultivation continued in the reporting period. The porous border with India facilitates the trafficking of cannabis. While the seizures of cannabis rose sharply over the period from 2011 to 2013, with a 15-year record of 47,086 kg of cannabis being seized in 2012, they decreased to 6,910 kg in 2014.

557.   A similar trend was reported for cannabis resin trafficked along land routes from Nepal to India and China, and by air to destinations such as Canada, Japan, the Russian Federation, the United States and Europe. In 2014, 2,053 kg of cannabis resin were seized in Nepal,

compared with 1,931 kg in 2013 and a record of 5,169 kg in 2012.

558. In 2014, in Nepal, the downward trend in heroin seizures continued: 3.8 kg of heroin were seized, against 12.42 kg in 2013 and 15.7 kg in 2012. Heroin from South-West and South-East Asia was smuggled into Nepal across the border with India and through Kathmandu international airport. Traffickers were also reported to use Nepal as a transit country through which they smuggled heroin to destinations such as Australia, China and the Netherlands. There were also seizures of low-quality heroin smuggled in small quantities from India, mainly intended for domestic consumption.

559. There is also evidence of illicit opium cultivation in Nepal. There have been no extensive surveys to determine its extent, but cultivation in small patches was reported in remote hilly areas that are difficult for enforcement agencies to access. No illicit heroin manufacturing facility has as yet been detected in Nepal. According to the Narcotics Control Bureau of Nepal, illicit opium is also being smuggled into India.

560. The first case of cocaine trafficking in Nepal was recorded in 2012. Since then there has been an increase. Instances of cocaine trafficking into the country by carriers from Namibia, Pakistan and Thailand via Brazil were identified in 2014. Reports indicated that Nepal was also being used as a transit point for cocaine smuggling. In 2014, 5.5 kg of cocaine were reported seized in the country. In April 2015, 11 kg of cocaine were seized at Kathmandu international airport, the largest cocaine seizure so far in Nepal.

561. In 2014, authorities in Nepal arrested 2,918 individuals for drug trafficking offences, against 2,673 in 2013. The Narcotics Control Bureau reported that an increasing number of Nepalese nationals were involved in drug trafficking. Previously, drug trafficking used to be dominated by foreign nationals.

562. Trafficking of heroin into Sri Lanka has been steadily increasing. The main trafficking routes were by sea, from southern India (for Indian heroin) and from Pakistan (for Afghan heroin). Heroin is smuggled into the island in sea containers and fishing boats. In 2014, 313 kg of heroin were seized, a decrease of about 11 per cent compared with the previous year.

563. Other than along the established sea routes, trafficking of drugs into Sri Lanka by air, largely through Colombo international airport, has been a regular occurrence. In recent years, the majority of the heroin seized

at the airport has been found on couriers arriving from Pakistan. They use various methods, including ingestion and concealment in body cavities and various kinds of equipment and luggage.

564. Cannabis and heroin are the major illicit drugs of abuse in Sri Lanka. Cannabis is illicitly cultivated in the country. The estimated land area under cannabis cultivation was nearly 500 ha in 2014. Cannabis abuse has become a significant problem. No cannabis resin production had been reported. In 2014, 19,644 kg of cannabis from India were seized. In 2014, cannabis seizures decreased by 76 per cent compared with 2013.

(b) Psychotropic substances

565. South Asia is increasingly being used for the illicit manufacture of amphetamine-type stimulants (ATS). ATS are also increasingly being abused. ATS in powder form is increasingly being smuggled from and illicitly manufactured in India, which is emerging as the main source in the region. Tablets containing ATS trafficked in India are also being smuggled into the country from Myanmar. In 2014, 196 kg of ATS were seized, more than twice the amount of 2013 (85 kg) and almost five times that of 2012 (41 kg). The number of ATS seizures and the quantities seized have been rising steadily. In 2014, 42 ATS seizures were reported, the highest number in five years. In 2014, the Narcotics Control Bureau of India reported the dismantling of five illicit manufacturing facilities, from which about 155 kg of amphetamines and 162 kg of ephedrine and pseudoephedrine were seized.

566. Seizures of methaqualone in India registered a sharp decrease, from 3,205 kg in 2013 to 54 kg in 2014, the lowest in five years. Methaqualone is often trafficked by means of courier parcels to Australia, Canada, Ethiopia, South Africa, the United Kingdom and countries in South-East Asia.

567. India and China are perceived as major sources of various new psychoactive substances. One of those is mephedrone,[38] whose increasing abuse has been reported globally in recent years. India was one of the source countries for mephedrone trafficked to various overseas destinations. After establishing its control over mephedrone and regulating it as a controlled psychotropic substance, India effected various seizures (1,106 kg from January to June 2015).

[38] The substance was brought under the control of the 1971 Convention by the Commission on Narcotic Drugs in March 2015.

568. In 2014, 109 grams of LSD were seized in India, which was the highest quantity in the past five years.

569. In Bangladesh, "yaba" (methamphetamine) continues to be smuggled from Myanmar across the south-eastern border. The quantities seized by Bangladesh law enforcement agencies have been rapidly increasing during the past five years. In 2014, 6.76 million "yaba" tablets were seized, compared with 2.8 million in 2013, a growth of 141 per cent. The quantity seized in 2014 was the highest since 2009. Sharp increases in seizures have been recorded since 2011. The proximity of Bangladesh to Myanmar and the surge in domestic demand made the country a big market for "yaba". "Yaba" is mainly smuggled from Myanmar by fishing boat. It is bartered for other drugs of abuse, such as buprenorphine and tranquillizers, that are then smuggled in the opposite direction, from Bangladesh to Myanmar.

570. Diazepam and buprenorphine ampoules were reported to be smuggled into Nepal from India. In 2014, 44,495 ampoules of diazepam and 37,000 ampoules of buprenorphine were seized in Nepal, slightly more than the 43,227 ampoules of diazepam and 30,887 ampoules of buprenorphine seized in 2013.

(c) Precursors

571. The diversion of ephedrine and pseudoephedrine from legal manufacture in India to illicit channels remains a major challenge for law enforcement agencies. Indian drug law enforcement agencies continued to report seizures of pharmaceutical preparations containing ephedrine and pseudoephedrine trafficked from India to Myanmar for the extraction of the precursors. Instances of ephedrine and pseudoephedrine trafficking to South-East Asia were also reported in 2014. The quantity of ephedrine and pseudoephedrine seized in India declined sharply, from 6,655 kg in 2013 to 1,662 kg in 2014.

572. Bangladesh has a growing chemical and pharmaceutical industry, and has recently emerged as a source and transit location for methamphetamine precursors such as ephedrine and pseudoephedrine. The drug-related challenges facing the authorities in Bangladesh in 2015 continued to be the diversion of precursor-based pharmaceutical preparations from the legitimate market, and the smuggling of shipments out of the country.

573. A comprehensive review of the situation with respect to the control of precursors and chemicals frequently used in the illicit manufacture of narcotic drugs and psychotropic substances in the region can be found in the 2015 report of the Board on the implementation of article 12 of the 1988 Convention.

(d) Substances not under international control

574. India continues to be a source country for ketamine trafficked to South-East Asia. Since February 2011, ketamine has been a controlled substance under the Narcotic Drugs and Psychotropic Substances Act, 1985. In 2014, Indian law enforcement agencies seized 32 kg of ketamine, a significant decrease from the 1,353 kg seized in 2013. Seizures indicate that ketamine trafficking may now be declining as a result of the authorities' stringency that followed the recent amendments to the Act.

5. Abuse and treatment

575. Most countries in South Asia do not regularly carry out national drug surveys; information on abuse and prevalence therefore needs to come from other sources. Cannabis is the most common drug of abuse in the region. According to the *World Drug Report 2015*, the annual prevalence rate for cannabis abuse in South Asia is estimated to be about 3.5 per cent of the population, or 33 million persons. According to UNODC, the annual prevalence of abuse of opioids remained stable at 0.3 per cent of the population and continued to be lower than the estimated world annual prevalence rate of 0.7 per cent.

576. The estimated prevalence of drug abuse by injection in South Asia in 2013 among the population aged 15 to 64 (the most recent information available from countries in the region) remained stable at 0.03 per cent, which was very low compared with the global average of 0.26 per cent. As mentioned above, the lack of reliable data on drug abuse in the region may be the reason why the reported prevalence is so low.

577. The abuse of "yaba" (methamphetamine) and codeine-based preparations continues to be widespread in Bangladesh, and is still increasing. Among street children, the abuse of glue and solvents by sniffing is common. Buprenorphine, mainly smuggled into the country from India, is one of the most popular drugs of abuse among those who inject drugs. Pethidine used to be the main drug of abuse among those who inject drugs in Bangladesh, but because of the emergence of buprenorphine over the past three decades and the high price of pethidine, the abuse of pethidine has decreased.

578. In 2014, Bangladesh stepped up its campaign against drug abuse and drug trafficking. The campaign included the distribution of posters, leaflets, stickers and booklets. Furthermore, speeches and discussion meetings were held in schools, and short films were produced with WHO. In 2014, a total of 10,364 patients were treated in private treatment centres, up from 8,108 patients in 2013. Women continued to make up a very small proportion of those receiving drug abuse treatment in Bangladesh, with only 25 female patients receiving treatment in 2014.

579. The Government of India accorded a high priority to the issue of drug abuse. The Prime Minister used many platforms to spread the message to parents that they should spend more time with their children. There was an emphasis on skill development, which was also encouraged among drug users.

580. In January 2015, the Government of India approved and launched a revised scheme of assistance for the prevention of alcoholism and substance (drug) abuse and for social defence services, which included the provision of financial assistance and grants for buildings and a toll-free national helpline for those with alcohol and drug abuse problems. The scheme was to provide a complete range of services such as awareness-raising and the identification, counselling, treatment and rehabilitation of addicts by voluntary and other organizations. Through preventive education programmes and whole-person recovery treatment of drug-dependent persons, its main pillars, the scheme was to reduce the demand for and consumption of alcohol and other dependence-producing substances.

581. Bangladesh, India and Nepal have implemented comprehensive packages for HIV prevention among drug users, including needle and syringe programmes and opioid substitution therapy.

582. Under its national AIDS control programme for 2013-2014, India established 45 new opioid substitution therapy centres for injecting drug users, thereby doubling the availability of such services in one year. The department of AIDS control of the Ministry of Health and Family Welfare is supporting the provision of opioid substitution therapy services through more than 150 dedicated centres across 30 states and union territories in India. After the successful completion of a pilot project in 2013, India decided to scale up the methadone maintenance treatment programme and its adoption by health clinics through the Ministry of Health.

583. In 2015, UNODC published the findings of the first study held among women in north-eastern India who use drugs. The study identified their drug use patterns, the adverse impact of their drug use, and the impediments that limited their access to services. The study included the recommendation to expand the nature and scope of services provided to women in the future.

584. Cannabis and heroin continued to be the two drugs most commonly abused in Sri Lanka. Opium, opiates and opioids such as morphine, methadone and tramadol, were also reported to be misused in Sri Lanka. However, they were not being manufactured in the country. In 2014, a total of 1,646 people received drug abuse treatment, of whom 1,414 were treated for opioid addiction and 915 for cannabis addiction.

585. Sri Lanka does not manufacture any synthetic drugs or precursor chemicals, but the use of ATS, including methamphetamine and MDMA ("ecstasy"), and of other synthetic drugs, such as LSD and ketamine, is reportedly on the rise.

586. In Nepal, the common pharmaceutical preparations containing controlled substances that were being trafficked and abused were codeine-based cough syrups, buprenorphine, diazepam, nitrazepam and morphine.

587. In the Maldives, the problem of drug abuse was growing, especially among young people, who constituted about one third of the total population. The authorities reported that almost half of those who abused drugs (46 per cent) were aged between 16 and 24 years. While the variety of drugs available in Maldives is increasing, heroin and liquid cannabis (hash oil) are the most commonly used drugs. Maldives has implemented opioid substitution therapy.

West Asia

1. Major developments

588. The continuing instability and climate of insecurity that prevail in some parts of the Middle East, in particular Iraq, the Syrian Arab Republic and Yemen, continue to undermine law enforcement efforts and pose a challenge to drug control efforts among countries in the region. Poor border controls and the intensified movement of the population across countries is certainly favourable to illicit drug trafficking destined for markets in the region and can lead to a greater number of individuals abusing drugs.

589. The significant and rapid deterioration of the humanitarian situation in some countries of the region continues to pose a grave risk to peace and security, with various implications, following the displacement of millions of inhabitants. The difficult and traumatic situation of refugees escaping conflict zones, in particular in Iraq and the Syrian Arab Republic, makes them particularly vulnerable to and at high risk of exposure to drug trafficking and addiction. Lack of governmental control and a general atmosphere of lawlessness in many areas make it virtually impossible to monitor drug control activities.

590. The armed conflict and refugee crisis situations have given rise to increased demands for emergency supplies, including internationally controlled substances for medical purposes. However, as supply is wholly dependent on emergency aid, delivery in certain areas has been inadequate or severely limited. In that context, INCB wishes to draw attention to the special topic published in its annual report for 2014 on availability of narcotic drugs and psychotropic substances in emergency situations[39] and remind all States that, under international humanitarian law, parties to armed conflicts have an obligation not to impede the provision of medical care to civilian populations located in territories under their effective control. This includes access to necessary narcotic drugs and psychotropic substances.

591. Against the backdrop of a long-standing lack of official sources of reliable information on illicit drug production, trafficking and abuse among countries in the region, there have been several media and anecdotal reports regarding the widespread abuse of counterfeit Captagon tablets (containing amphetamine) among all parties engaged in armed violence in the Syrian Arab Republic.

592. The drug control situation in the region remains complex. The most recent estimates reported in the executive summary of the *Afghanistan opium survey 2015* suggest that the situation concerning illicit opium poppy cultivation in Afghanistan, a significant factor for drug control efforts in the region, may be improving. Nevertheless, drug trafficking and illicit manufacture of heroin continue to be matters of concern for Governments in transit and destination countries. The completion in December 2014 of the International Security Assistance Force mission in Afghanistan may further affect the security situation in the country, which, in turn, could have implications for the drug control situation.

593. Significantly, for the first time in six years, the *Afghanistan Opium Survey 2015*, for which the executive summary is available, notes that there has been a decrease in the estimated total area under illicit opium poppy cultivation in Afghanistan, which in 2015 totalled 183,000 hectares (ha). That represents a decrease compared with 2014, when cultivation reached record levels, at 224,000 ha. However, the area of cultivation in 2015 remains the fourth highest amount reported since the beginning of estimations in 1994. The extent of the decrease (19 per cent) may have been augmented by a recent change in the estimation methodology: the reliability of data is said to have improved significantly from 2014 to 2015. However, the results of different years must be compared with caution. The estimated potential opium production in the country decreased from 6,400 tons in 2014 to 3,300 tons in 2015. Similarly, average opium yield decreased to 18.3 kilograms per hectare, compared with 28.7 kilograms per hectare in 2014. At the same time, the total verified Governor-led eradication of opium poppy increased to 3,760 ha eradicated in 2015 in comparison with 2,693 ha in 2014.

594. Central Asian countries reported a decrease in seizures in 2014 of opiates originating in Afghanistan. Nevertheless, for criminal groups engaged in drug trafficking, the subregion remains attractive as a channel for smuggling opiates from Afghanistan to markets in the Russian Federation and Europe. Further, the abolition of customs controls at the borders between the countries in the Eurasian Economic Union, comprising Armenia, Belarus, Kazakhstan, Kyrgyzstan and the Russian Federation, may pose an additional challenge for the drug law enforcement authorities.

595. Similar to previous years, almost all illicit drugs are available in the Middle East subregion, which drug trafficking networks mainly use as a transit area for the smuggling of cocaine, heroin and amphetamine-type stimulants (ATS). Various seizure reports suggest that a trend of increasing traffic in cocaine emerged in the Middle East in 2014. According to various reports, cocaine seizures increased, in particular in Jordan, Saudi Arabia and the United Arab Emirates.

2. Regional cooperation

596. The London Conference on Afghanistan, held on 4 December 2014, brought together representatives of more than 50 States, multilateral organizations, non-governmental organizations and representatives of Afghan civil society to discuss development, governance and

---

[39] E/INCB/2014/1, paras. 228-238.

stability in Afghanistan, including issues related to drug control. The Conference provided a platform for the Government of Afghanistan to set out its vision for reform and for the international community to demonstrate its support and solidarity for Afghanistan.

597. The summit of the Collective Security Treaty Organization (CSTO), held in Moscow on 23 December 2014 and attended by the Presidents of Armenia, Belarus, Kazakhstan, Kyrgyzstan, the Russian Federation and Tajikistan, adopted the CSTO anti-drug strategy for the period 2015-2020.

598. At a meeting in Dushanbe in May 2015, the heads of the drug law enforcement agencies of CSTO member countries discussed the situation in Afghanistan and decided to continue their cooperation in tackling the manufacture and distribution of new psychoactive substances and to prepare a plan of action for the period 2016-2017.

599. At its summit held in Ufa, Russian Federation, in July 2015, the Shanghai Cooperation Organization's Council of Heads of State decided to accept the accession of India and Pakistan to the Organization. The Organization's main goals are the provision and maintenance of peace, security and stability among its members, including drug control. At the summit, the Organization adopted a development strategy outlining priority areas until 2025, including issues related to regional stability and drug control, and plans to address drug challenges were incorporated into the declaration of the Council of Heads of State issued at the summit. The Organization's member States expressed concern at the scale of narcotic drug manufacture in Afghanistan, which posed a threat to development and security in the region.

600. The Central Asian Regional Information and Coordination Centre, a standing intergovernmental body for combating trafficking in narcotic drugs, psychotropic substances and their precursors, continues to serve as a regional platform for exchanging information and experiences on countering drug trafficking and promoting law enforcement cooperation.

601. Several regional and subregional organizations such as the Cooperation Council for the Arab States of the Gulf and its Criminal Information Centre to Combat Drugs and the League of Arab States, including its Council of Arab Ministers of the Interior and the Council of Arab Ministers for Health, continue to actively promote cooperation and harmonization of efforts among Arab countries, including in the area of drug control.

602. In June 2015, the Board participated in the 11th international conference on drug control, organized by the Dubai Police. The event, attended by representatives of Ministries of the Interior and counter-narcotics agencies from countries of the Middle East and North Africa and of the Gulf Cooperation Council, focused on access to controlled substances for licit purposes while preventing diversion and abuse, and conducted a workshop to guide national delegations in identifying recommendations for incorporation into national strategies.

603. The international anti-drug forum organized by the Qatari Ministry of Interior in Doha in May 2015 recommended measures to tackle emerging drug trafficking trends in the region through the establishment of an early warning observatory and the inclusion of legal provisions to criminalize the promotion of illicit drug use through the Internet.

3. National legislation, policy and action

604. In order to counter the rapidly developing illicit market for synthetic drugs and the emergence of new psychoactive substances, the abuse of which is becoming a matter of concern in West Asia, some countries in the region have amended their national legislation and have begun to place some new psychoactive substances under national control. The Government of Armenia amended its national legislation in May 2015, placing 114 new psychoactive substances on the list of nationally controlled substances.

605. In March 2014, the Government of Georgia adopted a package of legislative amendments, pursuant to which illicit trafficking in pharmaceutical preparations containing codeine, ephedrine, norephedrine or pseudoephedrine is now subject to criminal prosecution.

606. In Kazakhstan, the new penal code and the code of criminal procedure, which entered into force in January 2015, stipulate criminal liability for offences related to trafficking in analogues of narcotic drugs and psychotropic substances. In addition, the law on narcotic drugs, psychotropic substances and their analogues and precursors, the main drug control legislation of Kazakhstan, was also strengthened and supplemented with provisions on analogue scheduling in July 2014.

607. In 2014, the Government of Kyrgyzstan approved a counter-narcotics strategy and implementation plan which defined measures and activities in the field of drug control for the period 2014-2019. The strategy seeks to

promote healthy lifestyles among the country's young people through different types of activities, including awareness-raising campaigns. The strategy also aims to strengthen the law enforcement agencies of Kyrgyzstan and enhance drug demand reduction and prevention efforts, including the implementation of tertiary prevention measures such as needle exchange, counselling, the provision of health care, and educational activities, as well as treatment and rehabilitation programmes.

608. In order to prevent the abuse of substances not under international control, Turkey placed 246 new psychoactive substances under national control in 2014. In addition, article 19 of the national law on the control of drugs was supplemented with provisions on generic scheduling in January 2015.

609. The Government of Israel has taken legislative measures to curb the growing market for new psychoactive substances and their popularity among the youth in particular. In 2014, new synthetic cannabinoids and their derivatives were listed as narcotic drugs in the national legislation.

610. In June 2015, the United Arab Emirates health authorities recommended the inclusion of three plant materials, namely kava (*Piper methysticum*), kratom (*Mitragyna speciosa*) and *Salvia divinorum* in Table 4 of that country's Federal Law No. 14 of 1995 (article 2) on the countermeasures against narcotic drugs and psychotropic substances.

611. In the United Arab Emirates, efforts are also being made to standardize procedures for prescriptions involving controlled substances, restricted pharmaceuticals and psychoactive drugs, including innovative measures such as the establishment of an electronic system for the issuance of prescriptions and the dispensing of medicines containing controlled narcotic drugs and psychotropic substances.

612. In February 2015, Turkmenistan strengthened its main drug control law on narcotic drugs, psychotropic substances and precursors through an amendment establishing that amnesty may not be granted to individuals who have been convicted of crimes related to trafficking in narcotic drugs, psychotropic substances or precursors.

613. In Jordan, the Security Directorate and the Ministry of Labour entered into agreements to secure employment for inmates, including those incarcerated for drug-related sentences, upon completion of their sentence period or treatment period. Furthermore, some reforms within the

Jordanian social security institution will broaden the social security system to include rehabilitation centres.

4. Cultivation, production, manufacture and trafficking

(a) Narcotic drugs

614. Cannabis production, trafficking and abuse continue to be widespread in West Asia. Cannabis plants, seeds and oil are frequently seized in the region and remain the most widely abused substances. Afghanistan continues to be considered one of the largest illicit producers of cannabis resin worldwide. While the trend of illicit cannabis cultivation and production is believed to be stable in that country, on the basis of the results of annual surveys conducted by the United Nations Office on Drugs and Crime between 2009 and 2011, systematic data collection efforts have not been undertaken since. Further, there are continued reports of illicit cultivation of cannabis in the Bekaa valley of Lebanon, where eradication efforts have been sustained.

615. According to the data available to the Board, cannabis seizures increased in West Asia in 2014, with the exception of Israel, where quantities of both cannabis herb and cannabis resin seizures decreased from 2013 to 2014 (from 38 kilograms (kg) to 7 kg of cannabis herb and from 320 kg to 6 kg of cannabis resin). The countries reporting the largest seizures of cannabis in 2014 were, in descending order of seizure amount, Saudi Arabia, Jordan and Lebanon. According to the data provided to the Board by the authorities of Saudi Arabia, seizures of cannabis herb in the country have nearly doubled: from 23 tons in 2011 to nearly 38 tons in 2014.

616. Large shipments of cannabis destined for Libya are regularly stopped in Lebanon, where almost 3 tons of cannabis herb were seized in 2014, a considerable increase compared with the 164 kg seized in 2013. Furthermore, in early 2015, Lebanese police had already seized a total of 2 tons of cannabis on the way to Libya. Similarly, nearly 7 tons of cannabis, of which about 20 per cent was cannabis resin, were smuggled across land borders into Jordan, where they were seized in 2014.

617. The executive summary of the *Afghanistan Opium Survey 2015* estimated the total area under illicit opium poppy cultivation in that country to be 183,000 ha in 2015. Even taking into account the impact of methodological changes introduced between 2014 and 2015, this figure represents a marked decrease from the previous

year, when cultivation had reached record levels at 224,000 ha. While 2015 marked the first decrease since 2009, cultivation levels remained high in absolute terms. The estimated area of illicit opium poppy cultivation in 2015 was nevertheless the fourth highest since estimations began in 1994, surpassed only by the estimated amounts for 2007, 2013 and 2014. A corresponding decrease in Afghanistan's estimated potential production of opium was recorded: 3,300 tons (48 per cent less than in 2014). The low production estimates are believed to be a result of the reduction in total area under cultivation, combined with a significantly reduced average opium yield per hectare. The reduced average yield was reportedly owing to a lack of water in certain regions, which may have affected plant density. In 2015, the average opium yield was 18.3 kilograms per hectare, compared with 28.7 kilograms per hectare in 2014 (a 36 per cent decrease).

618.   In 2015, 97 per cent of the total illicit opium poppy cultivation in Afghanistan took place in the eastern, southern and western regions of the country, which include the country's most insecure provinces. The same three regions experienced the greatest relative decrease in opium poppy cultivation levels in 2015 (decreases of 40 per cent, 20 per cent and 10 per cent respectively, compared with 2014), while steep increases were observed in the central and northern regions (increases of 38 per cent and 154 per cent, respectively). Poppy cultivation levels in the north-eastern region of the country remained stable. The extent to which these comparative figures might be attributable to the recent change in estimation methodology must, however, be borne in mind. At the province level, Helmand continued to account for more than 47 per cent of all illicit opium cultivation in Afghanistan.

619.   The Government of Afghanistan continued its efforts to eradicate illicit opium poppy cultivation in the country, increasing total eradication of opium poppy to 3,760 ha in 2015. However, the total eradicated area remains very limited in absolute terms compared with the total estimated area under illicit opium poppy cultivation in Afghanistan (1-2 per cent).

620.   The route from Afghanistan through the Islamic Republic of Iran is one of the shortest trafficking routes from West Asia into Europe, with significant amounts of Afghan opiates seized there every year, primarily opium and heroin. Accordingly, the Islamic Republic of Iran has remained the country in the world with the largest quantity of opium seized: 393 tons in 2014. In total, the country's authorities seized 511 tons of illicit drugs in 2014, compared with 555 tons in 2013.

621.   Heroin smuggling routes through the southern Caucasus are marked by constant changes. According to data provided to the Board, seizures of heroin in Georgia increased from 117 kg in 2013 to more than 591 kg in 2014, and seizures of heroin in Azerbaijan totalled nearly 296 kg in 2014, compared with 101 kg in 2013. Significant increases in heroin seizures were also reported in Armenia, where over 850 kg were seized in 2014, in contrast to the low levels of seizures made in the country in the previous years (less than 5 grams were seized in 2012 and in 2013).

622.   Drug seizures in Central Asia have followed a decreasing trend. In particular, the amount of heroin seized in the subregion decreased by 24.6 per cent, from 1.6 tons in 2013 to 1.2 tons in 2014. The amount of heroin seized in Kazakhstan decreased by 48 per cent (from 754 kg to 392 kg) and by 12.4 per cent in Uzbekistan (from 121.6 kg to 106.5 kg). Only Kyrgyzstan and Tajikistan reported a moderate increase in seizures of heroin, from 247 kg to 285 kg and from 483 kg to 507 kg, respectively. In Turkmenistan, seizures of heroin decreased from 12.6 kg in 2013 to 1.8 kg in 2014.

623.   Countries in the region continued their cooperation in countering illicit drug trafficking within the framework of CSTO. In particular, the counter-narcotics operation "Channel Patrol", conducted on 18-22 May 2015, resulted in the seizure of more than 12 tons of narcotics, including over 7 tons of opium, approximately 3 tons of hashish, more than 1 ton of heroin and 126 kg of cannabis herb. The operation involved cooperation among the law enforcement agencies of Armenia, Belarus, Kazakhstan, Kyrgyzstan, the Russian Federation and Tajikistan, with the involvement of the agencies of Afghanistan, China and Iran (Islamic Republic of) and INTERPOL as observers.

624.   Similarly, the information available to the Board shows that heroin seizures decreased among countries in the Middle East in 2014. Heroin seizures, which increased significantly in several countries of the region in 2013, decreased in 2014, particularly in, in decreasing order of seizure amounts, Jordan, Lebanon, Saudi Arabia and Israel. In July 2015, a joint security operation of Pakistan and the United Arab Emirates resulted in the dismantling of a major heroin ring, the arrest of 40 drug traffickers and the seizure of 150 kg of heroin.

625.   Data available to the Board indicate that annual opium seizures in the Middle East subregion in 2014 were also small, ranging from 34 grams in Jordan to about 4 kg in Saudi Arabia.

626.   The extent of cocaine trafficking in West Asia continued to increase in 2014, with some countries in

the region reporting a marked increase in drug seizures. For example, Saudi Arabia reported an increase in seizures of cocaine, rising from 4.6 kg in 2013 to 533.5 kg in 2014, and Jordan reported an increase from 12 kg in 2013 to 319 kg in 2014.

627.   As in previous years, the territory of the United Arab Emirates served as a transit area for traffickers smuggling drugs from South America to Africa and Asia. In June 2015, cocaine traffickers who had transited Dubai, United Arab Emirates, were arrested in Nigeria, South Africa and Turkey.

628.   Further, increasing quantities of South American cocaine, in particular cocaine originating in Mexico and destined for Israel and Lebanon, are being seized while the drug is in transit through Jordan and Saudi Arabia; most of the cocaine is trafficked by sea, using containers, and seizures take place at seaports; 320 kg were seized by the Lebanese authorities during the first eight months of 2014, and 319 kg were intercepted by the Jordanian authorities in 2014, compared with 12 kg in 2013.

(b) Psychotropic substances

629.   According to seizure data, pharmaceutical preparations containing psychotropic substances are trafficked in most countries in West Asia. In particular, abuse of sedatives and anxiolytics (for example, diazepam and nitrazepam) in the form of tablets is widespread, which may indicate weaknesses in national systems for the control of the networks for licit distribution of prescription medicines containing controlled substances. **INCB calls upon the countries concerned to increase their vigilance with respect to diversion, trafficking and abuse of such preparations and to reinforce controls on domestic distribution channels for pharmaceutical preparations containing controlled substances.**

630.   Seizures of psychotropic substances in Central Asian countries remain relatively low. In 2014, authorities of Kazakhstan reported the seizure of 13,983 vials and 3,496 tablets of psychotropic substances. The law enforcement authorities of Tajikistan in the same year reported the seizure of 2,590 MDMA tablets, 2,025 phenobarbital tablets and 10 tablets of diazepam. The total amount of pharmaceutical preparations seized in Kyrgyzstan amounted to 3,604 grams in 2014.

631.   Trafficking and abuse of ATS have been reported by a growing number of countries in West Asia, particularly abuse of amphetamine, methamphetamine and

MDMA, with a marked increase in abuse of "ecstasy"-type substances noted in Lebanon in 2014. For 2014, there were reports of significant seizures of MDMA ("ecstasy") in Israel and amphetamine in Saudi Arabia.

632.   The quantity of reported seizures of ATS in the Islamic Republic of Iran decreased considerably. The amount of seized ATS was 2,644 kg in 2014, a decrease of 28 per cent compared with the previous year. The number of clandestine drug laboratories dismantled in the Islamic Republic of Iran in 2014 (340 laboratories) was a decrease of 24 per cent from 2013 (445 laboratories).

633.   Seizures of counterfeit Captagon tablets (believed to contain amphetamine) continue to be reported by most countries in the Middle East. In particular, Lebanon, Saudi Arabia and the Syrian Arab Republic reported that seizures of amphetamine illicitly manufactured under the brand name "Captagon" in 2014 were higher than in previous years. Most of the Captagon tablets are smuggled across the non-official border crossings between Jordan and the Syrian Arab Republic, transiting Jordan, with Saudi Arabia as the main final destination. In October 2015, 2 tons of Captagon destined for Saudi Arabia were reportedly seized at the international airport in Beirut.

634.   Trafficking and abuse of amphetamine among countries in the Middle East continued to be reported. Saudi Arabia is among the countries that registered a significant increase in the amount of amphetamine tablets seized, as the country seized more than 100 million tablets in 2014, compared with 57 million in 2013. Furthermore, almost 32 million amphetamine tablets were seized in Jordan in 2014.

635.   In March 2014, a special joint operation between the drug enforcement administrations of Saudi Arabia and Bahrain resulted in the dismantling of a trafficking ring and the seizure of 22 million amphetamine tablets.

636.   In 2014, Jordanian authorities seized more than 43 million tablets made using procyclidine, an antiparkinsonian agent, obtained from Kemadrin tablets; the seized tablets had originated in India and been smuggled by air. Kemadrin is apparently mixed with other substances to produce hallucinogenic effects. It appears that Jordan is used as a transit country as more than 98 per cent of the drug was destined for Iraq.

(c) Precursors

637.   Seizures of acetic anhydride, the key precursor chemical used in the illicit manufacture of heroin,

declined in Afghanistan in 2014. The change of trafficking routes and modi operandi used by traffickers were among the possible reasons for the decrease in seizures. Further, the black market price of acetic anhydride in Afghanistan, which is an indicator of the chemical's availability on the market, increased slightly in 2014, likely due to an increase in demand caused by the high levels of opium production in the country. INCB urges all relevant stakeholders of Member States in the region to increase the exchange of drug-related intelligence among their national competent law enforcement authorities, including through the relevant regional intelligence centres such as the Central Asian Regional Information and Coordination Centre, the Joint Planning Cell of Afghanistan, Iran (Islamic Republic of) and Pakistan and the Gulf Cooperation Council's Criminal Information Centre to Combat Drugs.

638.   The territories of Central Asian countries continued to be exploited by trafficking organizations involved in the diversion of and trafficking in precursor chemicals. The total amount of precursors seized in Kazakhstan reached 729 tons in 2014. The law enforcement authorities of Kyrgyzstan reported seizures of precursor chemicals totalling 6,197 tons.

639.   A comprehensive review of the situation with respect to the control of precursors and chemicals frequently used in the illicit manufacture of narcotic drugs and psychotropic substances in the region can be found in the report of the Board for 2015 on the implementation of article 12 of the 1988 Convention.

(d)   Substances not under international control

640.   Abuse of substances not under international control, such as ketamine and khat, have continued to be reported by some countries in the region. The abuse of tramadol, a synthetic opioid not under international control, continued to be reported by some countries in the region. New drug abuse patterns for *Salvia divinorum* and synthetic cannabinoids were also reported in Lebanon.

641.   Seizures of substances not under international control continued to be reported in Turkey in 2014. A total of 773 kg of synthetic cannabinoids were seized in the country. Georgia reported a 90 per cent decrease in consumption of new psychoactive substances, known locally as "bios" and "spices", in the period June-December 2014 following the adoption of the new law on new psychoactive substances in May 2014.

5.   Abuse and treatment

642.   According to latest available data, for 2012, the number of drug users in Afghanistan was estimated to be between approximately 1.3 million and 1.6 million, and 2.65 per cent of the total population were abusing opiates. In contrast to many other countries, drug abuse in Afghanistan appears to be highest among older segments of society (9 per cent among those aged 45 years and older). The overall annual prevalence of drug use in Afghanistan is estimated to be 6.6 per cent, while in urban areas drug use prevalence is estimated to be about 5.3 per cent. Although the number of treatment centres in Afghanistan increased from 43 in 2009 to 102 in 2012 and to 108 in 2013, drug treatment capacity in Afghanistan still covers less than 8 per cent of opium and heroin users.

643.   The number of drug users in the Islamic Republic of Iran was estimated to be about 1,325,000 in 2014, which is 2.26 per cent of the adult population of the country. The Government also estimated that some 750,000 persons had received treatment for drug-related problems. There are currently more than 4,500 private and around 600 public treatment and rehabilitation centres in the country.

644.   According to official statistics, in 2014 there were a total of 65,216 persons registered as drug users in Kazakhstan, Kyrgyzstan, Tajikistan and Uzbekistan, compared with a total of 73,345 persons in 2013. The number of officially registered drug-dependent persons in Kazakhstan in 2014 stood at 34,221 persons, which is a significant decrease compared with 40,224 persons in 2013. In Kyrgyzstan, 9,024 persons were officially registered as drug-dependent in 2014, which is 8.8 per cent less than in 2013. The number of people suffering from drug addiction remained stable in Tajikistan in 2014. According to official statistics, there were 7,279 registered drug-dependant individuals in the country, of which 80.8 per cent were abusing heroin. A total of 14,692 drug-dependent persons were officially registered in Uzbekistan in 2014, a decrease of 9.2 per cent from the previous year.

645.   Despite the lack of reliable estimates concerning the age range and the number of drug abusers, drug abuse in the Middle East is a growing problem. In Lebanon, for example, it is estimated that about 2,500 people need treatment for drug abuse. Among the 3,016 patients admitted in treatment centres in Lebanon in 2014, 89 per cent abused cannabis, 51 per cent abused heroin and 42 per cent reported abusing cocaine. Other substances of abuse of those patients included ATS, benzodiazepines, hallucinogens, GHB, ketamine, *Salvia divinorum* and tramadol.

646. In view of the lack of comprehensive and reliable data on the extent of drug abuse in the region, INCB urges the Governments concerned to assess the situation in their country by setting up drug monitoring systems and conducting population-based surveys on the extent of drug abuse, in order to develop and implement the appropriate prevention, treatment and rehabilitation programmes.

647. Access to drug dependence treatment is hampered by the limited number of specialized medical facilities in the region, in addition to the stigma associated with drug dependence. Nevertheless, the Board notes that a number of countries in the region established or are in the process of establishing treatment facilities and services to address the negative health and social consequences of drug abuse. INCB is hopeful that this will improve the availability of drug abuse treatment and rehabilitation services.

648. In May 2014, under the auspices of the Palestinian Ministry of Health, an opioid substitution therapy clinic was opened in Ramallah, in which methadone is provided under medical supervision. Prior to the opening of the centre, health professionals conducted a study visit to opioid substitution therapy in Jerusalem and training in collaboration with the Nazareth methadone centre. By mid-June 2015, there were 52 patients benefiting from the centre.

649. The Board also notes that the opioid substitution therapy programme launched in Lebanon in 2011 is now fully operational and serves 1,375 patients, double the number registered by mid-2013. Nearly 95 per cent of the patients are male and more than half are between the ages of 26 and 35. Comprehensive care is provided, including medical treatment, psychiatric evaluation, psychological and social assistance.

D. Europe

1. Major developments

650. Europe continues to be an important market for drugs produced locally and drugs smuggled from other regions, in particular Latin America, West Asia and North Africa. The synthetic drugs manufactured in Western and Central Europe supply illicit markets both in that subregion and in other parts of the world. In recent years, Eastern Europe has emerged as a transit and destination area for cocaine, although the amounts of cocaine seized in the subregion remain relatively small.

651. In Western and Central Europe, cannabis is the most commonly seized drug, accounting for about 80 per cent of all seizures. Cocaine ranks second overall, accounting for more than double the number of reported seizures of amphetamines or heroin. The number of seizures of MDMA ("ecstasy"), was relatively low in Western and Central Europe.

652. By March 2015, more than 450 new psychoactive substances were being monitored by the European Monitoring Centre for Drugs and Drug Addiction (EMCDDA). During 2014 alone, 101 new psychoactive substances were reported for the first time via the European Union early warning system. The increase in the trafficking and abuse of those substances continued to pose a public health challenge in many European countries.

653. Both the purity and the potency of all the drugs of abuse commonly found in Western and Central Europe have increased. The reasons for that increase are complex, and may include advances in technology and market competition. In some countries that produce high-potency cannabis, the share of that substance on the domestic market has increased in recent years. New data indicate that the potency of cannabis resin smuggled in the region has also increased. Recently, EMCDDA and Europol alerted the European Union community to health risks associated with the consumption of high-purity "ecstasy" and tablets containing *para*-methoxymethamphetamine (PMMA) but sold to users as "ecstasy". In some countries, high-quality synthetic cannabinoids and cathinones offered in the illicit market compete with low-quality and relatively more expensive most commonly abused drugs.

654. The Internet and social media have become important tools in marketing drugs. According to EMCDDA more than 600 websites selling new psychoactive substances, sometimes in amounts in the kilograms, were identified in the European Union in 2013 and 2014. Assessment of the size of the online drug market is not easy and there is a need for further awareness-raising regarding the growing potential role of the Internet and use of cryptocurrencies, such as bitcoin, in drug supply and marketing with respect to both established drugs and new psychoactive substances. There is also a need for a review of existing regulatory models to perform in a global and virtual context.

2. Regional cooperation

655. The countries of South-Eastern Europe continued to intensify their regional law enforcement cooperation

in the area of organized crime and drug control. All countries of the region are active participants in the UNODC regional programme for South-Eastern Europe (2012-2015).

656.   In September 2014, in Sarajevo, the Southeast European Law Enforcement Center held a workshop on tackling drug trafficking, at which experts from the Center's member States and the United States discussed forfeiture investigations and money-laundering related to drug trafficking. In March 2015, a meeting on facilitation of common and coordinated measures in the western Balkan region, at which the participants agreed on annual plans for common and coordinated operations in 2015, was held in Belgrade within the framework of the Border Security Programme of the Geneva Centre for the Democratic Control of Armed Forces.

657.   In 2014, the Russian Federation continued supporting the provision of law enforcement training in counter-narcotics at its national institutions to the Counter-Narcotics Police of Afghanistan as part of the UNODC regional programme for Afghanistan and neighbouring countries. That joint cooperation will be extended into 2016 and expanded to include assistance to the five countries of Central Asia. Moreover, the Russian Federation informed the Board about a number of initiatives to strengthen joint efforts to tackle the world drug problem, including the international conference of the Russian-African Anti-Drug Dialogue, held in Banjul on 23 July 2015, and the regional anti-drug operation, "Operation Channel", for the period 2014-2015.

658.   Large-scale international counter-narcotics operations were carried out in 2014 by the member States of CSTO and Afghanistan, in cooperation with the Federal Drug Control Service of the Russian Federation. As a result of those operations, 16.5 tons of narcotic drugs were seized.

659.   The European Union continued intensive cooperation among its member States and with third countries and other regions. The Horizontal Working Party on Drugs, a working group of the Council of the European Union, held talks with third countries, namely Brazil, the Russian Federation, the United States and the States of the Western Balkans and Central Asia.

660.   In July 2015, the European Union and the Government of Afghanistan signed a cooperation agreement on partnership and development, the first official contractual framework governing cooperation between the European Union and Afghanistan. The agreement builds on the European Union strategy for Afghanistan

for the period 2014-2016 and enshrines the Union's commitment to a partnership with Afghanistan in order to fulfil the Government's vision of "realizing self-reliance".

661.   "Shaping our common future: working for prosperous, cohesive and sustainable societies for our citizens" was the theme of the second European Union-Community of Latin American and Caribbean States (CELAC) summit, held in Brussels on 10 and 11 June 2015, which adopted a declaration on a "Partnership for the next generation", the Brussels declaration entitled "Shaping our common future" and an updated European Union-CELAC action plan.

662.   The Cooperation Group to Combat Drug Abuse and Illicit Trafficking in Drugs (Pompidou Group) of the Council of Europe, at its sixteenth Ministerial Conference, adopted its working programme for the period 2015-2018, entitled "Drug policy and human rights: new trends in a globalised context". The work programme establishes the following thematic priorities: bringing human rights to the forefront of drug policy; analysing policy coherence, costs, impact and potentially adverse effects of drug policy measures; addressing changing patterns and context of drug use, production and supply; and identifying opportunities and challenges for drug policies arising from the Internet. Furthermore, the States members of the Pompidou Group continued to foster the exchange of information on drugs and addictions with and within countries of the Mediterranean basin through the Mediterranean Network (MedNET).[40] The activities of MedNET network include the establishment of country profiles for Algeria, Egypt, Jordan, Lebanon, Morocco and Tunisia with a view to sharing information on the drug control situation in those countries, including information on the drug trafficking situation and drug prevention and treatment programmes.

3.   National legislation, policy and action

663.   During the reporting period, the European countries continued to adopt measures to counteract the spread of new psychoactive substances. Germany, Lithuania, Romania and Slovenia added 32, 31, 30 and 9 new psychoactive substances, respectively, to their lists of nationally controlled substances.

664.   In 2014, Belarus addressed the growing threat of new psychoactive substances to public health by adding

---

[40] MedNET countries include Algeria, Cyprus, Egypt, France, Greece, Italy, Jordan, Lebanon, Malta, Morocco, Portugal and Tunisia.

nine new substances to its National List of Narcotic Drugs, Psychotropic Substances, their Precursors and Analogues Subject to State Control. Sweden placed 11 substances under control as narcotic drugs and an additional 21 substances as "goods dangerous to health". In the same year, 36 substances were added to the list of substances subject to control in the Russian Federation, including 27 new psychoactive substances. In addition, Belgium adopted a law providing for the listing of controlled substances according to definitions for generic groups. In December 2014, Finland brought into force new legislation introducing a definition of "new psychoactive substance" and listing 294 substances as psychoactive substances banned from the consumer market. The new legislation prohibits the production and supply of those substances, although it does not establish criminal liability for their possession or use.

665. The Board recommends that countries continue to monitor trends and collect data on the use, abuse, illicit domestic and international distribution and manufacture of new psychoactive substances and share those data with the Board.

666. In March 2014, an action plan to prevent and suppress criminal activity relating to the cultivation of plants containing narcotic substances was approved by the State Police of Albania. The action plan provides for measures aimed at discouraging illicit cultivation of such plants and increasing awareness—among youth, State administration entities and locally elected officials—of illicit cultivation and State Police operations to eradicate such cultivation.

667. In Belarus, a system of measures to stabilize the drug situation and a comprehensive action plan to counter drug trafficking, prevent drug abuse and facilitate the social rehabilitation of drug abusers were approved in 2014.

668. The National Committee for the Coordination and Planning of Drug Responses of Greece drafted a new national strategy on drugs (for the period 2014-2020) and a new action plan (for 2014-2016).

669. In 2014, Italy launched a national action plan to address the threat posed by the illicit sale and distribution of new psychoactive substances via the Internet.

670. In Malta, the Drug Dependence (Treatment not Imprisonment) Act came into force in April 2015. Pursuant to the Act, drug possession for personal use is not a criminal offence and any person found in possession is tried before a Commissioner for Justice and subject to a fine. If the person reoffends within a two-year period, he or she is called before the Drug Offenders Rehabilitation Board, which determines whether the offender is drug-dependent and issues any necessary orders accordingly. Failure to comply with such orders is punishable by a fine or three months' imprisonment.

671. In September 2014, the Republic of Moldova adopted a national action plan to combat drug trafficking for the period 2014-2016. The plan provides for a wide range of measures aimed at reducing drug abuse, especially among youth, addressing the economic, health and social impact of drug abuse, strengthening prescription regulations and combating illicit cultivation and trafficking.

672. Several legislative acts were adopted in Romania with the aim of strengthening the drug control regime. Legislation on preventing and countering drug abuse and trafficking, together with provisions on the legal regime governing plants and preparations containing narcotic drugs and psychotropic substances, were amended with a view to the further protection of public health, especially the health of young people. The Government amended administrative regulations to optimize the licensing regime and improve the access of drug-dependent persons to medical and social programmes. In 2014, an interministerial office was established to coordinate drug policy and oversee the activities of the Ministry of Health and the Ministry of the Interior.

673. In December 2014, the Government of the Russian Federation approved legislative amendments setting out legal conditions facilitating the assistance provided by non-commercial organizations involved in drug demand reduction activities and establishing priority access to controlled substances for patients in need of pain relief. Furthermore, in response to increased trafficking of new psychoactive substances into the country, in January 2015, the Government adopted a law introducing criminal liability for offences involving new psychoactive substances and authorizing the drug control authorities to impose a temporary ban on any potentially dangerous psychoactive substances.

674. In December 2014, Serbia adopted a national drug strategy (for 2014-2021) and an action plan for its implementation (2014-2017).

675. The National Assembly of Slovenia adopted a new resolution on the National Programme on Drugs for 2014-2020. The goals of the Programme include reducing the number of new drug users among youth and the number of drug-related offences and reducing the number of deaths caused by overdose.

676.   In June 2015, the European Commission approved implementing Regulation (EU) 2015/1013 laying down rules for the monitoring of trade in drug precursors between the Union and third countries. The Regulation, which applies to all member States of the European Union, also establishes uniform procedural rules for the licensing and registration of operators and users and their listing in the European database on drug precursors.

4. Cultivation, production, manufacture and trafficking

(a) Narcotic drugs

677.   There are two main cannabis products found on the European illicit drug market: cannabis herb and cannabis resin. Cannabis is both illicitly cultivated in countries of the region and also trafficked, in sizeable amounts, within the region and from other regions. There is an increasing tendency for criminal groups operating in the region to run numerous small-scale cannabis plant cultivation sites, usually indoors, rather than fewer but large-scale outdoor plantations, in order to mitigate the risk of detection. Most cannabis resin destined for Europe is smuggled from Morocco.

678.   According to the *European Drug Report 2015*, in 2013, the European Union countries reported 431,000 individual seizures of cannabis herb and 240,000 seizures of cannabis resin.

679.   The total amount of cannabis resin seized in the European Union in 2013 (460 tons) was much higher than that of cannabis herb (130 tons). Spain, a major point of entry for cannabis produced in Morocco, reported more than two thirds of the total quantity of cannabis resin seized in Europe that year. Afghanistan, Lebanon, Morocco and Pakistan were among the countries of origin or departure of shipments of cannabis resin seized in Western Europe in 2014. Analysis of trafficking trends in those European countries that regularly report seizures of cannabis shows a large increase from 2006 to 2013 in the potency (level of THC) of both herbal cannabis and cannabis resin. Among the causes of that increasing potency may be the introduction of intensive production techniques in Europe and, more recently, the introduction of high-potency plants in Morocco.

680.   South-Eastern Europe continued to see an expansion in the trafficking of cannabis produced in Albania in 2014. The State Police of Albania continued its efforts to contain cannabis cultivation following its successful operations carried out in the southern region and other parts of the country. The Albanian authorities have intensified cooperation with their Italian counterparts in mapping illicit cultivation areas through aerial surveys. The quantity of cannabis seized in Albania in 2014 (101.7 tons) exceeded the total quantity seized during the previous nine years (96 tons).

681.   Seizures of cannabis plants in a country may indicate the production of the drug in its territory. According to EMCDDA, seizures of cannabis plants have significantly increased in Western and Central Europe since 2002. In 2013, Italy and Belgium each identified 1,100 illicit outdoor cannabis plant cultivation sites and eradicated 885,000 and 394,000 plants respectively. In the same year, the eradication of cannabis plants cultivated indoors was reported by Germany (94,000 plants), the Czech Republic (66,000 plants), Ireland (29,000 plants), Latvia (14,000 plants) and Italy (10,300 plants). In 2014, eradication of cannabis plants were reported by the United Kingdom (461,300 plants), Germany (131,800 plants), Greece (52,300 plants) and Finland (21,800 plants). According to the Finnish drug control authorities, small-scale domestic cultivation has recently become more common in Finland. Cannabis growers usually grow up to 20-30 cannabis plants in their homes for personal use.

682.   With the increasing involvement of organized criminal groups in the production and trafficking of cannabis, the drug plays a major role in drug-related crime in Western and Central Europe, where it accounts for 80 per cent of drug seizures and cannabis use or possession for personal use accounts for more than 60 per cent of all reported drug-related offences. However, there are considerable differences between European countries with respect to practice in sentencing for offences relating to cannabis supply; for example, the penalties for a first-time offence of supplying 1 kilogram of cannabis in Europe may range from less than 1 year to 10 years in prison.

683.   Since 2010, several Western and Central European countries have reported declining trends with respect to heroin, inter alia, in the number of seizures and the amounts of the drug seized, the number of offences relating to supply, heroin prices and scale of abuse. According to the latest EMCDDA report on opioid trafficking routes from Asia to Europe, published in 2015, there has been an overall increase in the purity of heroin in the region in recent years.

684.   According to EMCDDA, there is also evidence of an increased range of opioids appearing on the European market. Since 2005, 14 new synthetic opioids have been

reported via the European Union early warning system. In 2014, seizures of diverted or counterfeit pharmaceutical products containing opioids, such as methadone, buprenorphine, fentanyl and tramadol, were reported by competent national authorities of several European countries, including Austria, Finland, Greece and Sweden.

685.   According to the *World Drug Report 2015* heroin seizures have recently increased slightly in Eastern and South-Eastern Europe.[41] In particular, in 2013, heroin seizures in South-Eastern Europe increased slightly in comparison to 2012, although they remained below the levels observed in the subregion between 2007 and 2009. The amounts of heroin seized in Eastern Europe increased slightly in 2013, but remained stable from the long-term perspective.

686.   The three main routes used by trafficking rings to smuggle heroin to Europe are: *(a)* the traditional Balkan route, a major heroin trafficking route into the European Union that links Afghanistan and the Islamic Republic of Iran and passes through Turkey and the Balkans; *(b)* the southern route, which has been used in recent years to smuggle heroin to Europe directly from ports in the Islamic Republic of Iran and Pakistan, or via the Arabian Peninsula or Africa; and *(c)* the northern route, which, according to EMCDDA, is used for heroin trafficking by land from the northern borders of Afghanistan to supply illicit drug markets in Belarus, the Russian Federation, Ukraine and countries in Central Asia.

687.   The discovery of heroin processing laboratories in Europe, in particular two laboratories processing morphine into heroin, dismantled in Spain in late 2013 and early 2014, may indicate possible shifts in heroin supply channels. Greece reported that it had destroyed facilities involved in cutting and packaging heroin from Afghanistan or Pakistan that had been intended for illicit drug markets in other European Union countries.

688.   In December 2014, an extensive network engaged in trafficking heroin into the European Union was dismantled by a joint investigation team, facilitated by Eurojust and supported by Europol. Some 400 suspects were arrested and 100 kg of heroin were seized together with cocaine, cannabis and cash. The network, operating from Austria, Germany and the former Yugoslav Republic of Macedonia, brought heroin into the European Union along the Balkan route and distributed it in several European countries.

689.   According to figures released in 2015, cocaine and "crack" cocaine accounted for 10 per cent of the total number of seizures in Western and Central Europe. Overall, the purity of cocaine seized in the European Union has increased in recent years, while its price has remained relatively stable. In most parts of Eastern and South-Eastern Europe the availability of cocaine remained limited.

690.   Africa continued to be used as a trans-shipment area for the smuggling of cocaine across the Atlantic Ocean into Europe. An example of involvement of the African region in cocaine trafficking is the seizure, in April 2015, of 3 tons of cocaine on a vessel registered in Tanzania. The vessel was intercepted by the authorities of the United Kingdom 100 miles east of the coast of Scotland. The interdiction was conducted in cooperation with the French customs service and other international partners, and represents one of the largest cocaine seizures in the history of the United Kingdom.

691.   Of the European countries, Spain has seized the most cocaine in recent years. In 2013, Spain, Belgium, the Netherlands, France and Italy together accounted for more than 80 per cent of the 62.6 tons seized in the European Union. In 2014, seizures of cocaine in quantities exceeding 100 kg were reported by Spain, France, the United Kingdom, Germany, Greece, Lithuania and Sweden (listed in descending order).

692.   Organized criminal groups from South-Eastern Europe, closely connected with cocaine producers in South America, have been actively involved in trafficking cocaine to Western and Central European ports. Recent seizures of cocaine, albeit in small quantities, in ports on the eastern Mediterranean, Baltic and Black seas have provided new evidence of the diversification of cocaine trafficking routes into Europe.

693.   In 2013, a total of 478 kg of cocaine was seized in Eastern Europe and more than 100 kg in South-Eastern Europe. Seizure data show that cocaine traffickers continue to target many parts of those subregions, cocaine seizures being reported by almost all of the countries concerned in 2013. Eastern Europe is emerging both as a transit area and as a destination for cocaine, of which there has been an increased number of seizures (although only in small quantities) in recent years, which points toward the emergence of a cocaine market in the subregion.

(b)   Psychotropic substances

694.   Europe is a major illicit manufacturer of amphetamine-type stimulants; most of the amphetamine and

---

[41] Reported according to the regional groupings of the *World Drug Report*, annex II.

methamphetamine manufactured in Europe is destined for national illicit markets, although some is destined for other regions, particularly East and South-East Asia. Amphetamine manufacture in Europe mainly takes place in Belgium, the Netherlands, Poland and the Baltic States and, to a lesser extent, in Germany; illicit methamphetamine manufacture is concentrated in the Baltic States and Central Europe. Europe is also known as a transit hub for methamphetamine trafficked from Africa and the Islamic Republic of Iran to East and South-East Asia.

695.   In 2013, a total of 6.7 tons of amphetamine was seized in the European Union, exceeding the figure for the period 2010-2012. Germany, the Netherlands and the United Kingdom accounted for more than half of that amount. Both the number of methamphetamine seizures and the amount of methamphetamine seized in the European Union increased in 2013 compared with the previous year. In 2013, seizures of methamphetamine reported in the European Union amounted to 0.5 tons. In 2014, the following Western and Central European countries reported seizures of amphetamine exceeding 100 kg: Germany (1,336 kg), the United Kingdom (1,225 kg), Poland (783 kg), Spain (562 kg), the Czech Republic (442 kg), Sweden (412 kg), Finland (298 kg), Denmark (292 kg) and France (268 kg). Romania reported that the quantity of amphetamine-type stimulants seized in 2014 was almost 11 times greater than that seized in 2013.

696.   In 2014, Austria reported the detection of three amphetamine and nine methamphetamine laboratories, while German authorities dismantled 11 amphetamine laboratories and three laboratories that had been manufacturing methamphetamine from pseudoephedrine extracted from nasal decongestants. In the Czech Republic, the number of dismantled methamphetamine laboratories slightly increased to 272 in 2014, compared with 262 laboratories dismantled in 2013. An amphetamine-refining laboratory was also discovered in Sweden. Bulgaria continued to seize methamphetamine, which, according to the Bulgarian authorities, had been dispatched from the Netherlands and Turkey. It also dismantled 12 clandestine laboratories producing methamphetamine in 2014.

697.   There was a significant increase in the smuggling of amphetamine and methamphetamine into the Russian Federation in 2014, while the smuggling of "ecstasy"-type substances into that country has substantially decreased. The Russian Federation reported that amphetamine-type stimulants seized by its authorities had been illicitly manufactured in European Union countries, the Islamic Republic of Iran and China and were destined for illicit markets in the Russian Federation, Belarus and Kazakhstan.

698.   Ukraine observed an increase in illicit home-based production of amphetamine-type stimulants. At the same time, Ukraine reported that the amphetamine seized by its authorities had been sourced mainly from Poland and Belarus and had been intended for the illicit market in Ukraine.

699.   In Europe, illicit manufacture of "ecstasy" has for a number of years been associated mainly with two countries, Belgium and the Netherlands. European experts recently expressed concerns that high-purity "ecstasy" powder and tablets appearing on the European market had started replacing tablets that were previously being sold on the market as "ecstasy" but often contained only little or none of that substance and had consequently fallen out of favour with consumers on account of their poor quality and high adulteration.

700.   Seizures of "ecstasy"-type substances in South-Eastern Europe, while low in number compared to seizures of other substances, increased in 2014 compared with the previous year, reaching their highest number since 2006.

701.   Bulgaria reported that seizures of "ecstasy"-type substances, originating in the Netherlands and Bulgaria itself, increased in 2014. The trafficking of "ecstasy" via Bulgaria has been affected by the growing illicit markets in the Middle East. According to Bulgarian authorities, a proportion of the "ecstasy" smuggled through the country was exchanged for heroin in barter deals. In 2014, the country also observed an increasing trend in "ecstasy" trafficking via surface predominantly from the Netherlands via Bulgaria and Turkey along the Balkan route. In 2014, there were 37 seizures of "ecstasy"-type substances, a total of 148 kg (16,845 pills) being seized.

702.   Similarly, Moldova reported a large increase in seizures of "ecstasy"-type substances in 2014, those substances having been dispatched mainly from France, transiting Romania before entering Moldova.

703.   In 2014, seizures of "ecstasy" tablets exceeding 100,000 units were also reported by France, Germany, Spain, the United Kingdom, Ireland, Finland and Greece (listed in descending order).

(c)   Precursors

704.   For several years, large-scale trafficking in APAAN, a pre-precursor of amphetamine and methamphetamine, has been of concern to drug control authorities worldwide. In March 2014, the Commission on Narcotic Drugs

decided to include APAAN and its optical isomers in Table I of the 1988 Convention, that decision taking effect on 6 October 2014. In the European Union, following control measures implemented in member States from January 2014, both the number of seizures and the amounts of APAAN seized have decreased gradually from 34 seizures (a total of 28.7 tons) in 2012 to 9 seizures (8.1 tons) in 2014. In the first half of 2015, five incidents involving a total of 1,250 kg of the substance were reported.

705.   In December 2013, the European Union adopted new control measures aimed at preventing the large-scale diversion of acetic anhydride from the European Union market. Since then, the number of attempts to divert supplies from trade among European Union-based trading companies have decreased considerably, although they have not ceased altogether, as was evidenced by a seizure of 2.2 tons of the substance in Austria in April 2015. New control measures have also led traffickers to revert to other forms of crime to secure supplies. For example, in 2015, the Netherlands reported that 18,000 litres of acetic anhydride had been stolen during transportation between two companies in that country.

706.   In 2014 and 2015, Belgium, Germany, the Netherlands and Spain reported seizures of large amounts of diverse "designer" precursors, derivatives of internationally controlled precursors included in Table I of the 1988 Convention. Those seizures corroborate continued concerns that traffickers are attempting to trade in purpose-made precursor derivatives with a view to circumventing existing precursor control mechanisms and using those substances in the illicit manufacture of amphetamine-type stimulants.[42]

707.   In 2014, Bulgarian authorities prevented a number of attempts to smuggle pseudoephedrine (approximately 500 kg in total) in the form of pharmaceutical preparations. The preparations were legally produced in Turkey but then trafficked via Bulgaria for use in the illicit synthesis of methamphetamine in the Czech Republic and Poland.

708.   A comprehensive review of the situation with respect to the control of precursors and chemicals frequently used in the illicit manufacture of narcotic drugs and psychotropic substances in the region can be found in the report of the Board for 2015 on the implementation of article 12 of the 1988 Convention.

(d)   Substances not under international control

709.   Seizure data provided by Governments and information gathered through the European Union early warning system indicate the increased diversification and availability and continued proliferation of new psychoactive substances in Western and Central Europe. As at March 2015, more than 450 new psychoactive substances were being monitored by EMCDDA, 101 new substances being reported via the European Union early warning system for the first time during 2014. Most of those substances were synthetic cathinones (31 substances)—often sold as replacements for "ecstasy", amphetamine and cocaine—and synthetic cannabinoids (30 substances), which are sold as replacements for cannabis.

710.   Seizures of new psychoactive substances increased seven-fold across Europe between 2008 and 2013. In 2013, some 47,000 seizures of new psychoactive substances—a total of more than 3.1 tons—were reported by the 28 European Union member States, Norway and Turkey, including 21,500 seizures of synthetic cannabinoids (almost 1.6 tons) and 10,700 seizures of synthetic cathinones (more than 1.1 tons). Seizures of synthetic cannabinoids have risen sharply since 2011.

711.   In 2014, the Romanian authorities reported seizures of 5 kg of tryptamines and 75 kg of khat (*Catha edulis*). Nineteen incidents involving seizures of dried khat amounting to 664 kg were also reported by Bulgarian customs authorities in 2014. The khat seized in Bulgaria originated in Kenya and Uganda.

712.   Many of the new psychoactive substances that were destined for European markets were reported to have been manufactured, in bulk, by chemical companies established in China and India and shipped to Europe by air freight, where they were processed, packaged and then sold to consumers. In 2013, EMCDDA identified more than 600 websites selling new psychoactive substances to consumers in the European Union.

5.   Abuse and treatment

713.   Drug abuse is one of the major causes of mortality among European youth, both directly through overdose and indirectly through drug-related diseases, accidents, violence and suicide. Every year in the European Union, more than 6,000 drug users die as a result of overdose, most of those cases involving opioids. According to a recent EMCDDA paper entitled "Mortality among drug users in Europe: new and old challenges for public health",

---

[42] For more information, see E/INCB/2015/4.

published in 2015, the risk of death among problem drug users is at least 10 times higher than that among their peers in the general population.

714.   Almost a quarter of the adult population in the European Union, or over 80 million adults, have tried illicit drugs at least once in their lives. The most commonly used drug in the European Union (according to past-year prevalence among adults between 15 and 64 years of age) is cannabis (19.3 million), followed by cocaine (3.4 million), "ecstasy" (2.1 million) and amphetamines (1.6 million). Denmark, France and the United Kingdom are among the European Union countries with the highest lifetime prevalence of drug abuse among the general population.

715.   According to an EMCDDA report entitled "Drug use and its consequences in the Western Balkans 2006-14", the lifetime prevalence of illicit drug use among the general population in the Western Balkan region appears to be lower than the European average. There are no marked differences between the Western Balkan countries with respect to lifetime prevalence of drug abuse among school students aged 15-16 years, all estimates of lifetime illicit drug use falling between 4 per cent and 8 per cent, which is 2.5 times lower than the European average. The drug most commonly used is cannabis, between 2 per cent and 8 per cent of those surveyed reporting lifetime cannabis use—a range considerably lower than the 17 per cent European average.

716.   The relatively high annual prevalence of cannabis abuse (5.7 per cent) among the general population in Western and Central Europe has stabilized or in some cases decreased, in particular in countries where cannabis consumption is long-established. It is not clear, however, whether that decrease could be linked to the emerging use of synthetic cannabinoids or other new psychoactive substances.

717.   The overall number of first-time treatment admissions for cannabis abuse in the European Union increased from 45,000 to 61,000 between 2006 and 2013. The increase in demand for cannabis abuse treatment, however, has to be understood in the context of service provision and referral practice. For example, in some countries, direct referrals from the criminal justice system account for a high proportion of treatment admissions.

718.   The abuse of heroin and synthetic opioids remains relatively low in the European Union. The average annual prevalence of opioid use, mainly of heroin, among the general population between 15 and 64 years of age was estimated at about 0.4 per cent. Nonetheless, opioids continue to be the drugs associated with the greatest proportion of morbidity, mortality and treatment costs relating to drug abuse in the region.

719.   In 2013, opioids were the primary drug of abuse for 41 per cent of all those receiving drug abuse treatment in Western and Central Europe. While the number of new first-time treatment admissions for heroin abuse has more than halved from a peak of 59,000 in 2007 to 23,000 in 2013, the consumption of opioids other than heroin raises concerns. Eleven countries in Western and Central Europe reported that more than 10 per cent of all opioid users who received drug abuse treatment in 2013 were treated for problems primarily related to opioids other than heroin.

720.   The high prevalence of opioid abuse in Eastern Europe overall is mainly due to high levels of such abuse in the Russian Federation and Ukraine: an estimated 2.4 million persons, representing a prevalence rate of 2.3 per cent. According to the World Drug Report 2015, the proportion of persons in treatment for opioid abuse in Eastern Europe continues to be high, which reflects the extent of problem opioid abuse, particularly problem abuse of heroin, in the subregion. Ukraine reported that more than 25,000 persons received drug treatment for opioid abuse in 2014. Also of concern is the reported suspension of opioid substitution treatment in the Autonomous Republic of Crimea and the city of Sevastopol[43] since March 2014, which reportedly has had serious consequences on the patients who were receiving such treatment.

721.   Worldwide, the highest prevalence rates of persons who inject drugs continue to be found in Eastern and South-Eastern Europe. Approximately 40 per cent of the estimated global number of persons who abuse drugs by injection and are living with HIV reside in Eastern and South-Eastern Europe. For example, Ukraine reported a prevalence rate of HIV infection of 6.7 per cent among injecting drug users. According to WHO, the Russian Federation and Ukraine have rates of mortality due to HIV/AIDS of over 40 per 100,000 population. According to the European Centre for Disease Prevention and Control, 18 countries benefited from the 45 million dollars in aid that was provided by the European Commission to support national responses to HIV in the European Union and in European Neighbourhood Policy countries and the Russian Federation; of which the largest amount was allocated for Ukraine and the Russian Federation. There have also been epidemics of hepatitis C among persons who inject drugs in the Western Balkans, where the

---

[43] In accordance with General Assembly resolution 68/262 on the territorial integrity of Ukraine.

prevalence of that virus ranges from 12 per cent to more than 77 per cent.

722. Overall, the cocaine market in the European Union remained stable in 2013. The annual prevalence of cocaine abuse among the general population aged 15-64 remained high, at around 1 per cent, in Western and Central Europe. In some countries with high levels of abuse, such as Denmark, Italy and Spain, the prevalence of cocaine abuse has decreased since 2008. The demand for treatment for cocaine abuse in the region indicates an overall declining trend.

723. In many countries of Western and Central Europe, the abuse of amphetamines remained stable. EMCDDA estimates that 1.3 million (1.0 per cent) of young adults between 15 and 34 years of age have used amphetamine or methamphetamine in the past year. Methamphetamine abuse was predominant in the Czech Republic and, more recently, Slovakia, although there are also indications of increasing abuse of the substance in other countries. Between 2007 and 2013, the Czech authorities observed an increasing prevalence of high-risk methamphetamine abuse, including by injection. In 2014, an increase in amphetamine abuse was reported by Germany while stable or decreasing trends in amphetamine abuse were reported by Cyprus, Finland, Portugal and the United Kingdom.

724. It is estimated that some 1.8 million Western and Central European young adults between 15 and 34 years of age have used "ecstasy" in the past year. In 2014, a slight increase in "ecstasy" abuse was reported by Finland and Germany, while stable or decreasing trends were reported by Lithuania, Portugal and the United Kingdom. The demand for treatment for "ecstasy" abuse is not very high in Western and Eastern Europe, accounting for less than 1 per cent of reported first-time treatment entrants in 2013.

725. For a number of years the prevalence rates of hallucinogenic mushroom and LSD abuse in Europe have been low and stable; according to the latest national surveys, the past-year prevalence of abuse of both substances was estimated to be less than 1 per cent among young adults between 15 and 34 years of age.

726. Overall, estimating the prevalence of abuse of new psychoactive substances remains a challenge. A Flash Eurobarometer survey conducted in 2014, entitled "Young people and drugs", showed that 8 per cent of 13,000 respondents between the ages of 15 and 24 in the European Union member States had used a new psychoactive substance at least once in their lives, compared to 5 per cent in 2011, 3 per cent having used the substance in the past year. The highest levels of past-year prevalence of use were recorded in Ireland (9 per cent), Spain (8 per cent), France (8 per cent) and Slovenia (7 per cent).

727. Belarus reported that, in 2014, the number of individuals abusing cannabinoids increased by 9 per cent, mainly as a result of the increase in the number of persons using synthetic cannabinoids compared to the previous year. The main trend of 2014 was a significant increase in the number of persons abusing new psychoactive substances, mostly synthetic cannabinoids, and other psychoactive substances.

728. The number of persons who abuse drugs by injection residing in Eastern and South-Eastern Europe is estimated to be 2.91 million, which is 24 per cent of the global total number of persons who abuse drugs by injection.

729. The World Drug Report 2015 suggests that in Eastern and South-Eastern Europe, 1.27 per cent of the general population aged 15-64 years is estimated to use drugs by injection, a rate nearly five times the global average. The estimate for Eastern Europe is heavily influenced by the high prevalence of drug abuse by injection in the Russian Federation (2.29 per cent of the population aged 15-64 years). This high level of drug abuse continued to constitute a challenge to public health in the Russian Federation, despite a trend towards a stabilization of the situation. According to the State Anti-Drug Committee of the Russian Federation, in recent years the number of individuals abusing narcotic drugs and psychotropic substances has reached about 6 per cent of the country's population, or 8 million to 8.5 million people.

730. According to the EMCDDA report "Perspectives on drugs: injection of synthetic cathinones", the abuse of synthetic cathinones by injection has emerged among high-risk drug abusers in Austria, Belgium, the Czech Republic, France, Germany, Ireland, Poland, Romania, Spain and the United Kingdom, but is considered to be a relatively low-level and localized phenomenon.

E. Oceania

1. Major developments

731. The region of Oceania is vulnerable to the trafficking, manufacture and abuse of a wide range of drugs, with countries reporting significant seizures of many substances, including cocaine, heroin, MDMA ("ecstasy"), and precursor chemicals. Cannabis continues to be the most trafficked and abused drug in the region, mainly due to domestic cultivation.

732.   In its reporting period from July 2013 to June 2014, Australia recorded 93,000 drug seizures weighing more than 27 tons in total, the highest numbers on national record. Police and customs seizures of amphetamine-type stimulants in the country were also the highest on record. In 2014, New Zealand saw marked increases in seizures of certain substances, including cocaine. Countries in the region continue to focus on taking action to improve regional border security and the sharing of information on the flows and transhipments of drugs.

733.   Although cannabis is the most widely abused drug, amphetamine-type stimulants, particularly methamphetamine, pose a serious threat to the countries of Oceania. The region has also seen strong increases in the abuse of new psychoactive substances. The role of regional joint operations has been critical to the success of large methamphetamine seizures.

2.   Regional cooperation

734.   The Oceania Customs Organization held its seventeenth annual conference in Koror, Palau, in June 2015, at which it addressed the region's border security challenges. The keynote address was delivered by the President of Palau, who spoke about the importance of coordinating efforts to secure national borders. Coordination was necessary, given the Pacific Ocean's usefulness as a route for drug trafficking. The members adopted a three-year plan for the period 2015-2017, which sets out the strategic direction of the Organization and helps members' administrations to align their activities with the best international customs standards and practices, in order to foster greater economic prosperity and increased border security.

735.   In June 2015, the annual meeting of the Regional Security Committee of the Pacific Islands Forum was held in Suva. The Forum is a political group of States that works to promote regional cooperation and integration in the Pacific region. Also in June 2015, the Forum's Working Group on Counter-Terrorism and Transnational Crime held a meeting for members to discuss trends in and patterns of transnational crime, including illicit drug trafficking in the region.

736.   In December 2014, in Auckland, New Zealand, the UNODC Synthetics Monitoring: Analyses, Reporting and Trends (SMART) programme and the Pacific Islands Forum secretariat jointly hosted a forensic capacity-building training session that brought together law enforcement officials from the Cook Islands, Fiji, Niue, Palau, Papua New Guinea, the Marshall Islands, Samoa, Solomon Islands, Tonga and Vanuatu. The workshop included interactive and practical

sessions at which participants learned about methods for identifying drugs and precursors.

737.   A major regional achievement has been the completion and opening of a narcotics laboratory on the premises of the Scientific Research Organization of Samoa in late July 2013, and the subsequent training sessions, in 2014 and 2015 for Samoan scientists in New Zealand. The training sessions, which focused on examining cannabis and using equipment for testing drugs, was led by the Institute of Environmental Science and Research and the University of the South Pacific. This regional project makes the investigation and prosecution of narcotics-related offences more efficient and has continued in 2015 with the aim of developing testing methods for other drugs such as methamphetamine.

738.   The 2014 Pacific Islands Chiefs of Police Conference was held in Auckland, New Zealand. National police services of the Pacific island countries gathered to agree on a new strategic plan and to discuss regional issues, including illicit drugs and organized crime. In August 2015, the organization's forty-fourth annual conference was held in Alofi and hosted by the Niue Police Department.

3.   National legislation, policy and action

739.   On 5 March 2015, Australia adopted the Crimes Legislation Amendment (Psychoactive Substances and Other Measures) Act No. 12. The Amendment lays down measures to help the Government respond to new and emerging psychoactive substances by banning the importation of all substances, not banned or otherwise regulated, that have a psychoactive effect. The Amendment helps to ensure that new psychoactive substances cannot be imported until the Government has assessed their potential harmful effects and determined the appropriate controls to be applied. To prosecute an offence under the law, it will not be necessary to prove that a defendant knew or was reckless as to the particular identity of a substance or whether the substance had a particular psychoactive effect.

740.   New Zealand has released its national drug policy for the period 2015-2020, which sets out the Government's approach to alcohol and drug issues. The aim of the policy is to minimize harm and promote and protect health and well-being. Harm minimization will be a central feature of drug classification measures, and the regulation of controlled drugs for legitimate purposes will be reviewed. In the period 2017/18, New Zealand will commence a review of the policy and operation of the Psychoactive Substance Act 2013. An ongoing feature of the Government's

actions will be to conduct the national cannabis and crime operation as well as to work with authorities in source and transit countries to break supply chains into New Zealand for precursor chemicals and drugs.

741. In 2014, New Zealand announced that its drug enforcement relationship with China will be strengthened further to help identify members of organized criminal groups in China and to reduce the supply of precursors and methamphetamine from China trafficked into New Zealand. The move follows the signing of a memorandum of arrangement on precursor controls between China and New Zealand in April 2013.

742. New Zealand has also taken action to improve regional border security through cooperation with the authorities of Fiji. In 2015, New Zealand established a training programme for the Fiji Revenue and Customs Authority and the Fiji Police Force to focus on border security by introducing drug detector dogs in Fiji. In 2015, the Fiji Revenue and Customs Authority announced that it aimed to further strengthen its partnership with both Australia and New Zealand in order to carry out joint operations and share more information about the flow of drugs in the region.

743. In 2013, the Government of New Zealand introduced the Psychoactive Substances Act to control the importation, manufacture and sale of new psychoactive substances in the country—with interim approvals for 47 products by 150 licensed retailers. In 2014, an amendment Act came into effect that banned the use of animal testing in clinical trials, effectively bringing the industry and product development to a standstill. Retail regulations due to come into force in November 2015 would allow for the licensing of the sale, both wholesale and retail, of psychoactive substances, and the licensing of retail premises. As of 1 June 2015, approximately 37 local authorities had adopted local approved product policies, which provided directions about where psychoactive products may be sold in a particular area.

4. Cultivation, production, manufacture and trafficking

(a) Narcotic drugs

744. Cannabis is the most trafficked and widely abused drug throughout Oceania. The Australian Crime Commission has reported that, despite illicit domestic cultivation, the quantity of cannabis seized at the border in the 2013/14 reporting period was the highest in the past decade. In 2014,

the number of cannabis seizures in New Zealand remained about the same as in 2013, with approximately 4,800 instances of cannabis herb being seized. However, at the fifty-eighth session of the Commission on Narcotic Drugs, held in March 2015, New Zealand authorities stated that the previous 18 months had seen a resurgence in the visibility of cannabis. Data from the region also indicate that the potency of the available cannabis may be increasing.

745. Oceania in general, and Fiji, Papua New Guinea, Samoa, Tonga and Vanuatu in particular, continue to be used as illicit transit areas for various narcotic drugs. In December 2014, for example, the Fiji Police Force reported a significant heroin seizure worth around $15 million. The Force believed that the consignment was intended for onward trafficking to Australia or New Zealand.

746. Although the market for cocaine and heroin in Oceania remains limited, there are signs that trafficking in some countries may be increasing. Moreover, Oceania is considered a hub for the transhipment of cocaine. In 2014, New Zealand saw increases in both the quantity and the frequency of seizures of cocaine and heroin. Approximately 80 per cent of cocaine that was seized entered New Zealand by air, with about 59 per cent of that amount entering from Brazil. Therefore, in 2014, the cocaine market appeared to be expanding in New Zealand, with seizures more than doubling over 2013. The abuse of cocaine in New Zealand also has the potential to increase, at least partly because of the high market prices and profit margins, which can be an incentive for traffickers.

747. In Australia, one of the key findings in the 2013/14 reporting period was that the cocaine seized at the country's border had primarily come from Peru. Previously, the primary source country had been Colombia. Furthermore, for the first time an incident of heroin seized at the Australian border was identified as having originated in South America. Australia reported 3,121 domestic seizures of cocaine in the period 2013/14, a record number, although the total weight of the seizures had decreased by 70 per cent. While the number of seizures at the border had increased every year since 2009/10, in 2013/14 both the weight and number of border seizures of cocaine decreased.

(b) Psychotropic substances

748. In response to the increasing threats and regional interconnections in the methamphetamine market, as well as extensive domestic manufacture in some countries of the region, New Zealand continues to implement its multi-agency initiative entitled "Tackling methamphetamine: an

action plan", which has helped to improve resource targeting and thereby to gather more accurate data on methamphetamine abuse and trafficking. The increase in smuggling of small amounts of methamphetamine in 2014 may have occurred in response to increased law enforcement pressure on the diversion of precursors and on clandestine laboratories.

749.   The Fiji Revenue and Customs Authority has emphasized the role of joint regional operations in large methamphetamine seizures. For example, in July 2015, a sea container sent from South America to Fiji contained 80 kg of methamphetamine and was intercepted in a joint operation of Australia, New Zealand and Fiji.

750.   The Australian Crime Commission has also determined that, of all drug types, methamphetamine poses the greatest threat to the Australian public because of its increasing purity and the involvement of organized criminal groups. In its 2013/14 report, the Australian Customs and Border Protection Service asserted that seizures of amphetamine-type stimulants had increased by nearly 19 per cent from the previous year. Most of the amphetamine-type stimulants were detected in cargo and in postal consignments. In the 2014/15 reporting period, the Service maintained its focus on detecting and seizing amphetamine-type stimulants in postal consignments, while the country's law enforcement authorities expressed concern about the potential for transnational organized criminal groups to exploit the market for synthetic drugs.

751.   In 2014, law enforcement authorities in Australia reported "ecstasy" seizures of several tons each. The Australian Crime Commission indicated that a seizure of almost two tons made in November 2014 was indicative of the resurgence of the "ecstasy" market in both the country and the region. The Ecstasy and Related Drugs Reporting System reported that in 2014 the availability of "ecstasy" pills, powder, and capsules appeared to have increased significantly from 2013. In 2013, amphetamine-type stimulants, particularly methamphetamine, were the most detected drug at the Australian border.

(c)   Precursors

752.   Strong demand for methamphetamine in the region and the involvement of organized crime in its manufacture have had the result that the majority of precursors seized have been pseudoephedrine and ephedrine. The Australian Crime Commission has reported that China and India are the primary source countries of several precursor chemicals but that precursors are also diverted from licit domestic trade. In the period 2013/14, the number of clandestine laboratories detected nationally decreased to 744 compared with 757 in the period 2012/13, and although that was the third highest number on record, it is not indicative of abuse rates or availability. Methamphetamine was nevertheless the main drug produced in laboratories detected. Australia also saw a 10-ton seizure of benzaldehyde, a precursor used to produce methamphetamine. There were 1,035 detections of amphetamine-type stimulants precursors in the period 2013/14, a slight decrease from the detections in the previous reporting period.

753.   New Zealand has reported that although it still sees a large amount of pseudoephedrine, it appears that ephedrine is now the precursor preferred by traffickers. Ephedrine continues to be the main precursor seized at the border. Seizures of those substances were on the decline for a couple of years, but the amounts seized in 2013 were significantly higher, attributable to interceptions of ContacNT and ephedrine by the Organised and Financial Crime Agency of New Zealand and customs officers during Operation Ghost in 2013. However, New Zealand saw more finished methamphetamine trafficked in 2014, possibly in response to increased law enforcement pressure on precursor imports and on domestic clandestine laboratories.

754.   Although increasing methamphetamine abuse is of concern throughout the Pacific island States and territories, there is insufficient data region-wide on trafficking, transhipment and seizures of precursors and substances listed in Tables I and II of the 1988 Convention. Information on diversion of chemicals is limited despite the actions of transnational organized criminal groups in the region of Oceania. Moreover, only 1 of 16 countries in the region submitted form D (annual information on substances frequently used in the illicit manufacture of narcotic drugs and psychotropic substances) for 2014 to the Board by the annual reporting deadline of 30 June, thus affecting the Board's ability to analyse regional precursor trends and patterns.

755.   A comprehensive review of the situation with respect to the control of precursors and chemicals frequently used in the illicit manufacture of narcotic drugs and psychotropic substances in the region can be found in the report of the Board for 2015 on the implementation of article 12 of the 1988 Convention.

(d)   Substances not under international control

756.   New Zealand has reported that it continues to see new psychoactive substances, including a large number of

synthetic cannabinoids and other substances. Detected blotter paper increasingly contains new substances and not the more commonly abused substances such as lysergic acid diethylamide, making them significantly cheaper for consumers. At the fifty-eighth session of the Commission on Narcotic Drugs, New Zealand reiterated that the presence of new synthetic psychoactive substances necessitated changes to national legislation in 2013 and 2014 in order to address the widespread availability and constantly changing composition of those substances. Drug analogues and new psychoactive substances also continue to increase in availability and popularity in Australia. The number of seizures of these substances in Australia in the period 2013/14 increased by more than 64 per cent from the previous period, comprising synthetic cannabinoids, synthetic cathinones and different NBOMe compounds.

5. Abuse and treatment

757. Data on the extent and patterns of abuse of most drugs, as well as treatment figures and therapeutic options, remain limited throughout most of Oceania. Governments are encouraged to increase data collection on the prevalence of abuse and availability of treatment options as part of the region's approach to drug abuse as a serious public health issue.

758. As the Board has previously noted, the high prevalence of abuse of cannabis remains stable throughout the region; however, data on its abuse are generally limited to Australia and New Zealand. In the latter country, data from the 2012/13 survey indicated that 11 per cent of adults aged 15 years and over had reported using cannabis in the previous 12 months, while 34 per cent of people abusing cannabis had reported consumption of the drug at least weekly in the previous 12 months. In New Zealand, the 2012/13 survey indicated that past-year abuse of amphetamines, including methamphetamine, among adults aged 16-64 years was 0.9 per cent, which was roughly the same as prevalence found by the 2011/12 survey. However, rates of amphetamine abuse appeared to have declined since 2003, when the past-year prevalence rate was 2.7 per cent.

759. The National Drug and Alcohol Research Centre of Australia has released reports showing that deaths involving methamphetamine have been steadily increasing since 2010 and that abuse of methamphetamine among injecting drug users has increased by 52 per cent over the past 10 years. With respect to opioid drugs, the Australian Institute of Health and Welfare has indicated that heroin is the most common opioid drug of abuse leading to treatment, with the number of people receiving treatment for opioid dependence almost doubling between 1998 and 2014. Survey data published by the Institute in 2014 show that about 3.3 per cent of Australians aged 14 years or older had used painkillers/analgesics for non-medical reasons in the previous 12 months, and 1.2 per cent had used heroin at least once in their lifetime.

760. The Australian Crime Commission has stated that the order of prevalence of drug abuse in the country is cannabis, MDMA and then methamphetamine—with the prevalence of abuse for all illicit substances remaining stable during the period 2010-2013. The 2013 National Drug Strategy Household Survey in Australia showed that 7 per cent of the Australian population aged 14 years or older reported abusing amphetamine or methamphetamine at least once in their lifetime. Recent analyses of wastewater compared with household survey data, however, have indicated that in regions of Australia methamphetamine was potentially abused to a much greater extent than suggested by household surveys alone. Treatment data in Australia generally show that people aged 20-29 years have the highest rates of acute and chronic harm related to amphetamine and methamphetamine abuse. The proportion of recent methamphetamine abusers that abused crystal methamphetamine increased from 22 per cent in 2010 to 50 per cent in 2013, along with the tripling, since 2010, in the level of purity of methamphetamine detected in some Australian jurisdictions.

761. In New Zealand, it was reported that in 2014 more than 41,000 people received drug abuse treatment for substances other than alcohol or tobacco, and that more than 37 per cent of those people were entering treatment for the first time. It is estimated that about 20,000 people inject drugs in New Zealand, and that 10 per cent of those injecting drug abusers had shared needles at the time they last injected. New Zealand has also indicated that as many as 57 per cent of injecting drug users are infected with hepatitis C and 20 per cent with hepatitis B due to drug abuse at some time in their past.

Chapter IV.

Recommendations to Governments, the United Nations and other relevant international and national organizations

762. The following paragraphs contain the most significant observations contained in the present report and a number of related recommendations. The Board invites Governments and international organizations to provide it with any feedback and information they consider relevant regarding their achievements and difficulties in implementing these recommendations and the recommendations of previous years in fulfilling their obligations under the international drug control treaties.

Health and welfare as the main objectives of the international drug control treaties

Special session of the General Assembly on the world drug problem

763. States parties have made important strides towards implementing more cohesive and coherent drug control strategies as envisioned in the Conventions. However, the evolving nature of the complex social problem of drug abuse, drug trafficking and illicit drug cultivation and production requires that Governments be cognizant of the challenges and opportunities facing them. The special session of the General Assembly on the world drug problem to be held in 2016 is a timely opportunity to review drug control policies and practices grounded in evidence and science and based upon the principle of shared responsibility and a comprehensive, integrated and balanced approach. The international drug control system should

promote the application of scientific knowledge, respect for human rights and the principle of proportionality in dealing with the set of problems related to drugs. Legalization of the use of internationally controlled narcotic drugs and psychotropic substances for non-medical purposes is not an adequate response to the existing challenges.

Recommendation 1: INCB recommends that States approach the review to be undertaken through the special session of the General Assembly with the goal of reinforcing best practices, while modifying measures that have not worked and expanding the options used to cope with new drugs, social developments, the use of the Internet for illicit purposes and money-laundering.

764. Strong communities with rich economic potential are more capable of withstanding the corrupting influence of illicit crop cultivation or drug dealing. Poverty reduction measures within a framework for sustainable development that give farmers an economically viable, legal alternative to growing illicit crops are of fundamental importance for the success of the efforts to reduce illicit cultivation.

Recommendation 2: States should promote alternative livelihood programmes in order to support communities and provide farmers engaged in illicit drug crop cultivation with licit and sustainable income-generating activities that can reduce and eliminate their dependency on income from that illicit crop cultivation. Such programmes include, inter alia, services related to health, education, infrastructure, community development and security.

Demand reduction

765.   States are reminded of their obligation to implement effective drug abuse prevention, treatment and rehabilitation programmes.

Recommendation 3: Prevention of substance abuse in society at large, particularly among the youth, should remain the prime objective of government action. Such action is not limited to drug-specific policies: anything that strengthens social cohesion and individuals' capacity for self-determination and resilience can reduce the prevalence of drug abuse. Reducing the adverse health and social consequences of drug abuse is an essential element of a comprehensive demand reduction strategy. States should provide effective and humane assistance to people affected by drug abuse, including both medically appropriate and evidence-based treatment. States should ensure that sanctions for drug-related criminal offences are proportionate and, where such offences are committed by drug users, consider alternatives to conviction and punishment as provided for in the treaties, such as treatment, education, after-care, rehabilitation and social reintegration.

Availability

766.   The international drug control system, as established by the conventions and built upon in the relevant political declarations, provides a comprehensive framework for ensuring the proper provision of narcotic drugs and psychotropic substances to reduce pain and suffering while preventing their diversion into illicit use. However, about 75 per cent of the world population still has limited or no access to proper pain relief treatment. The supplement to the present report, *Availability of Internationally Controlled Drugs: Ensuring Adequate Access for Medical and Scientific Purposes*, demonstrates that the availability of internationally controlled drugs can be—and has been—improved within the framework of the international conventions.

Recommendation 4: Striking a balance between overprescribing and underprescribing requires continuous study and an ongoing review of policies. Drug abuse should and will remain a concern for society as a whole, including those in the medical profession and public health officials. Adequate access to narcotic drugs and psychotropic substances for medical purposes can be improved through corrective action by States that should address the regulatory, attitudinal, knowledge-related, economic and procurement-related aspects identified as the causes of inadequate availability. The Board urges Member States

to implement the recommendations made in the above-mentioned supplementary report on the availability of internationally controlled drugs.

International Import and Export Authorization System

767.   As part of its endeavours to ensure effective and efficient implementation of the import and export authorization system for licit international trade in narcotic drugs and psychotropic substances, the Board developed the International Import and Export Authorization System (I2ES). I2ES is an electronic platform that allows Governments to electronically generate import and export authorizations for narcotic drugs and psychotropic substances, to exchange those authorizations in real time and to instantly verify the legitimacy of individual transactions while ensuring full compliance with the requirements of the conventions. The system significantly reduces the risk of drug consignments being diverted into illicit channels.

Recommendation 5: The Board urges all competent national authorities that have not yet done so to register and start using I2ES as soon as possible, as only through its widespread application will Governments be able to avail themselves of all the advantages that the tool can provide. The Board reiterates the call made to Member States by the Commission on Narcotic Drugs, in its resolution 58/10, to provide the fullest possible financial support to enable the secretariat of the Board to continue administering and monitoring the System.

Psychotropic substances

768.   The status of control in some countries for many psychotropic substances included in Schedules II, III and IV of the 1971 Convention remains unknown.

Recommendation 6: The Board reiterates its call for Governments to review their laws and regulations to verify that they are fully in line with all the relevant provisions of the 1971 Convention and relevant resolutions of the Economic and Social Council. The Board reminds the Governments concerned of the treaty requirement of issuing import/export authorizations for Schedule II substances, and calls on them to submit the missing information regarding their national control over Schedules III and IV substances, in particular in view of the recent scheduling of six new substances and the change in the scope of control of GHB, which was transferred from Schedule IV to Schedule II of the Convention in 2013.[44]

769. The widespread prescription of benzodiazepines and unwarranted treatment, particularly among older people, with sedative-hypnotics and anxiolytics carries the risk of overuse of pharmaceutical preparations containing those substances and the resulting adverse and toxic reactions.

Recommendation 7: The Board calls on all Governments to remain vigilant to the consequences of misuse and overuse of benzodiazepines, particularly among older patients. Governments are urged to closely monitor the consumption levels of benzodiazepines and ensure that they are prescribed in accordance with sound medical practices and in line with the rational use of psychoactive drugs.

Precursors

770. Since the entry into force of the 1988 Convention, States have succeeded in substantively reducing the diversion of scheduled substances from international trade into illicit drug manufacture. To further support the monitoring of the licit trade in precursor chemicals and to prevent their diversion into illicit channels, INCB has developed electronic tools such as Pre-Export Notification Online (PEN Online) and the Precursors Incident Communication System (PICS).

Recommendation 8: All Governments are urged to make use of PEN Online and PICS to improve monitoring of the international trade in precursors and to exchange intelligence on related illicit activities in real time.

771. Insufficient attention has been given to national controls and the monitoring of domestic movements and the end use of precursor chemicals. Further challenges today are the emergence of non-scheduled substitute chemicals, including "designer precursors", and the increase in the sophistication, diversification and scale of illicit synthetic drug manufacturing operations. States have a shared responsibility to adopt a forward-looking strategy that addresses the limitations of the existing system, mainly in relation to non-scheduled chemicals.

Recommendation 9: In view of new developments, Governments should take the following set of actions:

(a) Use the opportunity provided by the special session of the General Assembly on the world drug

---

[44] Commission on Narcotic Drugs decision 56/1.

problem to reconfirm the importance of precursor control as a preventive component in a balanced drug control strategy;

(b) Make industry a critical partner in the prevention of chemical diversion and formalize the commitment to such partnerships;

(c) Review the effectiveness of national regulatory control systems and work to close any gaps in those domestic systems;

(d) Ensure that law enforcement authorities investigate seizures, stopped shipments and attempted diversions in order to identify the sources of diversion and the criminal organizations behind those activities, and share their findings globally to prevent future diversions using similar modi operandi.

New psychoactive substances

772. INCB notes the cooperation between WHO and UNODC to establish criteria for prioritizing new psychoactive substances that should be the subject of scrutiny for possible review and consideration for possible international control. In addition to scheduling at the international level, countries continue to bring new psychoactive substances under national control. New psychoactive substances have also been the subject of an increasing number of meetings and conferences worldwide; however, effective strategies are still forthcoming. The challenges posed by those substances and the diversification of the abuse market continue to grow, with a rising number of reports about new psychoactive substances as the cause of hospital emergency admissions and deaths.

Recommendation 10: INCB encourages all Governments to build on relevant resolutions of the Economic and Social Council and the Commission on Narcotic Drugs, regional experiences and the experiences of individual Member States, and use the upcoming special session of the General Assembly to explore and devise regulatory, practical and realistic measures to protect individuals and the public at large from the harmful effects of new psychoactive substances. INCB also urges all Governments to make full use of the global focal point network Project Ion and the related incident communication platform (IONICS), which support operational cooperation among Governments with a view to preventing new psychoactive substances from reaching markets of drug abuse. INCB also reiterates the importance of primary prevention in addressing the challenge posed by new psychoactive substances.

Promoting the consistent application of the international drug control treaties

773.   Africa continues to be one of the world's major drug trafficking hubs. While West Africa has traditionally been used to traffic drugs, such as cocaine, to Europe, the subregion has also been identified as a source of amphetamine-type stimulants. Furthermore, East Africa's prominence as a transit region for Afghan heroin has increased. Recent developments on the continent have also included a rise in domestic drug abuse in some countries, particularly among youth.

Recommendation 11: The Board requests Governments to enhance regional cooperation and the sharing of information in an effort to target established and emerging trafficking routes, bolster security throughout the region and combat the rise of drug abuse.

774.   The rates of intravenous drug abuse in Eastern Europe have not abated and now stand at almost five times the global average. According to UNAIDS, one third of global population infected with AIDS who contracted the virus due to injecting drug use reside in that subregion.

Recommendation 12: The Board recommends the implementation by Governments in the region of prevention mechanisms to dissuade individuals from engaging in intravenous drug abuse. Treatment facilities for sufferers of drug-related diseases should also be provided, in addition to comprehensive rehabilitation programmes designed to facilitate the cessation of drug abuse, recovery and the social reintegration of drug abusers into society.

775.   The Board notes the measures taken by Afghanistan concerning regional and international cooperation in an attempt to address the drug-related threats facing the country. The Government has also committed to implementing initiatives such as alternative livelihood programmes. Although, according to the latest UNODC opium poppy survey, the area of illicit cultivation in 2015 was the lowest since 2001, the Board expresses its continuing concern about illicit opium poppy cultivation, drug production and drug trafficking in the country, including the situation with respect to the illicit cultivation of cannabis in the country.

Recommendation 13: INCB calls on the Government of Afghanistan to continue its efforts to tackle illicit drug crop cultivation and the illicit production and manufacture of drugs and for the interdiction of drug trafficking and increased prevention, treatment, rehabilitation, social reintegration and recovery from drug abuse. INCB recommends that international partners continue to provide assistance to Afghanistan in this regard.

776.   A worrying trend has emerged in North America regarding the number of people who have developed opioid dependencies, often following prescribed courses of treatment with opioid analgesics. Such dependency has resulted in both the abuse of prescription opioids and other narcotic drugs such as heroin. The result has been a high loss of life in the region due to overdoses.

Recommendation 14: The Board urges Governments to ensure the training of prescribers and dispensers of narcotic drugs in best practices for the prescribing and dispensing of, in particular, opioid-based analgesics.

777.   The South American continent accounts for almost all the world's illicit cultivation of coca bush. Both Bolivia (Plurinational State of) and Peru registered decreases in the size of the total area under illicit coca bush cultivation in 2014. In contrast, Colombia had a 44 per cent year-on-year area increase in coca bush cultivation in 2014.

Recommendation 15: The Board urges the Governments of the Andean region to increase their sharing of information and best practices to tackle and reduce illicit drug crop cultivation. Colombian authorities should look at ways to reverse the trend in the country, and both Bolivia (Plurinational State of) and Peru should ensure the continuation of the decreasing trend of area under illicit coca bush cultivation.

778.   The 1961 Convention establishes that the parties to the Convention shall take such legislative and administrative measures as may be necessary to give effect to and carry out the provisions of the Convention and to limit exclusively to medical and scientific purposes the production, manufacture, export, import, distribution of, trade in, use and possession of controlled narcotic drugs. Likewise, the 1971 Convention requires States parties to adopt such legislative and administrative measures as may be necessary to give effect to the provisions of the Convention within their respective territories and to cooperate with other States and international organizations in the execution of the aims of the Convention.

Recommendation 16: The Board stresses the importance of the universal adherence to the international drug control treaties and urges all Governments to carefully review the implementation of their respective obligations under the international drug control treaties and to ensure that domestic legislation does not contravene the provisions of the international conventions to which they are parties. The Board will continue to monitor developments and looks forward to continuing its dialogue with all authorities on matters related to the implementation of the drug control conventions.

(*Signed*)
Werner Sipp
President

(*Signed*)
Bernard Leroy
Rapporteur

(*Signed*)
Andrés Finguerut
Secretary

Vienna, 13 November 2015

Annex I.

Regional and subregional groupings used in the report of the International Narcotics Control Board for 2015

The regional and subregional groupings used in the report of the International Narcotics Control Board for 2015, together with the States in each of those groupings, are listed below.

Africa

Algeria

Angola

Benin

Botswana

Burkina Faso

Burundi

Cameroon

Cabo Verde

Central African Republic

Chad

Comoros

Congo

Côte d'Ivoire

Democratic Republic of the Congo

Djibouti

Egypt

Equatorial Guinea

Eritrea

Ethiopia

Gabon

Gambia

Ghana

Guinea

Guinea-Bissau

Kenya

Lesotho

Liberia

Libya

Madagascar

Malawi

Mali

Mauritania

Mauritius

Morocco

Mozambique

Namibia

Niger

Nigeria

Rwanda

Sao Tome and Principe

Senegal

Seychelles

Sierra Leone

Somalia

South Africa

South Sudan

Sudan

Swaziland

Togo

Tunisia

Uganda

United Republic of Tanzania

Zambia

Zimbabwe

Central America and the Caribbean

Antigua and Barbuda

Bahamas

Barbados

Belize

Costa Rica

Cuba

Dominica

Dominican Republic

El Salvador

Grenada

Guatemala

Haiti

Honduras

Jamaica

Nicaragua

Panama

Saint Kitts and Nevis

Saint Lucia

Saint Vincent and the Grenadines

Trinidad and Tobago

North America

Canada

Mexico

United States of America

South America

Argentina

Bolivia (Plurinational State of)

Brazil

Chile

Colombia

Ecuador

Guyana

Paraguay

Peru

Suriname

Uruguay

Venezuela (Bolivarian Republic of)

East and South-East Asia

Brunei Darussalam

Cambodia

China

Democratic People's Republic of Korea

Indonesia

Japan

Lao People's Democratic Republic

Malaysia

Mongolia

Myanmar

Philippines

Republic of Korea

Singapore

Thailand

Timor-Leste

Viet Nam

South Asia

Bangladesh

Bhutan

India

Maldives

Nepal

Sri Lanka

West Asia

Afghanistan
Armenia
Azerbaijan
Bahrain
Georgia
Iran (Islamic Republic of)
Iraq
Israel
Jordan
Kazakhstan
Kuwait
Kyrgyzstan
Lebanon

Oman
Pakistan
Qatar
Saudi Arabia
State of Palestine
Syrian Arab Republic
Tajikistan
Turkey
Turkmenistan
United Arab Emirates
Uzbekistan
Yemen

Europe

Eastern Europe

Belarus
Republic of Moldova

Russian Federation
Ukraine

South-Eastern Europe

Albania
Bosnia and Herzegovina
Bulgaria
Croatia

Montenegro
Romania
Serbia
The former Yugoslav Republic of Macedonia

Western and Central Europe

Andorra
Austria
Belgium
Cyprus
Czech Republic
Denmark
Estonia
Finland
France
Germany
Greece
Holy See
Hungary
Iceland
Ireland
Italy
Latvia

Liechtenstein
Lithuania
Luxembourg
Malta
Monaco
Netherlands
Norway
Poland
Portugal
San Marino
Slovakia
Slovenia
Spain
Sweden
Switzerland
United Kingdom of Great Britain and Northern Ireland

Oceania

Australia

Cook Islands

Fiji

Kiribati

Marshall Islands

Micronesia (Federated States of)

Nauru

New Zealand

Niue

Palau

Papua New Guinea

Samoa

Solomon Islands

Tonga

Tuvalu

Vanuatu

Annex II.

Current membership of the International Narcotics Control Board

Wei Hao

Born in 1957. National of China. Professor of Psychiatry and Deputy Director of the Mental Health Institute, Central South University, Changsha, China. Director of the World Health Organization (WHO) Collaborating Centre for Psychosocial Factors, Substance Abuse and Health, Western Pacific Region. Currently serving as Chair, Education Committee of the Asian-Pacific Society for Alcohol and Addiction Research, and as President, the China Association of Drug Abuse Prevention and Treatment and Chinese Association of Addiction Medicine.

Bachelor of Medicine, Anhui Medical University; Master's and Doctorate degrees of Psychiatry, Hunan University of Chinese Medicine.

Previously held positions as Scientist, Substance Abuse Department, WHO, Geneva (1999-2000); Medical Officer, Department of Mental Health and Substance Abuse, WHO, Western Pacific Region, and President, the Chinese Psychiatrist Association (2008-2011). Membership in the Scientific Advisory Committee on Tobacco Product Regulation, WHO (2000-2004). Currently holding membership on the Expert Advisory Panel on Drug Dependence and Alcohol Problems, WHO (2006-present); and the national focal point for China for the implementation of the regional plan of action for the reduction of alcohol-related harm in the Western Pacific, WHO (2009-present); and member of the Working Group on the Classification of Substance Abuse for the eleventh revision of the International Classification of Diseases (ICD-11), WHO (2011-present).

Recipient of research support from various bodies at the national level (Ministry of Health, Ministry of Science and Technology, National Natural Science Foundation) and at the international level (WHO and the National Institute on Drug Abuse and the National Institute on Alcohol Abuse and Alcoholism of the United States). Coordinator of series of WHO/China workshops on addictive behaviour. Member of the Expert Committee of the national project on mental health service in communities in China. Consultant for the development, implementation and evaluation of China's mental health law, and for the development of the anti-drug law and regulations in China.

Published over 400 academic articles and 50 books on alcohol and drug dependence. Selected recent publications in peer-reviewed journals include the following: "Longitudinal surveys of prevalence rates and use patterns of illicit drugs at selected high-prevalence areas in China from 1993 to 2000", *Addiction* (2004); "Drug policy in China: progress and challenges", *Lancet* (2014); "Transition of China's drug policy: problems in practice" *Addiction* (2015); "Improving drug addiction treatment in China", *Addiction* (2007); "Stigmatization of people with drug dependence in China: a community-based study in Hunan province", *Drug Alcohol Dependence* (2013); and "Drinking and drinking patterns and health status in the general population of five areas of China", *Alcohol & Alcoholism* (2004).

Member of the International Narcotics Control Board (since 2015).[a] Member of the Committee on Finance and Administration (2015). Member of the Standing Committee on Estimates (2015).

---

[a] Elected by the Economic and Social Council on 17 November 2014.

David T. Johnson

Born in 1954. National of the United States. Vice-President, Sterling Global Operations; retired diplomat. Bachelor's degree in economics from Emory University; graduate of the National Defence College of Canada.

United States Foreign Service officer (1977-2011). Assistant Secretary for the Bureau of International Narcotics and Law Enforcement Affairs, United States Department of State (2007-2011). Deputy Chief of Mission (2005-2007) and Chargé d'affaires, a.d. (2003-2005), United States Embassy, London. Afghan Coordinator for the United States (2002-2003). United States Ambassador to the Organization for Security and Cooperation in Europe (1998-2001). Deputy Press Secretary at the White House and Spokesman for the National Security Council (1995-1997). Deputy Spokesman at the State Department (1995) and Director of the State Department Press Office (1993-1995). United States Consul General, Vancouver (1990-1993). Assistant National Trust Examiner, Office of the Comptroller of the Currency, United States Treasury (1976-1977).

Member of the International Narcotics Control Board (since 2012). Member of the Committee on Finance and Administration (since 2012). Chair of the Committee on Finance and Administration (2014).

Bernard Leroy

Born in 1948. National of France. Honorary Deputy Prosecutor General and Director of the International Institute of Research against Counterfeit Medicines.

Degrees in Law from the University of Caen, Institute of European Studies of Saarbrucken, Germany, and University Paris X. Graduate of the French National School for the Judiciary (1979).

Previously held positions of Deputy General Prosecutor, Versailles Court of Appeal, 2010-2013. Senior Legal Advisor, United Nations Office on Drugs and Crime (UNODC) (1990-2010). Advisor in charge of international, legislative and legal affairs in the French National Drug Coordination (1988-1990). Investigating judge specializing in drug cases, Evry High Court (1979-1988). Head of the Legal Assistance Programme, UNODC, and Coordinator of the decentralized team of legal experts, Bogota, Tashkent and Bangkok (1990-2010). Leader of the legal assistance team assisting the Government of Afghanistan in the drafting process of the new drug control law, 2004. Co-author of the preparatory study for the

law introducing community service sentencing as an alternative to imprisonment in France (1981). Co-founder of "Essonne Accueil", a non-governmental organization providing treatment services for drug addicts (1982). Member of the French delegation for the final negotiations of the United Nations Convention against Illicit Traffic in Narcotic Drugs and Psychotropic Substances, 1988. Chair of the study group on cocaine trafficking in Europe, Council of Europe (1989). Author of the report resulting in the first European political coordinating committee to combat drugs (1989). Chair of the World Bank and UNODC joint team (the Stolen Asset Recovery (StAR) Initiative) which organized the freezing and subsequent recovery in Switzerland of the assets stolen by the former dictator Jean-Claude Duvalier in Haiti (2008).

Organizer of the lifelong learning programme on combating drug trafficking and addiction for members of the French judiciary, French National School for the Judiciary (1984-1994). Lecturer for medical graduates in psychiatry in the field of forensic expertise and responsibility, Faculty of Medicine, Paris-Sud University (1983-1990). Lecturer in the field of social work, University of Paris 13 (1984-1988). Lecturer for second year Master's courses in Security and Public International Law, Jean Moulin Lyon 3 University (2005-2013).

Member of the Executive Board of the international section of the National Association of Drug Court Professionals (2006). External member of the Management Board of the French Monitoring Centre for Drugs and Drug Addiction (2013). Member of the committee of the Reynaud report (2013).

Selected publications include "Le travail au profit de la communauté, substitut aux courtes peines d'emprisonnement", *Revue de science criminelle et de droit comparé*, No. 1 (Sirey, 1983); *Drogues et drogués*, École nationale de la magistrature, studies and research (1983); *Étude comparative des législations et des pratiques judiciaires européennes face à la drogue* (Commission of the European Communities, 1991); Ecstasy, Inserm Collective Expertise series (Editions Inserm, 1997); *The International Drug Control System*, in cooperation with Cherif Bassiouni and J. F. Thony, in *International Criminal Law: Sources, Subjects and Contents* (Martinus Nijhoff Publishers, 2007); *Routledge Handbook of Transnational Criminal Law*, Neil Boister and Robert Curie, eds. (Routledge, 2014).

Member of the International Narcotics Control Board (since 2015).[b] Rapporteur (2015).

---

[b] Elected by the Economic and Social Council on 23 April 2014.

Richard P. Mattick

Born in 1955. National of Australia. Professor of Drug and Alcohol Studies at the National Drug and Alcohol Research Centre, Faculty of Medicine, University of New South Wales; Professor of Brain Sciences, University of New South Wales; Principal Research Fellow, Australian Government National Health and Medical Research Council (2013-2017), and Registered Clinical Psychologist.

Bachelor of Science (Psychology), Honours, Class 1, University of New South Wales, 1982; Master of Psychology (Clinical), University of New South Wales, 1989; Doctor of Philosophy, University of New South Wales, 1988; and Certificate in Neuroanatomy, Anatomy, University of New South Wales, 1992.

Director of Research, Australian National Drug and Alcohol Research Centre (1995-2001), and Executive Director, Australian National Drug and Alcohol Research Centre, Faculty of Medicine, University of New South Wales (2001-2009). Member, Australian National Expert Advisory Committee on Illicit Drugs (2002-2004), Australian national expert advisory group on sustained release naltrexone (2002-2004), Monitoring Committee of the Medically Supervised Injecting Centre for the New South Wales Government Cabinet Office (2003-2004), Australian Ministerial Council on Drug Strategy Working Party on Performance and Image Enhancing Drugs (2003-2005), Australian Government Department of Health and Ageing Expert Advisory Committee on Cannabis and Health (2005-2006), New South Wales Expert Advisory Group on Drugs and Alcohol for the New South Wales Minister of Health (2004-2013), Australian National Council on Drugs advising the Prime Minister (2004-2010), WHO/UNODC Technical Guidelines Development Group on Pharmacotherapy of Opioid Dependence (2004-2008), Australian Research Alliance for Children and Youth (2005-2015).

Served on the editorial and executive boards of the *Drug and Alcohol Review* (1994-2005), and as Deputy Editor (1995-2000) and Executive Editor (2000-2005). Assistant Editor of the international peer-reviewed journal *Addiction* (1995-2005). Editor, Cochrane Review Group on Drugs and Alcohol (1998-2003). Authored over 280 books, chapters in edited volumes on substance abuse, addiction and treatment, and peer-reviewed academic journal articles on those subjects. Recent articles include "Buprenorphine maintenance versus placebo or methadone maintenance for opioid dependence", "Young adult sequelae of adolescent cannabis use" and "The Pain and Opioids IN Treatment study: characteristics of a cohort using opioids to manage chronic non-cancer pain".

Recipient of academic and research support from the Australian Government Department of Health; the New South Wales Government Department of Health; the Australian National Drug Law Enforcement Research Fund; the Alcohol Education and Rehabilitation Foundation; UNODC; the National Institute on Drug Abuse of the United States; the Australian Research Council; and the Australian Government National Health and Medical Research Council.

Member of the International Narcotics Control Board (since 2015).[c] Member of the Standing Committee on Estimates (2015).

Alejandro Mohar Betancourt

Born in 1956. National of Mexico. Director General of the National Cancer Research Institute of Mexico (2003-2013) and member of the National System of Researchers of Mexico, the National Academy of Medicine, the Mexican Academy of Sciences and the American Society of Clinical Oncology.

Doctor of Medicine, National Autonomous University of Mexico (UNAM) (1980); Postgraduate studies in anatomical pathology, National Institute of Nutrition (1985), Master of Sciences (1986) and Doctor of Sciences in Epidemiology (1990), Harvard School of Public Health.

Recipient of academic and research support from the National Council on Science and Technology (CONACYT) and the Mexican Foundation of Health. Head of the Department of Epidemiology (1988-1989), Deputy Director of Clinical Research (1993-1999) and Director of Research (1999-2003), National Cancer Research Institute of Mexico. Lecturer and Research Associate, Harvard School of Public Health (1988-1990). Lecturer and Director of master's and doctoral dissertations at the Faculty of Medicine, UNAM (since 1991). Coordinator of the Unit for Biomedical Research on Cancer, Biomedical Research Institute, UNAM (1998). Author of more than 110 scientific and popular works, 70 of which appear in indexed journals, including "Intratypic changes of the E1 gene and the long control region affect ori function of human papillomavirus type 18 variants", "Screening breast cancer: a commitment to Mexico (preliminary report)", "Impact of diabetes and hyperglycemia on survival in advanced breast cancer patients", "Ovarian cancer: the new challenge in gynaecologic oncology?" and "Validation of the Mexican-Spanish version of the EORTC

---

[c] Elected by the Economic and Social Council on 8 April 2015.

QLQ-C15-PAL questionnaire for the evaluation of health-related quality of life in patients on palliative care".

Awarded various recognitions including the following: Miguel Otero Award for clinical research, General Health Council (2012); third place for best pharmacoeconomics work, Mexican College for Pharmacoeconomics and International Society for Pharmacoeconomics and Outcomes Research, Mexico chapter (2010); member of the Group of the 300 Most Influential Leaders of Mexico; recognition for participation in the meeting of the Global Health Strategic Operations Advisory Group of the American Cancer Society (2009); member of the Board of Governors of the National Autonomous University of Mexico (2008); Distinction of Edward Larocque Tinker Visiting Professor, Stanford University (2000); member of the External Advisory Group for the Mexico Report on Social Determinants of Health (2010); member of the jury for the Aaron Sáenz Annual Prize for Paediatric Research, Federico Gómez Children's Hospital of Mexico and the "General y Lic. Aarón Sáenz Garza, A.C." Association (2010); member of the Global Health Strategic Operations Advisory Group of the American Cancer Society (2010); Certificate of Achievement for dedication and commitment to establishing a national cancer plan for Mexico, American Cancer Society (2006); member of the Scientific Committee of the Mexican Association of Pathologists (1993-1995).

Member of the International Narcotics Control Board (since 2013). Member of the Standing Committee on Estimates (since 2014). Vice-Chair of the Standing Committee on Estimates (2015).

Jagjit Pavadia

Born in 1954. National of India. Graduate in English Honours (1974), Dhaka University, LL.B from Delhi University (1988), Master's Diploma in Public Administration, Indian Institute of Public Administration (1996). Completed dissertation "Forfeiture of Property under the Narcotics Drugs and Psychotropic Substances Act, 1985" towards completion of Master's Diploma.

Held several senior positions in Indian Revenue Service for 35 years in the Government of India, including Narcotics Commissioner of India, Central Bureau of Narcotics (2006-2012); Commissioner, Legal Affairs (2001-2005); Chief Vigilance Officer, Power Finance Corporation (1996-2001); Customs Training Adviser Maldives, deputed by the Commonwealth Secretariat (1994-1995); Deputy Director, Narcotics Control Bureau (1990-1994); and retired as Chief Commissioner, Customs, Central Excise and Service Tax, Nagpur, in 2014.

Recipient of Presidential Appreciation Certificate for Specially Distinguished Record of Service on the occasion of Republic Day (2005), published in the *Gazette of India Extraordinary*.

Member of the Indian delegation to the Commission on Narcotics Drugs, Vienna (2007-2012); introduced resolutions 51/15 (2008) and 53/12 (2010), adopted by the Commission on Narcotic Drugs, and organized a side event on the margins of the Commission's session (2011), presenting issues involved in the illegal movement of poppy seeds to producing, importing and exporting countries. As representative of the competent national authority, attended Project Prism and Project Cohesion task force meetings (2006-2012), and coordinated and organized the Project Prism and Project Cohesion meeting in New Delhi (2008). Participated in the Meeting of the Heads of National Drug Law Enforcement Agencies (HONLEA), Asia and the Pacific, held in Bangkok (2006), and organized the Meeting of HONLEA, Asia and the Pacific, held in Agra, India (2011). Member of the INCB advisory expert group on the scheduling of substances (2006), and member of the advisory group finalizing the INCB *Guidelines for a Voluntary Code of Practice for the Chemical Industry* (2008). Rapporteur of the forty-first session of the Subcommission on Illicit Drug Traffic and Related Matters in the Near and Middle East, held in Amman (2006); Chairperson of the forty-second session of the Subcommission, held in Accra, India (2007); organized the meeting of the Paris Pact Initiative Expert Working Group on Precursors, held in New Delhi (2011), and participated in the International Drug Enforcement Conferences hosted by the United States Drug Enforcement Agency, held in Istanbul (2008) and Cancún, Mexico (2011).

Member of the International Narcotics Control Board (since 2015).[d] Second Vice-President and Chair of the Standing Committee on Estimates (2015).

Ahmed Kamal Eldin Samak

Born in 1950. National of Egypt. Graduated with a Law and Police Licence in 1971. Worked in the field of anti-narcotics for more than 35 years, until becoming the Minister Assistant of Police and Head of the Anti-Narcotics General Administration of Egypt, which is considered the first organization of anti-narcotics in the world and was founded in 1929. Independent adviser in the field of anti-narcotics and crime. First-rank badge of honour on the occasion of the police festival (1992). Contributed

---

[d] Elected by the Economic and Social Council on 23 April 2014.

to several missions, such as to Jordan, for anti-narcotics training (1988); India, for the signing of an agreement between India and Egypt to strengthen anti-narcotics and security cooperation to combat crime and terrorism (1995); France, for cooperation between Egypt and the International Criminal Police Organization (INTERPOL) relating to drugs and money-laundering (1996); Palestine,[e] to participate in a regional anti-narcotics workshop (1999); Saudi Arabia, to participate in a training programme related to drug cases (2001); United Arab Emirates, to represent the Ministry of the Interior at the thirty-sixth session of the committee concerned with illegal trade in drugs (2001); Libyan Arab Jamahiriya,[f] to participate in the celebration of the International Day against Drug Abuse and Illicit Trafficking (2002); Kenya, to participate in the twelfth and seventeenth conferences of African national anti-narcotics department leaders (2002 and 2007); Mauritius, for the second ministerial anti-narcotics meeting (2004); Lebanon, to participate in the conference "Drugs are a social epidemic", organized by Lebanese organizations for human rights (2004); Tunisia, to participate in the seventeenth to twenty-first Arab conferences of anti-narcotics department leaders (2003-2007); United States (2004); Austria, to represent the Ministry at the forty-fifth, forty-sixth and forty-eighth to fiftieth sessions of the Commission on Narcotic Drugs (2002-2007); Saudi Arabia, as a member of a scientific organization to prepare an article about arrest and investigation procedures (2007); United Arab Emirates, for the Regional Seminar for Strategic and Cooperative Planning in the Field of Anti-Narcotics (2007). Member of the National General Trust Fund for Anti-Narcotics and Addiction; and the Committee of National Strategy Planning on Anti-Narcotics.

Member of the International Narcotics Control Board (since 2012). Member of the Standing Committee on Estimates (2012, 2014 and 2015).

Werner Sipp

Born in 1943. National of Germany. Lawyer (Universities of Heidelberg, Germany, and Lausanne, Switzerland, University Institute of European Studies, Turin, Italy).

Assistant lecturer in Public Law, University of Regensburg (1971-1977). Senior administrative posts in several federal ministries (1977-2008). Head of the Division for Narcotic Law and International Narcotic Drugs Affairs in the Federal Ministry of Health (2001-2008); Permanent Correspondent of Germany in the Pompidou Group of the Council of Europe (2001-2008); Legal Correspondent of Germany in the European Legal Database on Drugs, Lisbon (2002-2008); Chairman of the Horizontal Working Party on Drugs of the Council of the European Union (2007); Coordinator of the German delegation to the Commission on Narcotic Drugs (2001-2009).

Expert Consultant to the German Federal Ministry of Health and Drug Commissioner of the Federal Government in international drug matters (2008-2009); Expert Consultant on drug issues to the Deutsche Gesellschaft für Internationale Zusammenarbeit (2008-2011); Expert on several European Union drug projects such as "Implementing the national strategy to fight drug abuse in Serbia" and the Central Asia Drug Action Programme.

Member of the International Narcotics Control Board (since 2012). Member of the Standing Committee on Estimates (2012-2014). Rapporteur (2013). First Vice-President of the Board (2014). President of the Board (2015).

Viroj Sumyai

Born in 1953. National of Thailand. Retired Assistant Secretary-General of the Food and Drug Administration, Ministry of Public Health of Thailand, and clinical pharmacologist specializing in drug epidemiology. Professor, Mahidol University (since 2001).

Bachelor of Science degree in chemistry (1976), Chiang Mai University. Bachelor's degree in pharmacy (1979), Manila Central University. Master's degree in clinical pharmacology (1983), Chulalongkorn University. Apprenticeship in narcotic drugs epidemiology at St. George's University of London (1989). Doctor of Philosophy, Health Policy and Administration (2009), National Institute of Administration. Member of the Pharmaceutical Association of Thailand. Member of the Pharmacological and Therapeutic Society of Thailand. Member of the Thai Society of Toxicology. Author of nine books in the field of drug prevention and control, including *Drugging Drinks: Handbook for Predatory Drugs Prevention* and *Déjà vu: A Complete Handbook for Clandestine Chemistry, Pharmacology and Epidemiology of LSD*. Columnist, *Food and Drug Administration Journal*. Recipient, Prime Minister's Award for Drug Education and Prevention (2005).

[e] Pursuant to General Assembly resolution 67/19 of 29 November 2012, Palestine has been accorded the status of a non-member observer State. The name "State of Palestine" is now used in all United Nations documents.

[f] Since 16 September 2011, "Libya" has replaced "Libyan Arab Jamahiriya" as the short name used in the United Nations.

Member of the International Narcotics Control Board (since 2010). Member (since 2010) and Chair (2012 and 2014) of the Standing Committee on Estimates. Chair of the Committee on Finance and Administration (2011 and 2013). Second Vice-President of the Board (2012 and 2014).

Sri Suryawati

Born in 1955. National of Indonesia. Professor and Head, Division of Medicine Policy and Management, Faculty of Medicine, Gadjah Mada University, Yogyakarta. Educational background includes pharmacy (1979), specialist in pharmacology (1985); doctoral degree in clinical pharmacokinetics (1994), certificate in medicine policy (1997). Lecturer in pharmacology/clinical pharmacology (since 1980); supervisor for more than 150 master's and doctoral theses in the areas of medicine policy, essential medicines, clinical pharmacology, pharmacoeconomics and pharmaceutical management.

Member of the WHO Expert Advisory Panel for Medicine Policy and Management (since 1999). Member of the Executive Board of the International Network for the Rational Use of Drugs (INRUD). Member of the WHO Expert Committee on the Selection and Use of Essential Medicines (2002, 2003, 2005 and 2007). Member of the WHO Expert Committee on Drug Dependence (2002 and 2006). Member of the United Nations Millennium Project Task Force on HIV/AIDS, Malaria and Tuberculosis and Access to Essential Medicines (Task Force 5) (2001-2005). Consultant in essential medicine programmes and promoting rational use of medicines in Bangladesh (2006-2007), Cambodia (2001-2008), China (2006-2008), Fiji (2009), the Lao People's Democratic Republic (2001-2003), Mongolia (2006-2008) and the Philippines (2006-2007). Consultant in medicine policy and drug evaluation in Cambodia (2003, 2005 and 2007), China (2003), Indonesia (2005-2006) and Viet Nam (2003). Facilitator in various international training courses in medicine policy and promoting the rational use of medicines, including WHO and INRUD courses on promoting the rational use of medicines (1994-2007), training courses on hospital drugs and therapeutics committees (2001-2007) and international courses on medicine policy (2002-2003).

Member of the International Narcotics Control Board (2007-2012 and since 2013). Member (2008-2011 and since 2013), Vice-Chair (2009) and Chair (2010 and 2013) of the Standing Committee on Estimates. Second Vice-President of the Board (2010 and 2013). Rapporteur (2011 and 2014). First Vice-President of the Board (2015).

Francisco E. Thoumi

Born in 1943. National of Colombia and the United States. Bachelor of Arts and Doctor of Philosophy in Economics. Senior member of the Colombian Academy of Economic Sciences and Corresponding Member of the Royal Academy of Moral and Political Sciences (Spain).

Professor at the University of Texas, Rosario University (Bogotá) and California State University, Chico. Worked for 15 years in the research departments of the World Bank and the Inter-American Development Bank. Founder and Director, Research and Monitoring Center on Drugs and Crime, Rosario University (August 2004-December 2007); Research Coordinator, Global Programme against Money-Laundering, Proceeds of Crime and the Financing of Terrorism; Coordinator for the *World Drug Report*, UNODC (August 1999-September 2000); Researcher, Comparative Study of Illegal Drugs in Six Countries, United Nations Research Institute for Social Development, Geneva (June 1991-December 1992); Fellow, Woodrow Wilson International Center for Scholars (August 1996-July 1997); Research Coordinator, Research Programme on the Economic Impact of Illegal Drugs in the Andean Countries, United Nations Development Programme, Bogota (November 1993-January 1996).

Author of two books and co-author of one book on illegal drugs in Colombia and the Andean region. Editor of three volumes and author of over 60 academic journal articles and book chapters on those subjects.

Member of the Friedrich Ebert Foundation Observatory of Organized Crime in Latin America and the Caribbean (since 2008) and the World Economic Forum's Global Agenda Council on Organized Crime (2012-2014).

Member of the International Narcotics Control Board (since 2012). Rapporteur (2012). Member of the Standing Committee on Estimates (2013). Member of the Committee on Finance and Administration (2014 and 2015).

Jallal Toufiq

Born in 1963. National of Morocco. Head of the National Centre for Drug Abuse Prevention and Research; Director of the Moroccan National Observatory on Drugs and Addictions; Director of the Ar-razi University Psychiatric Hospital and Professor of Psychiatry at the Rabat Faculty of Medicine.

Medical Doctor, Rabat Faculty of Medicine (1989); Diploma of Specialization in Psychiatry (1994); and lecturer at the Rabat Faculty of Medicine (since 1995). Undertook specialized training in Paris at the Sainte-Anne Psychiatric Hospital and Marmottan Centre (1990-1991); and at Johns Hopkins University as a National Institute on Drug Abuse research fellow and Clinical Observer (1994-1995). Conducted research at the University of Pittsburgh (1995); and gained Clinical Drug Research certificates at the Vienna School of Clinical Research (2001 and 2002).

Currently holding positions in Morocco as Head of the Harm Reduction Programme, National Centre for Drug Abuse Prevention and Research; teaching and residency training coordinator, Ar-razi Hospital; Director of the National Diploma Programme on Treatment and Prevention of Drug Abuse, Rabat Faculty of Medicine; Director of the National Diploma Programme on Child Psychiatry, Rabat Faculty of Medicine and Member of the Ministry of Health Commission on Drug Abuse.

At the international level, Representative of the Mediterranean Network (MedNET) for Morocco (MedNET/Pompidou Group/Council of Europe); former permanent correspondent of the Pompidou Group for Morocco (Council of Europe) on drug abuse prevention and research and former member of the Reference Group to the United Nations on HIV and Injecting Drug Use. Founding member and steering committee member, Middle East and North Africa Harm Reduction Association (MENAHRA); Director of Knowledge Hub Ar-razi for North Africa, MENAHRA; Member, Mentor International Scientific Advisory Network (drug abuse prevention in youth); former focal point/expert on prevention, United Nations Office on Drug Control and Crime Prevention (local network for North Africa); founding member, MedNET (advisory group on AIDS and drug abuse policies) of the Council of Europe, and member of the Reference Group to the United Nations on HIV and Injecting Drug Use.

Held consultancy roles with the WHO Regional Office for the Eastern Mediterranean, UNODC and other international institutions, research fellowships and the National Institute on Drug Abuse of the United States. Published widely in the field of psychiatry, alcohol and drug abuse.

Member of the International Narcotics Control Board (since 2015).[g] Member of the Standing Committee on Estimates (2015).

Raymond Yans

Born in 1948. National of Belgium. Graduate in Germanic philology and in philosophy (1972).

Belgian Foreign Service: Attaché, Jakarta (1978-1981); Deputy-Mayor of Liège (1982-1989); Consul, Tokyo (1989-1994); Consul, Chargé d'affaires, Luxembourg (1999-2003); Head of the Drug Unit, Ministry of Foreign Affairs (1995-1999 and 2003-2007); Chairman of the Dublin Group (2002-2006); Chairman of the European Union Drug Policy Cooperation Working Group during the Belgian Presidency of the European Union; charged with the national coordination of the ratification and implementation process of the Convention on Psychotropic Substances of 1971 and the United Nations Convention against Illicit Traffic in Narcotic Drugs and Psychotropic Substances of 1988 (1995-1998); liaison between the Ministry of Foreign Affairs and the National Police for drug liaison officers in Belgian embassies (2003-2005); participation in the launching by the European Union Joint Action on New Synthetic Drugs of an early warning system to alert Governments to the appearance of new synthetic drugs (1999); active in the creation of the Cooperation Mechanism on Drugs between the European Union, Latin America and the Caribbean (1997-1999). Author of numerous articles and speeches, including: "The future of the Dublin Group" (2004) and "Is there anything such as a European Union Common Drug Policy" (2005). Member of the Belgian delegation to the Commission on Narcotic Drugs (1995-2007); all the preparatory sessions (on amphetamine-type stimulants, precursors, judicial cooperation, money-laundering, drug demand reduction and alternative development) for the twentieth special session of the General Assembly; European Union Seminar on Best Practices in Drug Enforcement by Law Enforcement Authorities, Helsinki (1999); Joint European Union/Southern African Development Community Conferences on Drug Control Cooperation, Mmabatho, South Africa (1995) and Gabarone (1998); UNODC/Paris Pact round tables, Brussels (2003), Tehran and Istanbul (2005); meetings of the High-level Dialogue on Drugs between the Andean Community and the European Union, Lima (2005) and Vienna (2006).

Member of the International Narcotics Control Board (since 2007). Member of the Standing Committee on Estimates (2007-2010). Member (2007-2009) and Chair (2015) of the Committee on Finance and Administration. Rapporteur (2010). First Vice-President of the Board (2011). President of the Board (2012 and 2013).

---

[g] Elected by the Economic and Social Council on 23 April 2014.

About the International Narcotics Control Board

The International Narcotics Control Board (INCB) is an independent and quasi-judicial control organ, established by treaty, for monitoring the implementation of the international drug control treaties. It had predecessors under the former drug control treaties as far back as the time of the League of Nations.

Composition

INCB consists of 13 members who are elected by the Economic and Social Council and who serve in their personal capacity, not as government representatives. Three members with medical, pharmacological or pharmaceutical experience are elected from a list of persons nominated by the World Health Organization (WHO) and 10 members are elected from a list of persons nominated by Governments. Members of the Board are persons who, by their competence, impartiality and disinterestedness, command general confidence. The Council, in consultation with INCB, makes all arrangements necessary to ensure the full technical independence of the Board in carrying out its functions. INCB has a secretariat that assists it in the exercise of its treaty-related functions. The INCB secretariat is an administrative entity of the United Nations Office on Drugs and Crime, but it reports solely to the Board on matters of substance. INCB closely collaborates with the Office in the framework of arrangements approved by the Council in its resolution 1991/48. INCB also cooperates with other international bodies concerned with drug control, including not only the Council and its Commission on Narcotic Drugs, but also the relevant specialized agencies of the United Nations, particularly WHO. It also cooperates with bodies outside the United Nations system, especially the International Criminal Police Organization (INTERPOL) and the World Customs Organization.

Functions

The functions of INCB are laid down in the following treaties: the Single Convention on Narcotic Drugs of 1961 as amended by the 1972 Protocol; the Convention on Psychotropic Substances of 1971; and the United Nations Convention against Illicit Traffic in Narcotic Drugs and Psychotropic Substances of 1988. Broadly speaking, INCB deals with the following:

(a)   As regards the licit manufacture of, trade in and use of drugs, INCB endeavours, in cooperation with Governments, to ensure that adequate supplies of drugs are available for medical and scientific uses and that the diversion of drugs from licit sources to illicit channels does not occur. INCB also monitors Governments' control over chemicals used in the illicit manufacture of drugs and assists them in preventing the diversion of those chemicals into the illicit traffic;

(b)   As regards the illicit manufacture of, trafficking in and use of drugs, INCB identifies weaknesses in national and international control systems and contributes to correcting such situations. INCB is also responsible for assessing chemicals used in the illicit manufacture of drugs, in order to determine whether they should be placed under international control.

In the discharge of its responsibilities, INCB:

(a)   Administers a system of estimates for narcotic drugs and a voluntary assessment system for psychotropic substances and monitors licit activities involving drugs through a statistical returns system, with a view to assisting Governments in achieving, inter alia, a balance between supply and demand;

(b)   Monitors and promotes measures taken by Governments to prevent the diversion of substances frequently used in the illicit manufacture of narcotic drugs and psychotropic substances and assesses such substances to determine whether there is a need for changes in the scope of control of Tables I and II of the 1988 Convention;

(c)   Analyses information provided by Governments, United Nations bodies, specialized agencies or other competent international organizations, with a view to ensuring that the provisions of the international drug control treaties are adequately carried out by Governments, and recommends remedial measures;

(d)   Maintains a permanent dialogue with Governments to assist them in complying with their obligations under the international drug control treaties and, to that end, recommends, where appropriate, technical or financial assistance to be provided.

INCB is called upon to ask for explanations in the event of apparent violations of the treaties, to propose appropriate remedial measures to Governments that are not fully applying the provisions of the treaties or are encountering difficulties in applying them and, where necessary, to assist Governments in overcoming such difficulties. If, however, INCB notes that the measures necessary to remedy a serious situation have not been taken, it may call the matter to the attention of the parties concerned, the Commission on Narcotic Drugs and the Economic and Social Council. As a last resort, the treaties empower INCB to recommend to parties that they stop importing drugs from a defaulting country, exporting drugs to it or both. In all cases, INCB acts in close cooperation with Governments.

INCB assists national administrations in meeting their obligations under the conventions. To that end, it proposes and participates in regional training seminars and programmes for drug control administrators.

Reports

The international drug control treaties require INCB to prepare an annual report on its work. The annual report contains an analysis of the drug control situation worldwide so that Governments are kept aware of existing and potential situations that may endanger the objectives of the international drug control treaties. INCB draws the attention of Governments to gaps and weaknesses in national control and in treaty compliance; it also makes suggestions and recommendations for improvements at both the national and international levels. The annual report is based on information provided by Governments to INCB, United Nations entities and other organizations. It also uses information provided through other international organizations, such as INTERPOL and the World Customs Organization, as well as regional organizations.

The annual report of INCB is supplemented by detailed technical reports. They contain data on the licit movement of narcotic drugs and psychotropic substances required for medical and scientific purposes, together with an analysis of those data by INCB. Those data are required for the proper functioning of the system of control over the licit movement of narcotic drugs and psychotropic substances, including preventing their diversion to illicit channels. Moreover, under the provisions of article 12 of the 1988 Convention, INCB reports annually to the Commission on Narcotic Drugs on the implementation of that article. That report, which gives an account of the results of the monitoring of precursors and of the chemicals frequently used in the illicit manufacture of narcotic drugs and psychotropic substances, is also published as a supplement to the annual report.

Since 1992, the first chapter of the annual report has been devoted to a specific drug control issue on which INCB presents its conclusions and recommendations in order to contribute to policy-related discussions and decisions in national, regional and international drug control. The following topics were covered in past annual reports:

1992: Legalization of the non-medical use of drugs

1993: The importance of demand reduction

1994: Evaluation of the effectiveness of the international drug control treaties

1995: Giving more priority to combating money-laundering

1996: Drug abuse and the criminal justice system

1997: Preventing drug abuse in an environment of illicit drug promotion

1998: International control of drugs: past, present and future

1999: Freedom from pain and suffering

2000: Overconsumption of internationally controlled drugs

2001: Globalization and new technologies: challenges to drug law enforcement in the twenty-first century

2002: Illicit drugs and economic development

2003: Drugs, crime and violence: the microlevel impact

2004: Integration of supply and demand reduction strategies: moving beyond a balanced approach

2005: Alternative development and legitimate livelihoods

2006: Internationally controlled drugs and the unregulated market

2007: The principle of proportionality and drug-related offences

2008: The international drug control conventions: history, achievements and challenges

2009: Primary prevention of drug abuse

2010: Drugs and corruption

2011: Social cohesion, social disorganization and illegal drugs

2012: Shared responsibility in international drug control

2013: Economic consequences of drug abuse

2014: Implementation of a comprehensive, integrated and balanced approach to addressing the world drug problem

Chapter I of the report of the International Narcotics Control Board for 2015 is entitled "The health and welfare of mankind: challenges and opportunities for the international control of drugs".

Chapter II presents an analysis of the operation of the international drug control system based primarily on information that Governments are required to submit directly to INCB in accordance with the international drug control treaties. Its focus is on the worldwide control of all licit activities related to narcotic drugs and psychotropic substances, as well as chemicals used in the illicit manufacture of such drugs.

Chapter III presents some of the major developments in drug abuse and trafficking and measures by Governments to implement the international drug control treaties by addressing those problems.

Chapter IV presents the main recommendations addressed by INCB to Governments, UNODC, WHO and other relevant international and regional organizations.

United Nations system and drug control organs and their secretariat

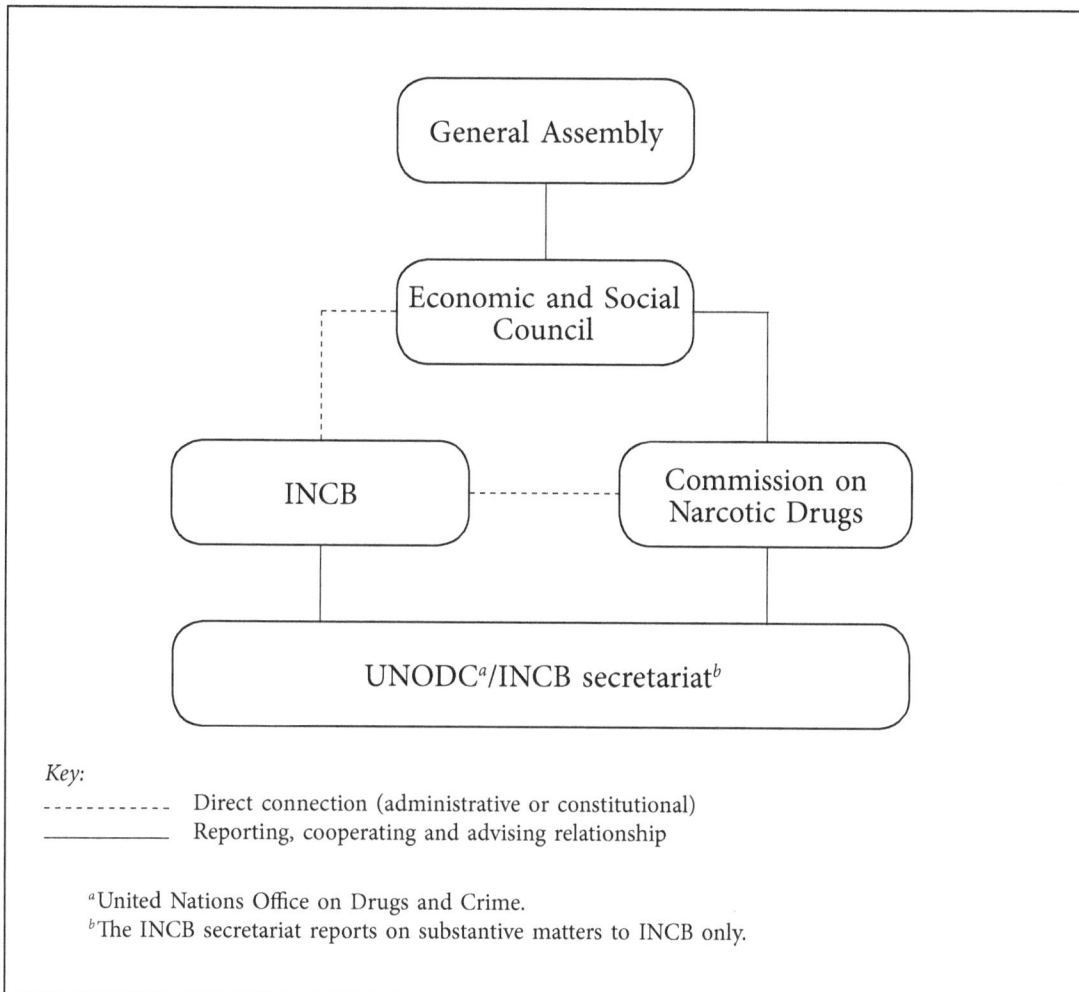

```
                        ┌─────────────────────┐
                        │   General Assembly   │
                        └──────────┬──────────┘
                                   │
                        ┌──────────┴──────────┐
                ┌ ─ ─ ─ │ Economic and Social │
                ¦       │      Council         │──────────┐
                ¦       └─────────────────────┘          │
                ¦                                         │
        ┌───────┴──────┐     ┌───────────────────────┐   │
        │     INCB     │─ ─ ─│    Commission on      │   │
        │              │     │   Narcotic Drugs      │   │
        └───────┬──────┘     └───────────┬───────────┘   │
                │                        │               │
        ┌───────┴────────────────────────┴───────────────┘
        │         UNODCᵃ/INCB secretariatᵇ               │
        └─────────────────────────────────────────────────┘
```

Key:

- - - - - - - - - - Direct connection (administrative or constitutional)
─────────── Reporting, cooperating and advising relationship

[a] United Nations Office on Drugs and Crime.
[b] The INCB secretariat reports on substantive matters to INCB only.

www.ingramcontent.com/pod-product-compliance
Lightning Source LLC
Chambersburg PA
CBHW080852300326
41935CB00041B/1554